PIERO DI COSIMO

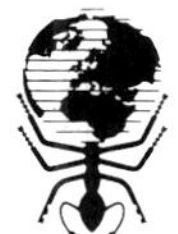

Books in the RENAISSANCE LIVES series explore and illustrate the life histories and achievements of significant artists, rulers, intellectuals and scientists in the early modern world. They delve into literature, philosophy, the history of art, science and natural history and cover narratives of exploration, statecraft and technology.

Series Editor: François Quiviger

Already published

Albrecht Dürer: Art and Autobiography *David Ekserdjian*
Aldus Manutius: The Invention of the Publisher *Oren Margolis*
Artemisia Gentileschi and Feminism in Early Modern Europe *Mary D. Garrard*
Blaise Pascal: Miracles and Reason *Mary Ann Caws*
Botticelli: Artist and Designer *Ana Debenedetti*
Caravaggio and the Creation of Modernity *Troy Thomas*
Descartes: The Renewal of Philosophy *Steven Nadler*
Donatello and the Dawn of Renaissance Art *A. Victor Coonin*
Erasmus of Rotterdam: The Spirit of a Scholar *William Barker*
Filippino Lippi: An Abundance of Invention *Jonathan K. Nelson*
Giorgione's Ambiguity *Tom Nichols*
Hans Holbein: The Artist in a Changing World *Jeanne Nuechterlein*
Hieronymus Bosch: Visions and Nightmares *Nils Büttner*
Isaac Newton and Natural Philosophy *Niccolò Guicciardini*
Jan van Eyck within His Art *Alfred Acres*
John Donne: In the Shadow of Religion *Andrew Hadfield*
John Evelyn: A Life of Domesticity *John Dixon Hunt*
Leonardo da Vinci: Self, Art and Nature *François Quiviger*
Leon Battista Alberti: The Chameleon's Eye *Caspar Pearson*
Lucas Cranach: From German Myth to Reformation *Jennifer Nelson*
Machiavelli: From Radical to Reactionary *Robert Black*
Michelangelo and the Viewer in His Time *Bernadine Barnes*
Paracelsus: An Alchemical Life *Bruce T. Moran*
Petrarch: Everywhere a Wanderer *Christopher S. Celenza*
Piero della Francesca and the Invention of the Artist *Machtelt Brüggen Israëls*
Piero di Cosimo: Eccentricity and Delight *Sarah Blake McHam*
Pieter Bruegel and the Idea of Human Nature *Elizabeth Alice Honig*
Raphael and the Antique *Claudia La Malfa*
Rembrandt's Holland *Larry Silver*
Rubens's Spirit: From Ingenuity to Genius *Alexander Marr*
Salvator Rosa: Paint and Performance *Helen Langdon*
Thomas Nashe and Late Elizabethan Writing *Andrew Hadfield*
Titian's Touch: Art, Magic and Philosophy *Maria H. Loh*
Tycho Brahe and the Measure of the Heavens *John Robert Christianson*
Ulisse Aldrovandi: Naturalist and Collector *Peter Mason*

PIERO DI COSIMO

Eccentricity and Delight

SARAH BLAKE McHAM

REAKTION BOOKS

Published by Reaktion Books Ltd
Unit 32, Waterside
44–48 Wharf Road
London N1 7UX, UK
www.reaktionbooks.co.uk

First published 2024

Copyright © Sarah Blake McHam 2024

Printed and bound in India by Replika Press Pvt. Ltd

A catalogue record for this book is available from the British Library

ISBN 978 1 78914 842 8

COVER: Piero di Cosimo, *Vulcan and Aeolus*, or *The Return of New Life to Lemnos*, 1490–1500, oil and tempera on canvas. National Gallery of Canada, Ottawa, photo Bridgeman Images.

CONTENTS

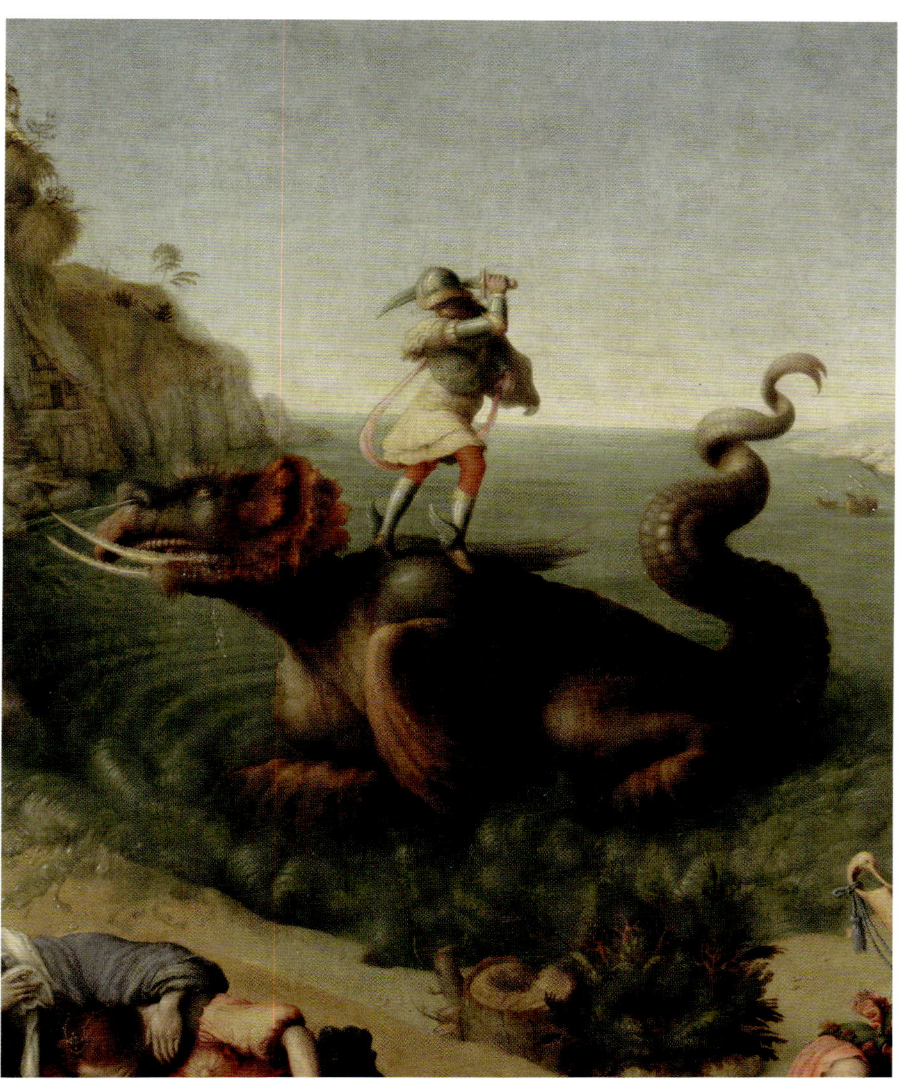

Introduction

He was very strange.

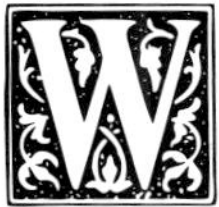
hy a book on Piero di Cosimo? The Florentine painter, who lived from 1462 to 1522, is nowhere near as famous as some of his peers, such as Botticelli, Leonardo and Michelangelo. However, his consistently and self-consciously unusual persona fascinated his contemporaries and later generations. His famed diet, restricted to eggs boiled fifty at a time in the water in which he had prepared glue, and commitment to living amid wild nature, never pruning the bushes and vines of his garden, point to the idiosyncratic life he deliberately espoused and hint at his independent mind. Piero was the favourite of sophisticated patrons of his day who were eager to decorate their residences with the new subjects of Graeco-Roman myths and legends. His vividly imagined visual interpretations led him to corner the market in the type of commission known as *spalliere*. These usually secular narratives were displayed horizontally, embedded into a room's woodwork or mounted on a large piece of furniture (usually at shoulder height, *spalla* in Italian), often in the bedrooms or bedroom antechambers of private residences. Sometimes they imparted didactic messages specific to the location, such as about the bonds of matrimony

1 Detail of Piero di Cosimo, *Perseus Liberating Andromeda*, c. 1510–13, oil on panel (illus. 6).

or civic duties, to an audience of family and close friends. The type was especially popular during the years of Piero's working career (*c.* 1480–1520), and he had the gift of reinterpreting their typically learned literary subjects as delightful fairy tales.

Even when he took on standard religious themes, Piero peppered them with slyly witty details that enlivened and extended their serious message. As Giorgio Vasari (1511–1574), the preeminent biographer of Italian Renaissance artists, characterized Piero in his *Lives of the Most Excellent Painters, Sculptors and Architects* (1550, 1568), 'he was very strange' and hard to teach because he did not pay attention, owing to how 'far had his brain wandered after some other fancy of his own'.[1] Vasari was writing more than a generation after Piero's death and had to rely chiefly on hearsay for his biography. Little contemporary evidence has survived about Piero, and consequently, largely because of Vasari's reaction, Piero's reputation did not survive the period. It took the novelist George Eliot in the nineteenth century to recognize the fictional potential of the irascible, odd fellow recorded by Vasari. She included him as a colourful character in her *Romola* (1862–3), a historical novel about late fifteenth-century Florence. As one of Piero's patrons in that book says perceptively, 'You seem to love the blending of the terrible with the gay.'[2] In the early twentieth century Piero achieved fleeting fame for a very different reason: the Surrealists touted him as one of their artistic ancestors because of his clever and challenging unorthodoxy.[3]

Serious interest in the artist did not revive until a pioneering scholarly monograph by Robert Langton Douglas in 1946. Given the limitations imposed by the post-war period, it was an impressive effort. Douglas briefly covered Piero's career and took advantage of his own location in the USA, where many of Piero's paintings had migrated, to view the works. His book inspired a little-known essay on Piero by the writer Jean-Louis Vaudoyer, a member of the French Academy and a correspondent of Marcel

Proust.[4] In 1968 it was published in a posthumous collection of Vaudoyer's essays about art.[5] Although its original date is uncertain, Vaudoyer refers to Douglas's book, and therefore his essay must have been written after 1946. Vaudoyer's essay treats only a few of Piero's paintings that he had seen in person in Europe, but he responded to Piero's interpretations of animals and humans with a more deeply sensitive appreciation than any previous writer. Decades later, in 1993, Sharon Fermor wrote the first modern monograph on Piero, skilfully pulling together the literature about Piero into a balanced text. Her volume was followed by a much more comprehensive scholarly volume by Dennis Geronimus, which to date remains the most authoritative guide to the artist's career.[6] More recently, Piero was introduced to a broader public by the major exhibition that Geronimus masterminded at the National Gallery of Art in Washington, DC, in 2014, followed by an exhibition at the Galleria degli Uffizi in Florence in 2015.[7] These exhibitions converted me into a fan: in decades of university teaching, I had never included Piero in my Renaissance courses. He seemed too much of an outlier to fit into any of the categories that I used to clarify for undergraduates the organization of my classes. However, I became intrigued by the extent to which his secular painting was rooted in Graeco-Roman literature and philosophy. I also recognized that no book intended for a wide audience had been written about Piero since the exhibitions and that this universally intriguing artist had been relegated to specialists' attention. This study takes advantage of the discoveries made at those exhibitions and subsequent scholarly conferences and aims to recover the pleasures Piero offers to everyone who loves to look at art.

To get a sense of his visual magic, let us begin with the enterprises for which Vasari reserved his greatest enthusiasm. They were ephemeral productions of which no traces remain. Such losses explain a good deal about Piero's diminished legacy. It is known that Lorenzo and the younger Filippo Strozzi commissioned Piero for the carnival of 1507.[8] What is unclear is whether the woodcut refers to it. The design seems a clear reference to another carnival design Piero supervised dated 1512; Piero and two students provided costumes and staging for the Triumph of Death procession, a masquerade and pageant in which chariots were shrouded in black and pulled by black buffalos carrying tombs. A colossal figure of Death surmounted one of the cars; from all of them, actors disguised as skeletons emerged at intervals to frighten and titillate onlookers. As Vasari recorded:

> Nor will I refrain from saying that Piero, in his youth, being fanciful and extravagant in invention, was much employed for the masquerades that are held during the Carnival; and he became very dear to the young noblemen of Florence, having improved their festivals much in invention, adornment, grandeur, and pomp . . .
>
> Among these spectacles, which were numerous and ingenious, it is my pleasure to give a brief description of one, which was contrived mostly by Piero, when he was already of a mature age, and which was not, like many, pleasing through its beauty, but, on the contrary, on account of a strange, horrible, and unexpected invention, gave no little satisfaction to the people . . . This was the Car of Death . . . This triumphal chariot was an enormous car drawn by buffaloes, black all over and painted with skeletons and white crosses; and upon the highest point of the car stood a colossal figure of Death, scythe in hand, and right round the car were a number of covered tombs; and at all the places where the procession halted for the chanting of dirges, these tombs opened, and from them issued figures draped in black cloth, upon which were painted all the bones of a skeleton, over their arms, breasts,

flanks, and legs; which, what with the white over the black, and the appearing in the distance of some figures carrying torches, with masks that represented a death's head both in front and behind, as well as the neck, not only gave an appearance of the greatest reality, but was also horrible and terrifying to behold. And these figures of the dead, at the sound of certain muffled trumpets, low and mournful in tone, came half out of their tombs, and seating themselves upon them, sang to music full of melancholy that song so celebrated at the present day: 'Dolor, pianto, e penitenzia' . . . as they walked, the whole company sang in unison, with trembling voices, that Psalm of David that is called the Miserere.

This dread spectacle, through its novelty and terror, as I have said, filled the whole city with fear and marvel together . . . Piero, the creator and inventor of the whole, gained consummate praise and commendation for it; and for holding similar festivals, this city has never had an equal. And in those old men who saw it there still remains a vivid memory of it, nor are they ever weary of celebrating this fantastic invention.[9]

Although Vasari admits that he did not attend this carnival procession himself, he knew others who did. He described the parade at length probably because it fit the sometimes terrifying, but captivating, weirdness that he saw as the key to Piero's character and creations. He also intended the passage to convey how Piero's pageant won the enthusiastic notice of Florentines and spurred his being awarded other commissions. The pageant featured singing, an innovation Piero had introduced, of the powerful dirge known as the *Miserere*. The lyrics derive from Psalm 50 (51), attributed to King David, and were closely associated with Girolamo Savonarola, the fire-and-brimstone Dominican preacher

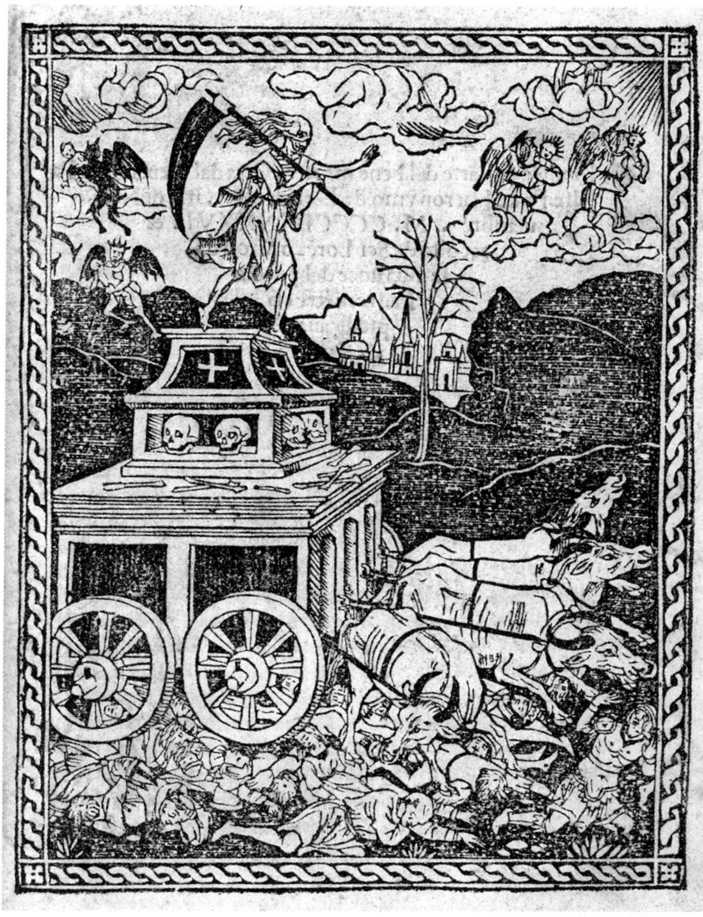

who used its words in several sermons to warn of the end of the
world unless humans repented their sins. Savonarola enjoyed
enormous popularity in Florence until his criticisms of the pope,
clergy and Medici rulers, among others, led to his execution in
1498. The frontispiece (illus. 2) of Savonarola's *Sermon on the Art
of Dying Well* shows a chariot drawn by four oxen and surmounted

2 Frontispiece to Girolamo Savonarola, *Sermon on the Art of Dying Well* (*Predica
del arte del bene morire*), *c.* 1502, woodcut on paper.

by a figure of Death holding a scythe, much like that which Vasari describes as the main feature of Piero's pageant. The oxen are not painted black with white crosses, but they do trample sinners underfoot. No doors open to reveal skeletons, but skulls decorate the chariot beneath the wild figure of Death. The choice of this subject strongly suggests the pageant's link to Savonarolan imagery, and not to the return of the Medici as Vasari later claimed.[10] Whether it means that Piero was influenced by the charismatic preacher, or that the clever artist knew a good subject when he saw one, cannot be said without more evidence.[11]

Despite this triumph of religious art, secular commissions constitute almost 40 per cent of Piero's extant production, which otherwise included religious subjects and portraits. His career extended over almost four decades, but fewer than fifty securely attributed paintings survive. He primarily worked alone, although towards the end of his career Piero taught artists who went on to become famous in sixteenth-century Florence, such as Pontormo and Andrea del Sarto.

Our surprisingly idiosyncratic painter was the son of a blacksmith and born Piero di Lorenzo. At some point in his career he adopted the surname Ubaldini, presumably because of some connection to that famous noble family, and thus became, like Michelangelo Buonarroti, one of the few artists to be associated with the prestige of a surname.[12] He trained in a conventional apprenticeship with a Florentine master named Cosimo Rosselli (1439–1507). Piero became so close with his master that he took the latter's name and was called thereafter Piero di Cosimo. In 1481, at approximately the age of twenty, Piero accompanied Rosselli to Rome, where Pope Sixtus IV had summoned Botticelli, Rosselli and others to decorate the Sistine Chapel with a series of wall scenes of Christ and Moses. Piero's master rightly calculated that expensive materials would most impress the pope: he walked off with the pope's prize for best painting because he lavishly

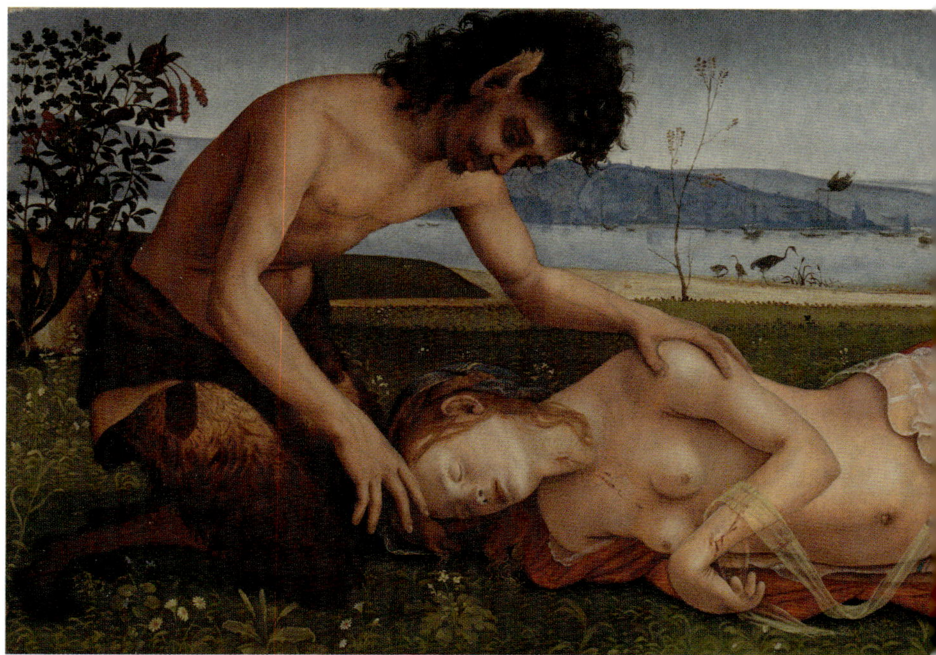

embellished his with gold and lapis lazuli. It was an auspicious beginning for Piero, even though it has proved impossible to identify a specific contribution he may have made to Rosselli's frescoes in Rome. Despite Piero's initiation into fresco painting, he seems to have never again worked in that medium, a favourite choice among his contemporaries.

Piero joined the expected Florentine organizations for painters, the Compagnia di San Luca (Company of St Luke) in 1482 and, later, the Arte dei Medici e Speziali (Guild of Doctors and Apothecaries). In the list of witnesses in two recently discovered documents he is recorded as Piero Laurentii Pieri miniatore, a manuscript painter, although no miniature paintings by his hand have been identified.[13] That background may account for

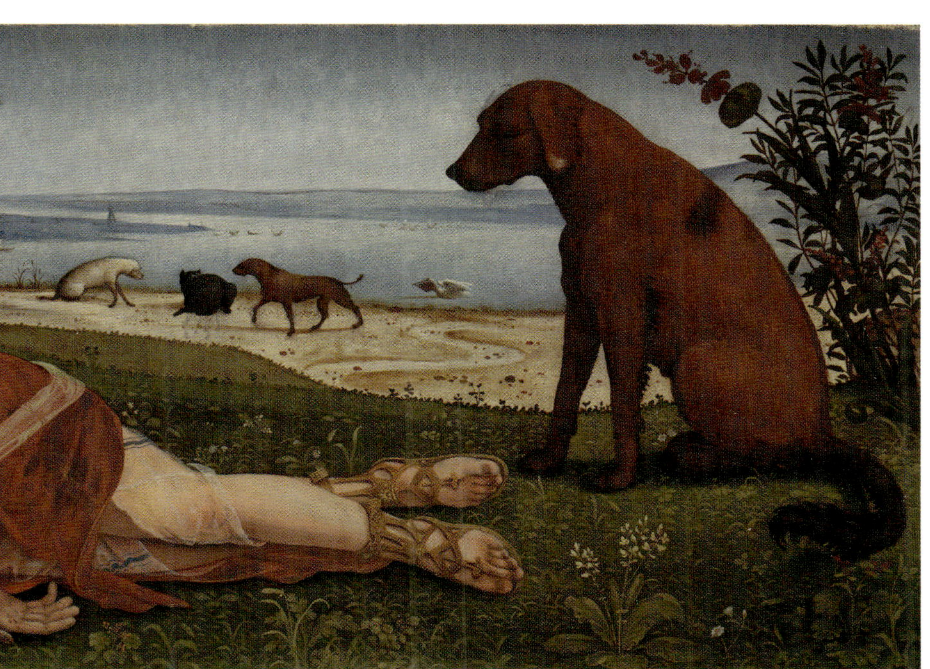

the painstaking details that strike the eye even in his large-scale productions. The exacting eye of a miniaturist has been astutely noted in items such as the lacing of the nymph's sandals in the panel painting *A Satyr Mourning over a Nymph* (*c.* 1495, illus. 3).[14] Many ancient sculptures were fragmentary, and sandaled feet were among the most common survivals, providing Renaissance art- ists with models of Graeco-Roman footwear. Piero's experience as a miniature painter could also have played a role in his acquaint- ance with ancient authors, as in the late fifteenth century their texts were often copied by hand or printed and hand-illustrated. He may have contributed to their embellishment and studied the solutions of his rivals in other illuminated illustrations of Graeco-Roman authors.

3 Piero di Cosimo, *A Satyr Mourning over a Nymph*, *c.* 1495, oil on panel.

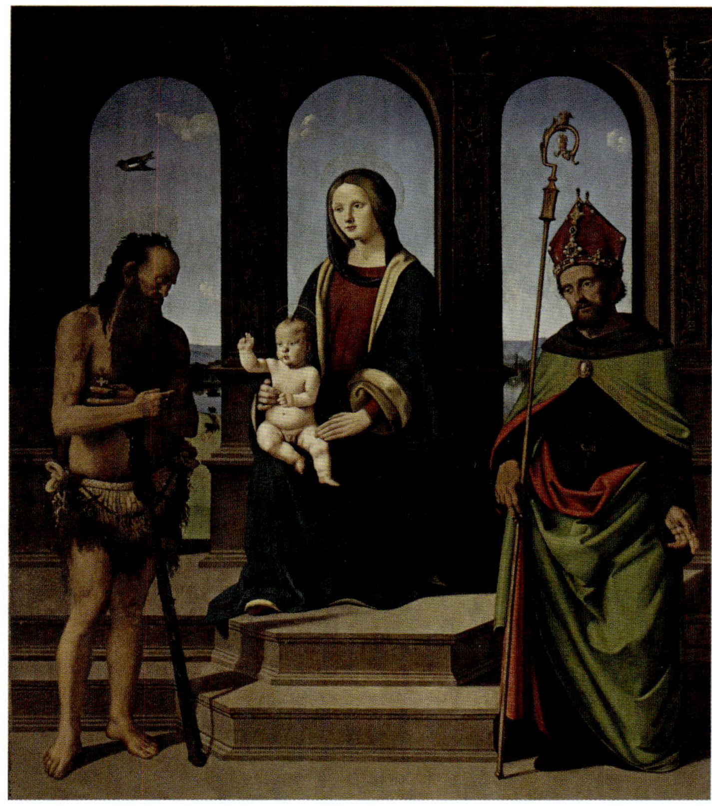

The hypothesis that he was commissioned to decorate new editions of ancient texts may suggest an explanation for Piero's route away from Cosimo Rosselli and towards his domination of the market in domestic panel paintings of Graeco-Roman subjects. Little documentary evidence has been uncovered that otherwise explains Piero's departure from a predictable path and his transformation into a radically different artist from his master.

We can, however, trace this evolution in his paintings. Piero's *Madonna and Child with Sts Onuphrius and Augustine* of about 1480

4 Piero di Cosimo, *Madonna and Child with Sts Onuphrius and Augustine*, c. 1480, oil and tempera on panel.

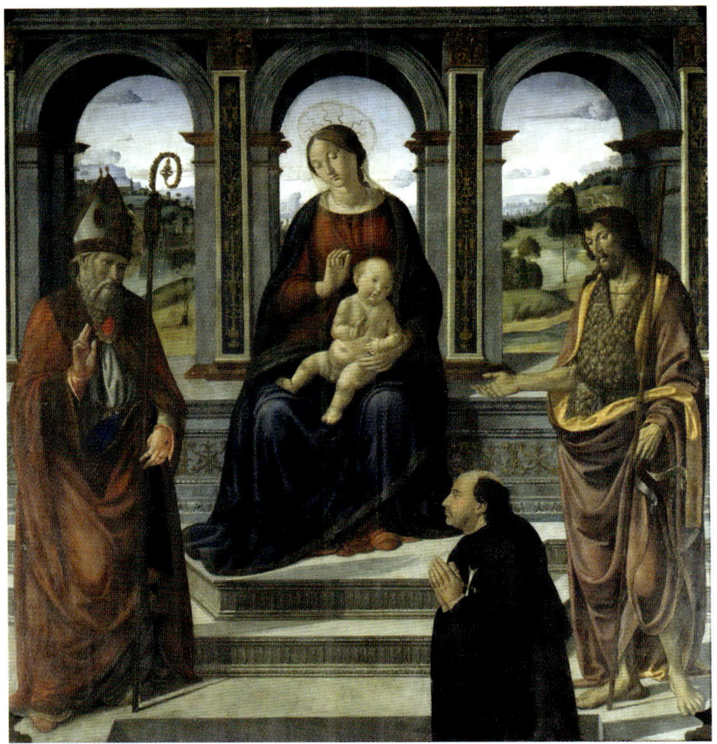

(illus. 4), once at Radda a Chianti, depicts the enthroned Madonna and Child between the hermit saint Onuphrius, standing on the left, and the bishop saint Augustine on the right. Their background is a dark brown, triple-arched arcade with pilasters on high plinths between the arches, the open spaces between leaving each saint outlined against a light-filled skyscape. The light from the outdoor setting casts prominent shadows in the foreground that reinforce the gestures exchanged by Christ and Onuphrius. Many features of the composition relate to a painting by Rosselli (illus. 5) of about 1480, leading to the recently raised question of whether Piero borrowed ideas from Rosselli or vice versa.[15]

5 Cosimo Rosselli, *Madonna and Child with Bishop Saint Eufrosino, John the Baptist and Niccolò Canigiani, c.* 1480, tempera on panel.

Whichever way the influence flowed, the result is that the painting by Piero's master seems, in comparison, woodenly symmetrical and lacking in luminosity and focus. Rosselli diminished the holy figures' importance by emphasizing the decorative detail and contrasting colours of his painting's architectural backdrop, whereas Piero's version, with its vibrant blue sky, monochrome background architecture and emphatically cast shadows, imparts more energy to the composition and directs attention to the Virgin and Child and the saints who venerate them. Although both compositions are similar, Piero's is much more dynamic and engaging.

Primary sources about Piero are scarce and unreliable, offering little information as to his development. Vasari is the sole significant one, and he wrote his first biography of Piero almost thirty years after the artist died. Aware of the lack of primary material, he apparently embroidered his account and invented the outlandish tales that underscored Piero's strange behaviour and came to be always associated with him. It is Vasari who contended that Piero simplified his existence by living exclusively on hard-boiled eggs cooked in batches of fifty in the water in which he had prepared glue. According to Vasari, Piero was often lost in daydreaming, oblivious to the world around him, and let everything in his garden grow wild to match his own inner state.[16] The historian decried Piero's eccentricities and pinpointed them as the cause of his not having achieved the reputation he deserved. Vasari, who knew well at least one of Piero's students, is the source of most of our basic information about the artist, such as his teacher, patrons and commissions, and so we necessarily depend on his account. We must do so with caution, however, given his bent for blending truth and fanciful fiction.

Despite his clear misgivings about Piero, Vasari named him a founder of the last and perfect phase of Italian art, what is now often called the High Renaissance, an epoch identified with such masters as Leonardo, Raphael, Michelangelo and Titian. Vasari conceded that Piero created a series of well-received standard subjects, including altarpieces, private devotional paintings, portraits, mythologies and legends. He acknowledged that Florence's leading families offered him patronage and collected his paintings, a pattern that continued in Vasari's day, fifty years later. The biographer himself owned one of them. He recorded that Piero was never hired by the Medici, Florence's ruling family, but that he gave an image he created of a marine monster to Giuliano de' Medici (1478–1516), a scion of the family, perhaps hoping for commissions that never materialized. The creature was said to be so convincing in its strangeness that it surpassed nature, much like its counterpart in Piero's *Perseus Liberating Andromeda* (*c.* 1510–13, illus. 6; detail, illus. 1). Vasari furthermore listed the prominent Florentine churches in which Piero's altarpieces stood and recorded that, in 1504, he served on the committee debating the placement of Michelangelo's *David*. These are all telling markers of prestige.

Less convincing is Vasari's claim that Leonardo influenced Piero to switch from tempera painting (mineral pigments bound

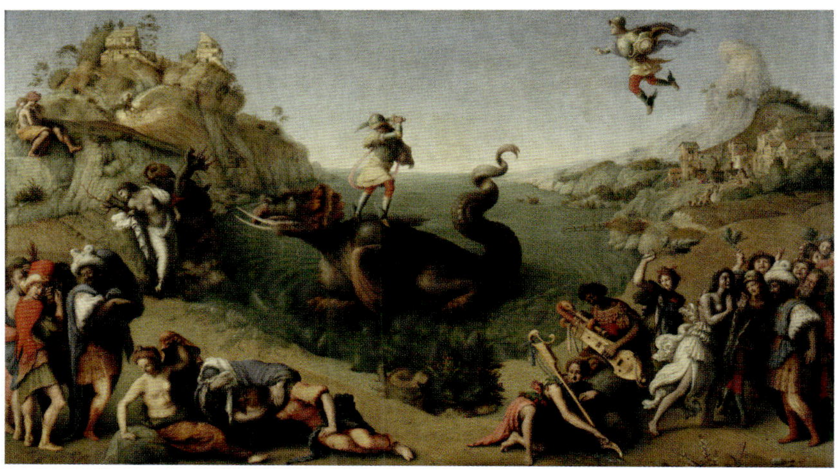

6 Piero di Cosimo, *Perseus Liberating Andromeda*, *c.* 1510–13, oil on panel.

with egg) to oil.[17] That change in medium happened widely in Italian painting in the last quarter of the fifteenth century and is more reasonably tied to the northern artists living in Florence teaching the Italians, as will be developed below. Vasari may have manufactured the connection to link Piero to the more famous artist, although, as we shall see, there are many instances he could have developed to convey Leonardo's impact on Piero.

How do we reconcile Piero's record of accomplishment with Vasari's reports of Piero's self-defeating actions? One way this book approaches Vasari's testimony is by recognizing that to a large extent he was writing historical fiction. He seems to have been informed about Piero indirectly, so his biography provides what should be counted as valuable information when it seems reasonable or can be corroborated by documents. However, when the historian lacked data, he derived his interpretation of the artist from the subjects and details of his paintings. Vasari also turned to earlier famous authors like the Roman Pliny the Elder (23–79 CE) and borrowed what he considered to be appropriate anecdotes about Greek artists to describe Piero and his other subjects. Ferreting out the inspiration for Vasari's fabrication of Piero's life in Pliny and other ancient authors is an important goal of this book. No less significant will be sifting the residue of substantiated biographical information to assess the version of Piero's life that pertains to him.

Finally, how do we square the fact that Piero, who is documented as having died without a book in his possession, created impressively learned interpretations? These themes were usually derived from ancient Greek and Roman mythologies, poetry and legends, some of them only recently recovered. His paintings bristle with relevant narrative details that cry for our attention by their (sometimes awkward) prominence and exactitude. Only occasionally were the sources filtered through more popularly known modern texts, such as those by Giovanni Boccaccio

(1313–1375). Did Piero invent his paintings from verbal accounts of written sources provided by his patrons or their literary colleagues? Did they hire him, delighted by the imaginative leap he could make between the arts? Or did he depend on earlier visual interpretations by other painters or print artists, and to what extent?

This book is organized according to the type of commission – whether mythologies, legends, portraits, religious altarpieces or small devotional paintings. Although both mythologies and legends tend to derive from sources in Graeco-Roman literature and to be commissioned for domestic settings, they sometimes result in different types of compositional and technical solutions. With that in mind, they have been evaluated separately, but discussion of each category is in roughly chronological order, for clarity's sake. Most of Piero's paintings are not precisely dated and his artistic style does not develop predictably. So, with a focus more on content than on style, each chapter considers three to six paintings, allowing for a careful assessment of what is conventional or not about Piero's interpretations.

ONE
Mythologies

Piero painted, for the elder Filippo Strozzi, a picture
with little figures of Perseus delivering Andromeda
from the Monster . . . Piero never made a more lovely
or more highly finished picture than this one, seeing
that it is not possible to find a more bizarre or more
fantastic sea-monster.

GIORGIO VASARI, *Lives*

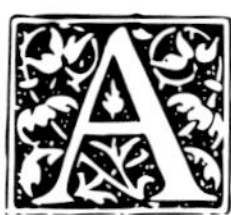s Vasari indicates, Piero di Cosimo's mythological
paintings for private residences were prized in his day
for their fantasy and facture. Along with legendary
scenes, they were the most popular genres in which he worked.
It is easy to see why: he took subjects like time-honoured
Graeco-Roman myths or newly discovered secular writings and
responded to them with verve and originality. He always added
an innovative, captivating twist of subject or interpretation.

The six paintings discussed in this chapter were all probably
intended as *spalliere*. Here Piero invented diverting and playful
interpretations of ancient myths whose mood seems to have
mitigated the more typical dour moral admonitions of this type
of painting and pleased patrons with their wit and fantasy. The
legends, to be discussed in the following chapter, usually depicted
scenes drawn from Graeco-Roman philosophy and literature.

The first two to be considered here are a pair of scenes regarding Vulcan. Whether they were originally part of a larger group is an open question. The seminal art historians Erwin Panofsky and Carlo Gamba first connected them with *A Hunting Scene* (*c.* 1485–1500, illus. 7), *The Return from the Hunt* (*c.* 1485–1500, illus. 9) and *The Forest Fire* (*c.* 1495–1505, illus. 10). These three scenes portray the role of fire in the earliest history of humans. Gamba argued that the five paintings were part of a more extensive group including *The Battle of the Lapiths and Centaurs* (*c.* 1500–1510, illus. 8) and the pair of *Bacchanals*, dated circa 1500, made for the Palazzo Vespucci, not discussed here. Gamba based his idea on unarticulated connections he perceived to the Roman poet Ovid. The sole source, Vasari, offered few clues in his unspecific, but enthusiastic, identification as bacchanalian the scenes that Piero painted for Giovanni Vespucci. Vasari provided even less help about the content of a second cycle painted for Francesco del Pugliese, calling it full of small figures and fantastic things drawn from fables.[1]

Panofsky's hypothetical group was restricted to the first five mentioned above, plus a lost scene of Venus, Mars and Vulcan mentioned by Vasari.[2] His theory has proved the more influential. Panofsky's limited series seems more reasonable because the paintings' themes are more connected to the themes of fire in civilization's origins, and he, unlike Gamba, provides a lengthy, erudite literary explanation underpinning his argument. The Vulcan scenes, according to Panofsky, represent stages of more advanced civilization, in which men worked metal, and hence they complete a series that began with the earliest beast-like humans. He cites Boccaccio's identification in his *De genealogia deorum gentilium* (On the Genealogy of the Pagan Gods, 1360–74) of Vulcan as the founder of human civilization, since he enabled the purposeful keeping alive of fire, which made possible cooking, metalworking and other valuable skills (XII, 70). Boccaccio had

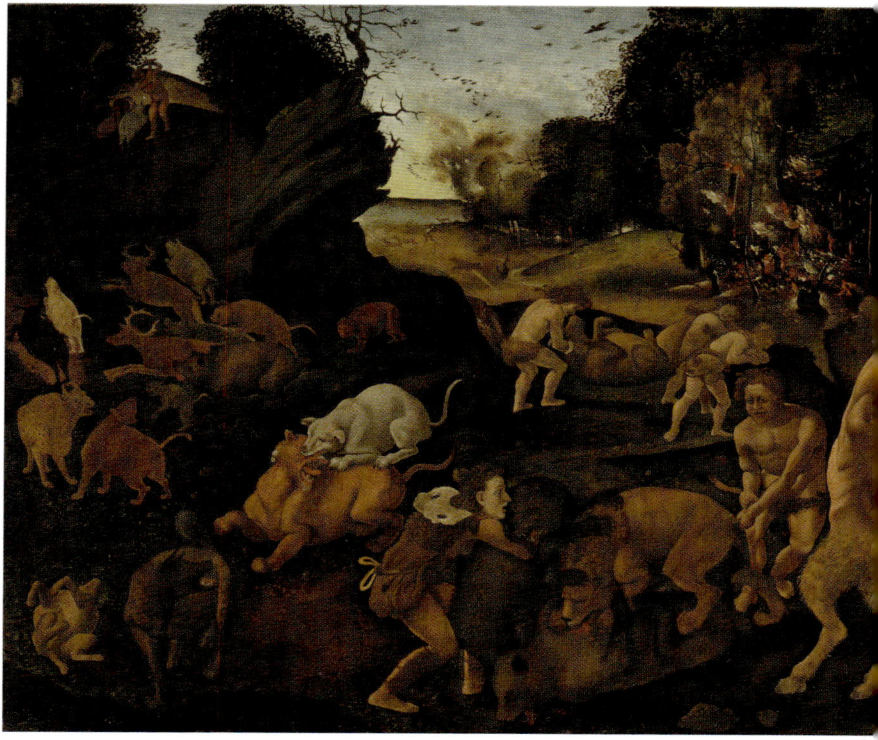

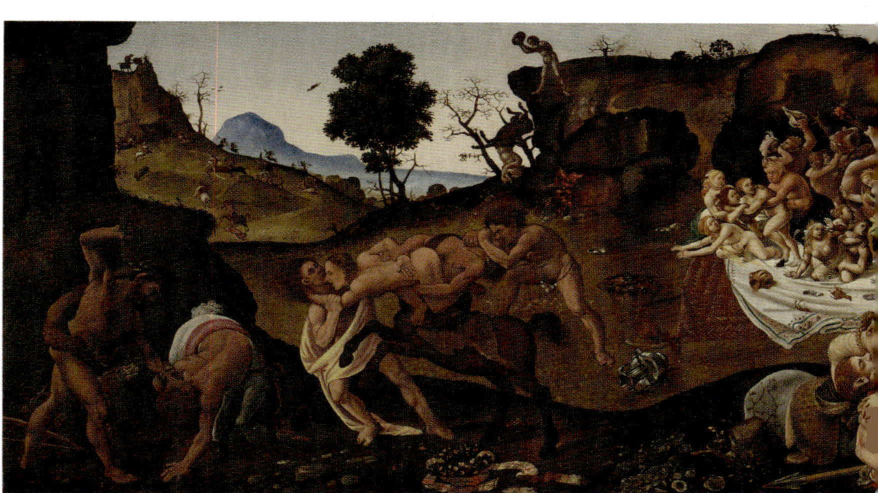

above: 7 Piero di Cosimo, *A Hunting Scene*, c. 1485–1500, oil and tempera on panel.
8 Piero di Cosimo, *The Battle of the Lapiths and Centaurs*, c. 1500–1510, oil on panel.

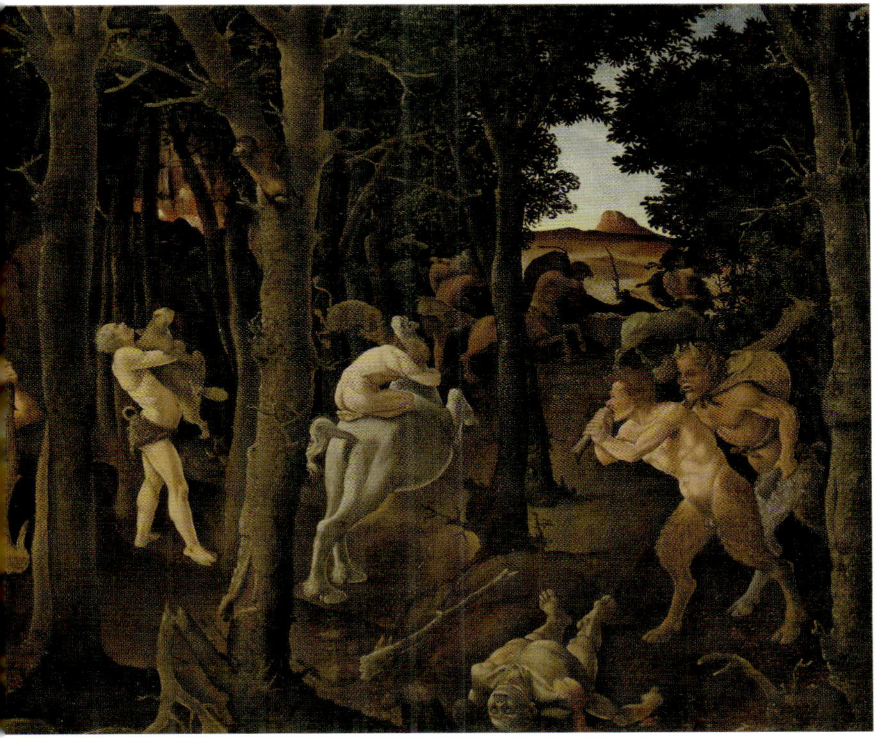

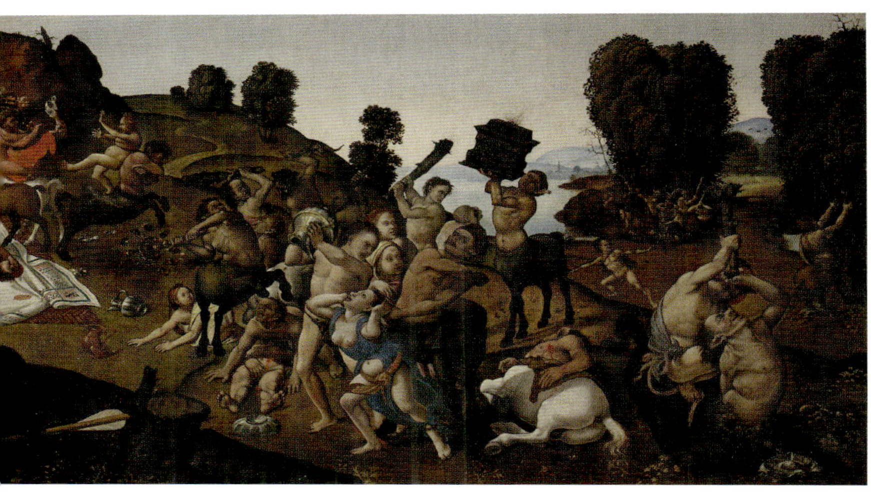

overleaf: 9 Piero di Cosimo, *The Return from the Hunt*, c. 1485–1500,
oil and tempera on panel, transferred onto a Masonite support.
10 Piero di Cosimo, *The Forest Fire*, c. 1495–1505, oil on panel.

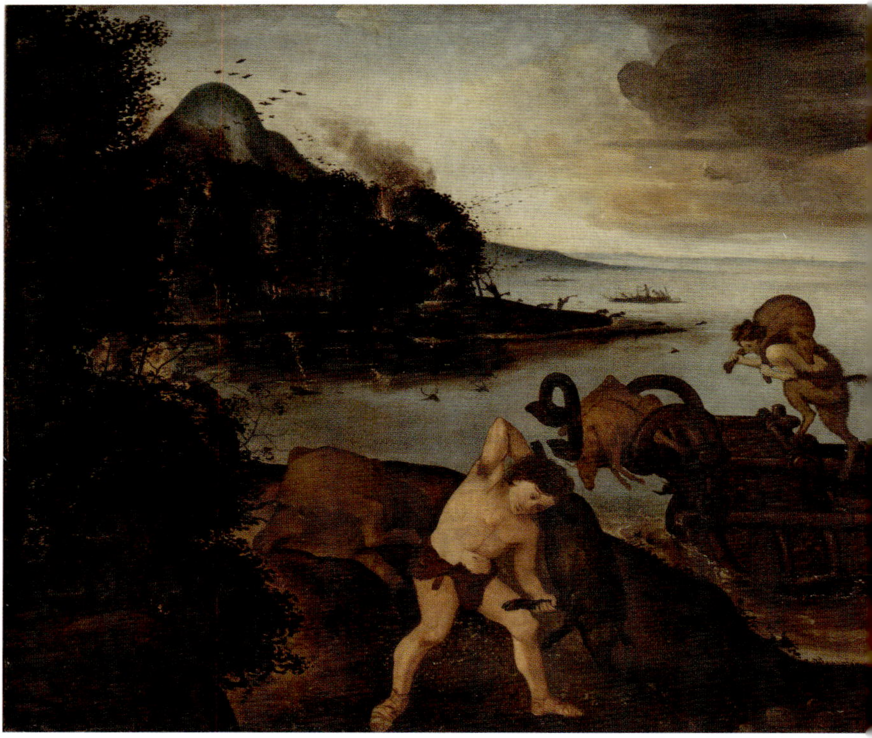

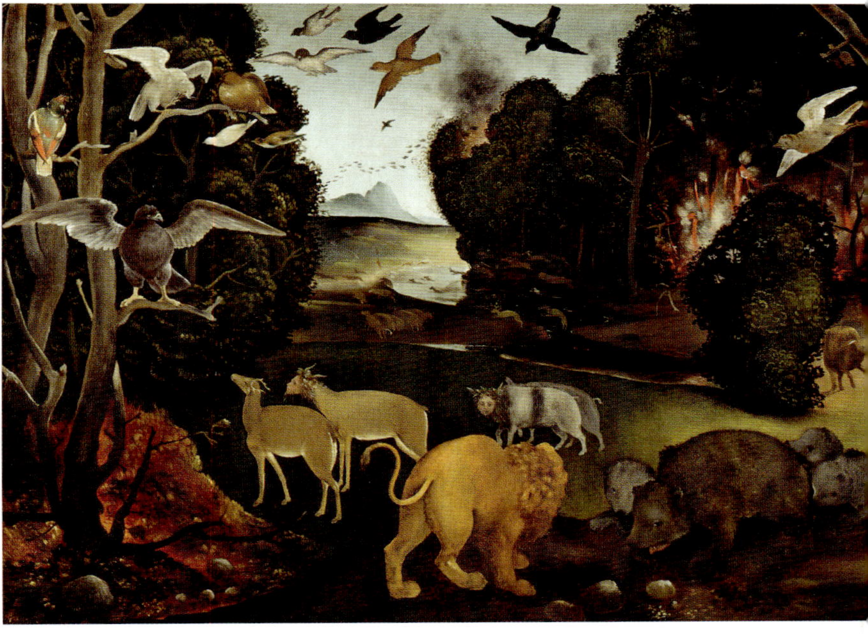

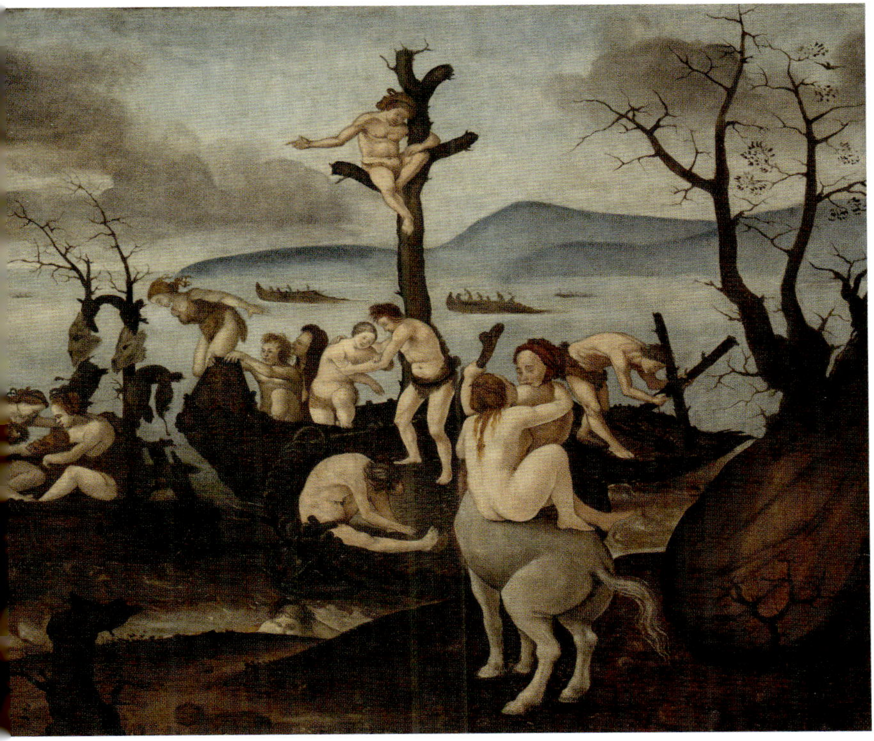

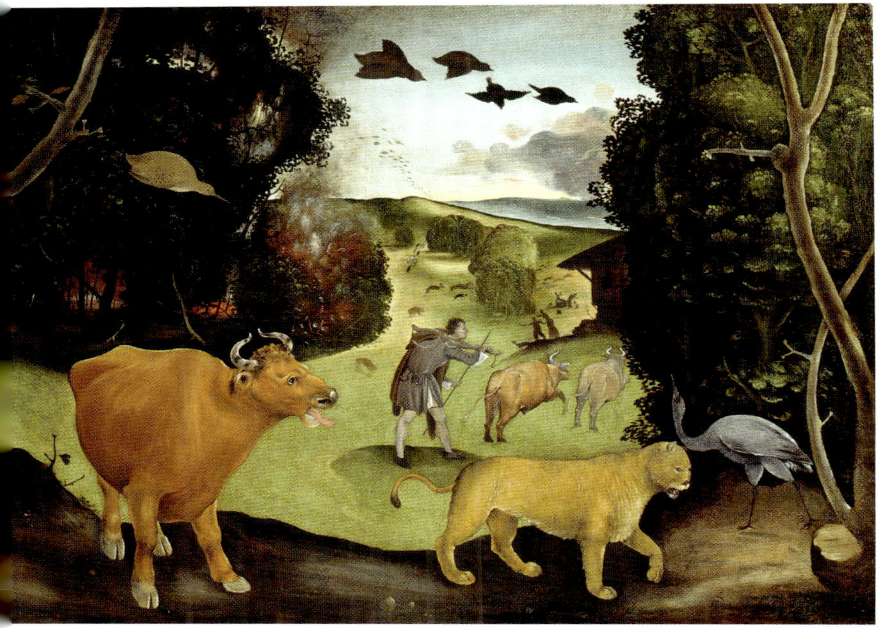

in turn drawn on the description by Vitruvius in *De architectura* (On Architecture, *c.* 30–20 BCE) of how earliest man had learned the advantages of fire through spontaneous lightning strikes.[3] Historians are still arguing in favour of and against Gamba's and Panofsky's conclusions about combining these paintings into a series. Most no longer accept their arguments. For example, Claudia Cieri Via contends that *The Forest Fire* panel should be excluded, considering it instead part of a commission by another patron who was impressed by the original series. She substitutes *The Battle of the Lapiths and Centaurs* and the *Construction of a Building* (illus. 11) of circa 1514–18.[4] Whereas Gamba's and Panofsky's theories are based on similarities in the paintings' subject-matter, most of the organizers of the exhibition of Piero at the Uffizi in 2015 argued in favour of an original grouping comprising the Vulcan panels as well as *A Hunting Scene, Return from the Hunt, Forest Fire, Battle of the Lapiths and Centaurs* and *Construction of a Building*. In doing so, they considered the relation of the paintings' themes to the evolution of civilization but also the similarly sized humans and animals, and the comparable compositional layouts.[5]

Rather than delving into that knotty and unresolved issue, I shall focus first on the two narratives, which concern Vulcan and Aeolus on the Greek island of Lemnos. Vasari makes an

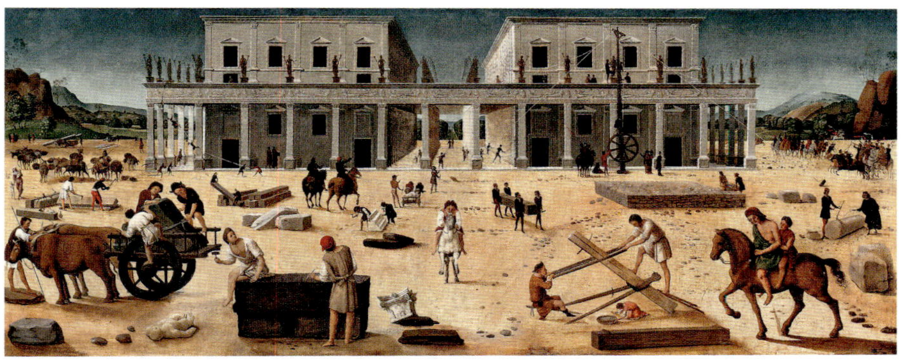

11 Piero di Cosimo, *Construction of a Building*, c. 1514–18?, oil on wood.

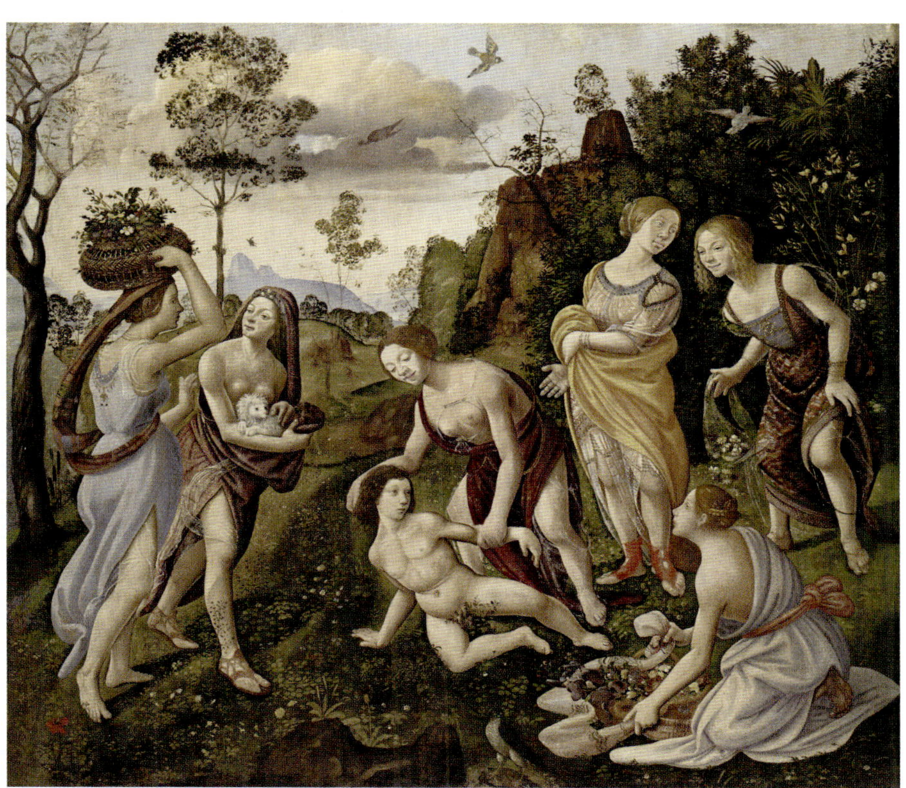

ambiguous reference to a painting of Vulcan intended for the
Pugliese family.[6] Francesco del Pugliese and his uncle Piero del
Pugliese shared a common residence and were known patrons
of the artist, so Vasari's identification has some corroboration.
The Finding of Vulcan on Lemnos (illus. 12) and its companion, *Vulcan
and Aeolus* (illus. 13), which is sometimes called *The Return of New
Life to Lemnos*, were probably executed between 1490 and 1500.
Both are outliers among Piero's mythological depictions in several
ways. They were executed in egg tempera and oil on canvas, an
unusual support for *spalliere*, which were predominantly on panel.

12 Piero di Cosimo, *The Finding of Vulcan on Lemnos*, 1490–1500, oil and tempera
on canvas.

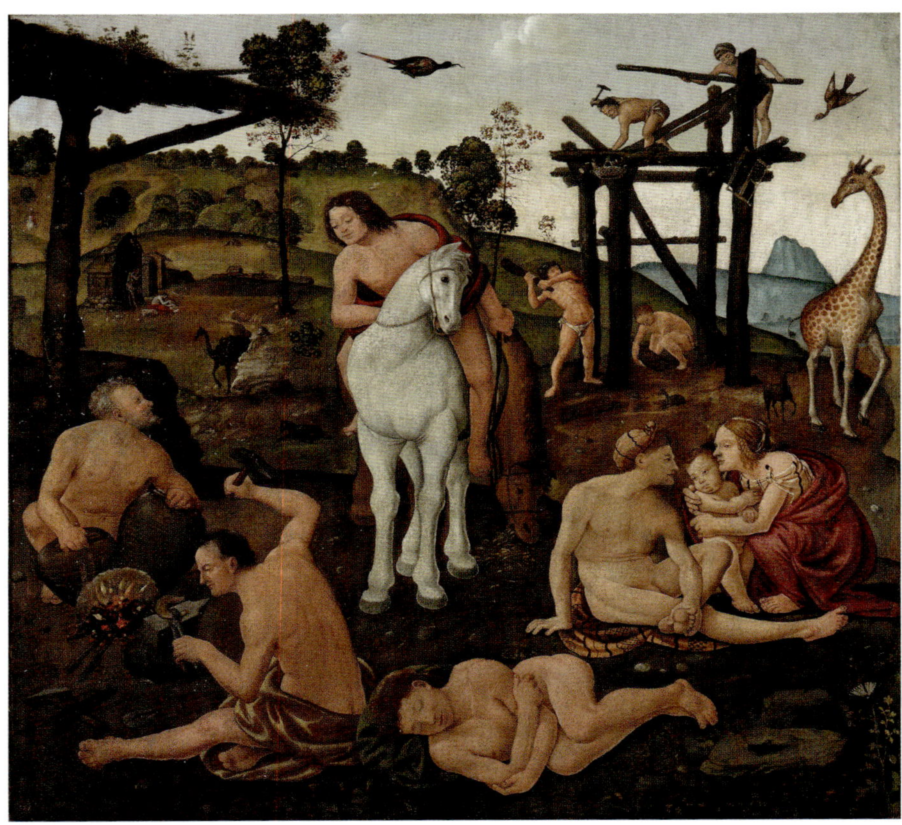

They have a nearly square format, unlike the typical horizontal arrangement (perhaps because they were placed over the room's doors). Such a placement – more distant from viewers' eyes – would also account for the figures' larger size, their placement in the foreground and the narrative focus on a single scene in *The Finding of Vulcan on Lemnos*, all so different from most *spalliere*. The *Vulcan and Aeolus* has large figures, with most of them positioned in the foreground, but lacks a sequential narrative. This is very unusual in this sort of domestic decoration.

13 Piero di Cosimo, *Vulcan and Aeolus*, or *The Return of New Life to Lemnos*, 1490–1500, oil and tempera on canvas.

The two paintings are not based even loosely on a standard source such as the *Metamorphoses* by the Roman poet Ovid (43 BCE–17 CE). On the contrary, there seems to have been no well-known literary origin for these episodes in the Renaissance, and their visual depictions are virtually unprecedented. The originality of subject-matter suggests that a learned literary adviser proposed the combination of narratives and Piero brought them to visual life. They may have constituted a pair or originally been part of a series of three related paintings about Vulcan and Jason, the leader of the Argonauts, connected by their experiences on the island of Lemnos.[7] Historians, beginning with Panofsky, have even argued that they were intended to be part of a larger series of five paintings about fire and the origins of civilization, as we have seen. These complexities of subject-matter immediately introduce us to recurring interrelated problems in studying Piero's paintings: their topics can be unusual, even unprecedented, and his patrons' motivations in asking for them unknown. Piero had few or no artistic models from which to develop his visualizations of the texts, and there is no evidence that he read about them himself. The judgement that he could not or did not read much (and certainly not in Latin, the language in which many Graeco-Roman texts were transmitted) seems corroborated by the fact that he left no library on his death. In addition, Piero turned to a public scribe to prepare his tax declaration in 1498, raising the possibility that he could not write.[8] Part of his genius seems to have been in leaping between media. Piero rendered into paint verbal summaries of Greek and Latin literature conveyed to him by learned figures. Patrons chose him as a painter because he could skilfully and imaginatively visualize subjects. They provided the 'what'.

In the case of the paintings about Vulcan, there seems to have been another series on the same subject. Vasari alludes to such a cycle by Domenico Ghirlandaio (1449–1494), which is today lost but was once in Lorenzo de' Medici's villa at Spedaletto.[9] Vasari briefly describes one of the murals as representing the *Forge of Vulcan*, so it was a generally similar scene to Piero's *Vulcan and Aeolus*. According to Vasari, Ghirlandaio's version of the scene included many nude figures hammering to create thunderbolts for Jove and was roughly contemporary with Piero's paintings, so it was unlikely to have been a precedent.[10] *The Finding of Vulcan on Lemnos* depicts Vulcan's awkward landing on earth after being kicked out of Olympus for the second time, on this occasion by his father, Jupiter, in anger at Vulcan's mother, his wife. The light-filled opening in the middle of the clouds above alludes to his erstwhile heavenly home, and the twisted splay of Vulcan's legs suggests their lame state. Nymphs, who had been gathering flowers, regroup around Vulcan and try to comfort him. This group of large-scale characters set in a flower-filled landscape recalls the *Primavera* by Botticelli (illus. 14), a contemporary whom Piero must have known since their days working together on the Sistine Chapel wall paintings. Comparison with Botticelli's painting shows that, while Piero kept up with his peer's inventions,

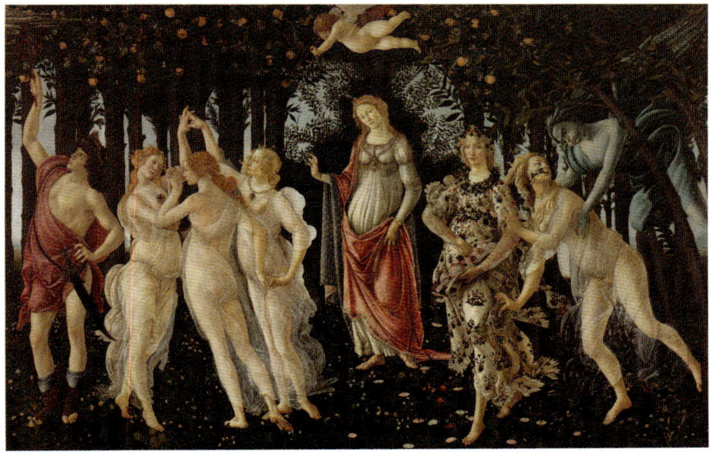

14 Sandro Botticelli, *Primavera*, c. 1480, tempera on panel.

he chose not to imitate Botticelli's elongated and idealized figures. The falcon, the symbol of the Strozzi family, prominently posed in the centre foreground, has led to the hypothesis that a member of that clan commissioned it, but there is no confirmation of the theory.

The two prominent figures in the lower left foreground lead to the painting usually being called *Vulcan and Aeolus*. Vulcan is taking on his role as a blacksmith by forging a horseshoe while a helper, who could be Aeolus, a god of wind who reigned over the island site of Vulcan's workshop, manoeuvres the bellows. The force of his air currents likely powered the movement of the bellows. The forge is on the ground, which is apparently a more comfortable position for the crippled Vulcan. A man on horseback behind them holds a second horse on a tether, awaiting Vulcan's completion of the shoe. It is a composition like no other in the Renaissance. The meanings of the approximately one dozen additional figures and the juxtaposition of their disjointed episodes prove puzzling, even disconcerting.

The most recent explanation is that the scene concerns an arcane tale by Philostratus (*c.* 170–247 CE) about Lemnos, the island of his birthplace. The text was known to Renaissance intellectuals and provides a telling indication of the patrons and thinkers who influenced Piero di Cosimo. Philostratus' *Heroïkos* (On Heroes) recounted how life returned to the island after a yearly ritual in which its women extinguished all fire there for nine days and sacrificed offerings for the dead to the gods. They were atoning for their misdeeds to the men of Lemnos. Following that purification, they brought back fire, families were reconstituted and new homes constructed. The legend seems to explain the otherwise startling nude boy curled up on the ground in foetal position, a haunting emblem of the return of life. The figures of a woman holding a baby and talking to a man could symbolize the revitalization of family life. In the background, four men in loincloths bang together the wood and metal frame for a house as an indication of new construction under way. In this reading, Vulcan and Aeolus working the forge appear in their roles as patrons of craftsmen rebuilding the island. The composition is not tightly unified, perhaps because the episodes are neither sequential nor causally related. All are simultaneous consequences of the yearly cleansing. Piero's method of visualizing this striking story is as sophisticated and unusual as its literary source. The stories may have held moral messages suitable for their domestic setting. The dangers of women placing themselves before their vows to husbands and family are countered by the warnings to men not to ignore their wives.[11]

Many visually delightful birds and animals inhabit both scenes. The most eye-catching is the giraffe loping forwards from the background of the *Vulcan and Aeolus* with a tiny calf alongside her. Two other calves, one laden with bags and emerging from an improbably short grotto, the other reclining, are spotted within the landscape. Such animals are unlikely finds on a Greek island. Their inclusion reflects instead the contemporary fascination felt in Florence with the giraffe that Qaitbay, the Mamluk Sultan of Egypt, had given in 1487 to the city's ruler, Lorenzo de' Medici. We can deduce therefore that the painting must date after 1487. The gifted giraffe had no offspring, so Piero had never seen a giraffe calf and inaccurately coloured it a uniform brown. Another notable detail from nature is the single outsized locust in the foreground.[12] This author earlier identified it as a cricket, a related insect from the Orthoptera order.[13] Pliny had mentioned locust invasions in Lemnos, so, on one level, the insect may serve to identify the island.[14] One locust is not a swarm, and Pliny noted the different means of trapping locust swarms in several locations, not just Lemnos, so it is likely to have another meaning (*Natural History*, XI, 105–6). It seems to pun on the name of 'cricket' in Latin, *gryllus* (in Italian, *grillo*), which Pliny, in his widely circulated *Natural History*, used to refer to the praiseworthy ancient Greek painters who interpreted small-scale secular subjects with humour, whimsy and imagination.[15] It is easy to see why Piero might have felt he merited such a flattering veiled reference.[16]

Venus, Mars and Cupid (c. 1495–1505, illus. 15) and *The Battle of the Lapiths and Centaurs* (see illus. 8) represent variants on well-known subjects by Botticelli and Michelangelo and make clear that Piero paid attention to his famous contemporaries. In the case of the *Venus, Mars and Cupid*, Botticelli's painting of *Venus and Mars* (c. 1485, illus. 16) is thought to be about ten years earlier, which suggests that Piero was deliberately riffing on Botticelli's subject of the post-coital Venus and Mars. Both artists created long, rectangular wooden panels whose probable function was as *spalliere*. The erotic themes betray their likely origin as wedding gifts meant to inspire lovemaking and guarantee future generations.

Botticelli's and Piero's very similar paintings are early versions of this subject not represented before 1450 but which became popular in the seventeenth century.[17] Piero seems clearly influenced by Botticelli, but both works are unusual depictions in the fifteenth century of the illicit love affair between Mars and Venus. They relate in a significant way to the *De rerum natura* (On the Nature of Things) by Lucretius (c. 100–50 BCE), a lengthy philosophical poem that was recovered in Florence only in the fifteenth century. The poet opens his verses with a hymn to Venus: 'Life-stirring Venus . . . you make all things beneath the dome/ Of sliding constellations teem, you throng the fruited earth/ And the ship-freighted sea – for every species comes to birth/ Conceived through you' (1, 1–5). The hymn's last lines describe the beneficial effects of her sexual unions with Mars:

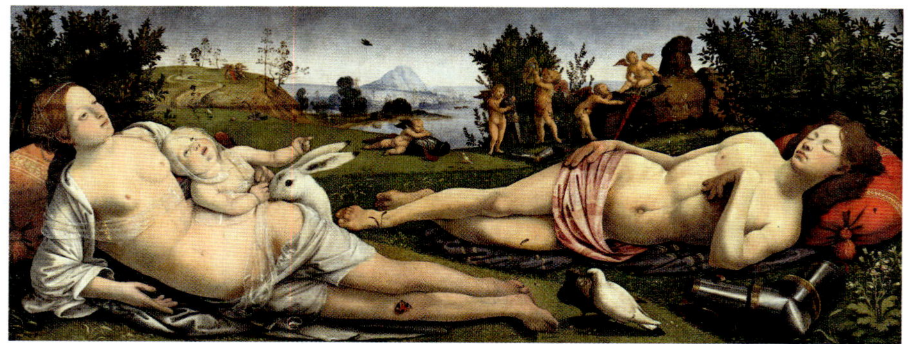

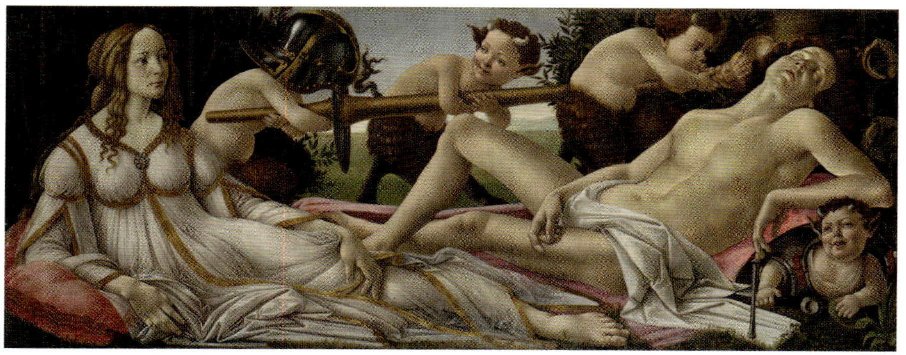

Holy One . . .
Make the mad machinery of war drift off to sleep.
For only you can favour mortal men with peace, since
    Mars,
Mighty in Arms, who oversees the wicked works of wars,
Conquered by Love's everlasting wound, so often lies
Upon your lap, and gazing upwards, feasts his greedy eyes
On love, his mouth agape at you, Famed Goddess . . .
Lady, sweet-talk him with honeyed speech,
Pleading for a quiet peace for Romans . . .
(I, 29–40)[18]

15 Piero di Cosimo, *Venus, Mars and Cupid*, c. 1495–1505, oil on panel.
16 Sandro Botticelli, *Venus and Mars*, c. 1485, oil and tempera on panel.

Lucretius went beyond the Neoplatonic argument current in late fifteenth-century thought that the universe could thrive in fruitfulness and harmony only when Venus, or love, prevailed over Mars, or strife.[19] An illuminated Renaissance manuscript of the *De rerum natura* in the Vatican Library displays a frontispiece representing the opening hymn to Venus.[20] A fully clad Mars reclines across the lap of an equally covered-up Venus.[21] In contrast, Piero and Botticelli represent the deities in a more frankly sexual way. They recline on the foreground grass and face each other. Both show Mars nearly nude and sound asleep while Venus watches him. The confrontation of the comatose god of war and the more alert goddess of love in both paintings conveys the victory of love. Piero's rendition of Venus is very unlike Botticelli's: his Venus reclines with an awkward twist of the torso, and her high, small breasts and wide lower body are far from the Graeco-Roman idealized standard that Botticelli imitates. Piero's lovers, unlike Botticelli's, are strangely disconnected: their bodies do not touch in any way. Furthermore, Piero is more explicit than Botticelli and depicts Venus barely covered by drapery and luxuriating in pleasurable sexual somnolence. The gold-threaded, diaphanous girdle below her breasts, the *strophion* that was untied by the groom on the wedding night in ancient Greece, is undone and loosely wound around Cupid's head and body. Mars, not her husband, Vulcan, has untied it.[22] Piero converts the baby satyrs playing with Mars' armour in Botticelli's version into putti and relegates them to the middle-ground. Piero may have taken this vignette directly from Botticelli's painting or from the description of a similar scene involving Alexander the Great and Roxana by the ancient painter Aetion and displayed at the Olympic games. The renown of the painting was recounted in the second-century Roman poem *Herodotus* by Lucian (*c.* 125–after 180 CE), which was well known in the Renaissance. Piero's idea to turn to the poem could have come from his patron verbally. In both paintings, Mars has virtually passed out after his and Venus' lovemaking and is blissfully unaware of his armour's potential loss: love conquers war.

Comparison with Botticelli also underscores the originality of Piero's interpretation, which overloads the panel with iconographic details such as the moth on Venus' knee, the pair of doves, and Cupid's bared-teeth expression as his eyes roll up to his mother and he points to Mars' cuirass, stolen by another cupid in the middle-ground; the latter is a sign of the god of war's undefended state. Piero's careful examination of the natural world is clear in the 'rabbit's' long, prominent ears with black fur insides, which reveal that this is no rabbit, the traditional symbol of fruitfulness, but a hare (which reproduces equally rapidly). The outsize animal may visualize a well-known licentious pun on *cuniculus*, the animal's Latin name, and *cunnus*, Latin for the female sex organ, to suggest the couple's large sexual appetites.[23] Such vignettes of ribald humour embedded in a learned literary painting offered levity and delight amid edification.

The brown and white rock doves in the foreground, cooing and billing each other, echo in avian terms the love of Venus and Mars.[24] On the other hand, the colourful moth on Venus' knee is readily identifiable as a Jersey tiger moth. Widely known as having a foul taste if ingested, the moth may be intended to warn the painting's audience against the dangers of an illicit love such as that of Mars and Venus.[25] Like the loosened *strophion*, it underscores the adultery that led to this sexual pleasure. Vasari betrays his admiration for Piero in this case: he admits that he owned the *Venus, Mars and Cupid*, which he kept in his home because it pleased him so much.[26]

The Battle of the Lapiths and Centaurs is another original interpretation of a famous Graeco-Roman literary subject. It situates a grieving female centaur cradling her dying lover in her arms at the centre foreground of the battle turmoil, in what seems a unique addition to a frequently depicted artistic theme. They are the centauress Hylonome, the beloved wife of the centaur Cyllarus, whom she adored and followed everywhere, even into battle. Piero increases the pathos of this pitiful pair by isolating them atop a dark hillock away from the lighter ground of the battle scenes. Her face touches his, a poignant intimacy that Piero likely borrowed from paintings of the mourning of Christ, for example Botticelli's *Lamentation* (*c.* 1490–92), in which the Magdalene presses her living cheek against Christ's dead one.[27] Piero makes the vignette of Hylonome and Cyllarus, which is not stressed by Ovid, a centrepiece to the oft-depicted tale of the Lapiths and centaurs from his *Metamorphoses* (XII, 393–428). Focus was usually exclusively on the ferocious battle that ensued when unruly, drunken centaurs invited to a Lapith wedding tried to abduct Lapith females. Piero features the violent consequences but, surprisingly, expresses unusual sympathy for the brawling troublemakers who caused the fracas and stresses the gentle side of their nature. He chose to highlight them compassionately, rather than the Lapiths, the wronged humans with whom he might have been expected to side. It has been argued that the emphasis on the loving, tragic couple again reveals the influence of Lucretius, and that Piero or his adviser is aiming to convey that Ovid's version of the myth has absorbed Lucretius' *De rerum natura*.[28] Ovid, however, engaged critically with Lucretius' views, particularly challenging his argument that centaurs did not exist, although he followed Lucretius' other theories. Lucretius had recounted how humans progressed from random, short-lived couplings to organized, enduring partnerships akin to marriage and family. For Lucretius, and other writers like Ovid who agreed with him on this point, this was important because the pairing of humans and the establishment of family structures were a bedrock of human civilization. Ovid changed the protagonists to centaurs and displayed them as a devoted couple, which enacts the potential that Lucretius had argued was a factor exclusive to the development

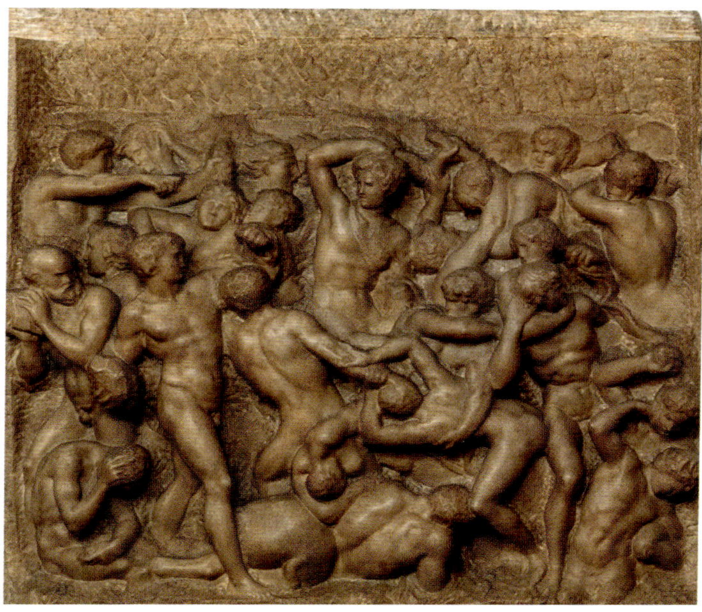

of human civilization.[29] It is on the basis that the panel represents
the later phase of civilization, and of its approximately similar
dimensions, that Cieri Via included it in the series with the
Hunt scenes.

While Michelangelo was a student in the Medici sculpture
garden, where promising carvers were trained under the court
sculptor Bertoldo di Giovanni (*c.* 1420–1491), he had taken on
the subject in a relief sculpture (illus. 17). Michelangelo represented it in a more traditional way than Piero, omitting the tragic
centaur couple. Although Michelangelo's sculpture represents
the battle as a tight group of overlapping warriors condensed
into a compact frieze and Piero separates the combatants into
several groups, the latter had clearly seen the former's depiction.
What drew Piero to the Michelangelo sculpture was the artist's
muscular, twisting warriors posed in many directions and postures.

17 Michelangelo, *Battle of the Lapiths and Centaurs*, *c.* 1492, marble relief.

We can see the results particularly in the left-hand group of Lapiths and centaurs, but they are evident all over Piero's painting. In addition, Michelangelo provided Piero with foreshortened poses to study, as in the figure at the lower right. The assumption of Michelangelo's primacy has been countered with the maverick view that the young sculptor instead depended on Piero, with the art historian Vincenzo Farinella arguing that the painter was, by the early 1490s, a notable artist and Michelangelo a tyro.[30] Piero also looked carefully at the frescoes of the renowned Florentine painter Paolo Uccello (1397–1475). In the Genesis frescoes (1420–25) in the Green Cloister at Santa Maria Novella in Florence, Uccello had painted the harrowing sight of foreshortened bleeding and dead bodies lying on their backs on the ground (illus. 18). Piero poses two Lapiths and one centaur in similar dramatic postures, but his Lapith at the lower right, seen feet first, is most akin to Uccello's.

A Satyr Mourning over a Nymph (see illus. 3) is painted in oil on panel and is shaped in the typical long, horizontal format of a *spalliera*. The low viewpoint of the composition confirms that its original installation was rather high on the wall, either as the backboard to a large chest or bench or at shoulder level in the woodwork. The painting's function and composition with just

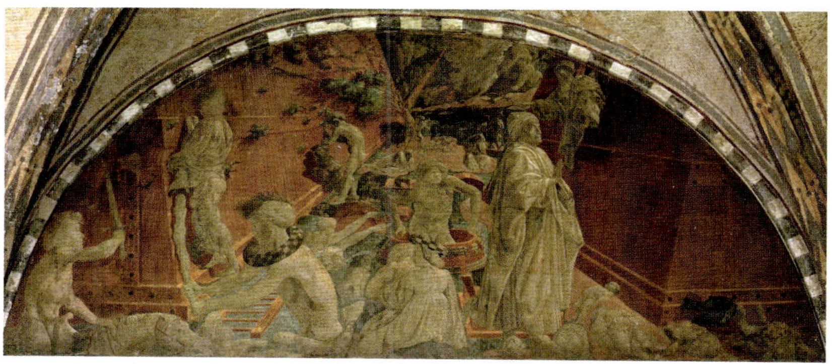

18 Paolo Uccello, *Flood and Waters Subsiding*, c. 1447–8, fresco, Green Cloister, Santa Maria Novella, Florence.

a few large foreground figures relate it to the *Venus, Mars and Cupid*. It has been traditionally identified as representing the story of the nymph Procris and her husband, Cephalus, most famously told by Ovid in the *Metamorphoses* (VII, 665–875). The tale was taken up by several other ancient authors, as well as by Ovid in other writings. If that tale is Piero's subject, it illustrates the cascading disasters caused by a lack of marital trust and fidelity, the sort of moralizing scene often chosen for domestic paintings commissioned to celebrate a wedding. Ovid's narrative begins with Cephalus agreeing to a goddess's suggestion that he test his wife's faithfulness. He disguises himself and attempts to seduce her, revealing himself as she begins to yield. To seal a reconciliation, Procris gives Cephalus a magical dog and a lance that never misses its prey. Cephalus afterwards goes out hunting with the dog and spear. Procris grows suspicious that he is unfaithful and follows him into the forest. When Cephalus hears her movements in a nearby thicket, he confuses her for a wild animal and accidentally kills her with his unerring lance. According to Ovid, the remorseful husband is left to cradle the dying Procris in his arms. Piero instead depicts a moribund woman lying on her side with blood spurting from a wound in her neck, trickling from her grazed forearm and smeared on the hand she used to staunch the flow.

Piero introduces many more discrepancies with this tale's literary sources. He omits the lance that never misses its target. And, even more surprising, he also leaves out Cephalus – clearly a necessary protagonist as he mistakenly killed her with that lance. A dog, which is an unusual choice of protagonist in Italian painting of the period, sits close to the nymph's feet. The dog has left behind its playmates in the background to mourn over her dead body with obvious affectionate melancholy, as if willing her to come back to life. It could be the magical hunting dog that Procris gave to her husband. Piero complicates the identity of the figures further by adding a grief-stricken satyr, who supports the nymph's head against his thigh as he crouches and caresses her tenderly. The dejected dog frames the dead woman's feet and mirrors the pose of the satyr at her head; their twinned positions intensify their relation to the dead woman and their shared sorrow. This supplemental character may have been inspired by a late fifteenth-century play staged at Ferrara that included a satyr in love with Procris, who deliberately misleads her into believing that Cephalus has been unfaithful. In this reading, the moment painted by Piero would depict that prior to Cephalus' arrival at his dead wife's body or be a visual epitome of the tragedy, in which Cephalus' dog stands in for him.[31]

This painting exemplifies the tendency of Piero's paintings to depart from orthodox narratives or current interpretations derived from customary sources. At this point it is unclear whether his learned patrons consulted additional literary sources not so far adduced and stimulated Piero's unprecedented interpretations, or whether they set free Piero to follow his own *fantasia* and create the sort of imaginative visual interpretation they had learned to expect from him.[32]

It may be that the painting represents a different tale. The dying female could be a nymph, if not specifically the nymph Procris. Nymphs were closely linked to water and vegetation and were the companions of satyrs and the protectors of animals.[33] These characteristics account for the dying female's bereaved mourners and the scene's setting. Based on her apparently swollen abdomen, she has recently been identified as the pregnant nymph Callisto, who in one version of the myths about Artemis, the goddess of the hunt, was shot dead by the arrow of the goddess, because she disobeyed her vows of chastity.[34] The curved contour, highlighted emphasis and gossamer girdle that dips before it all stress the abdomen's importance. The untied veil may well be the *strophion*, which, as in the *Venus, Mars and Cupid*, would indicate her loss of virginity. Visual clues point tentatively to the interpretation that

this is an image of the death of the nymph Callisto, rather than
her fellow nymph Procris.

As in *The Battle of the Lapiths and Centaurs* (see illus. 8), where
Piero emphasized empathy with the gentle, loving side of the
half-horse centaurs, here too he chooses two animal interlocutors,
the half-goat satyr and the dog, to epitomize sorrow at the nymph's
horrible death. They are clearly interpreted with deeply felt
sensibilities akin to a human's purposeful agency and emotional
reactions. As Vasari recorded, presumably based on the testimony
of Piero's students, 'He [Piero] set himself often to observe such
animals, plants, or other things as Nature at times creates out of

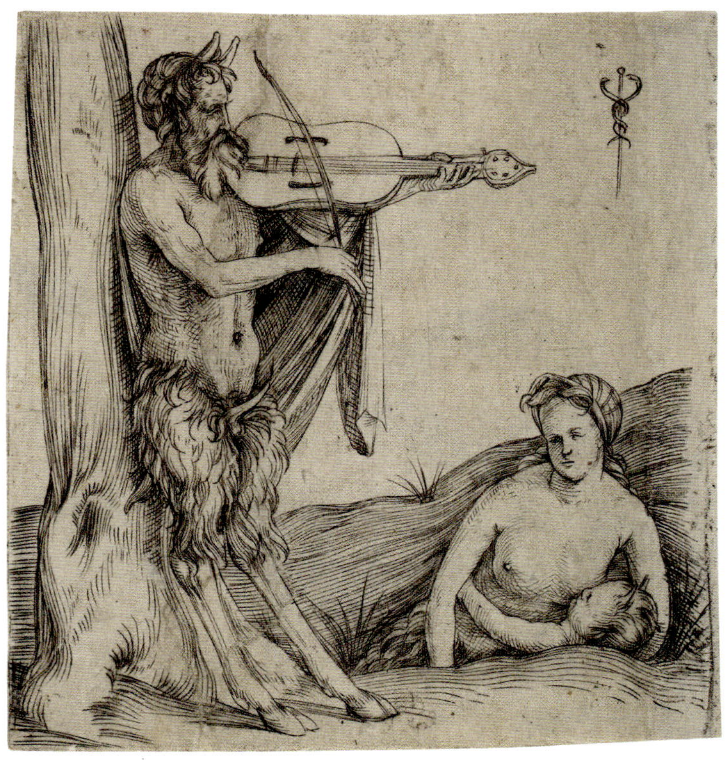

19 Jacopo de' Barbari, *Satyr's Family*, c. 1503–4, engraving.

caprice, or by chance; in which he found a pleasure and satisfaction that drove him quite out of his mind with delight.'[35] At another point in his text, Vasari claims: 'in all that there is to be seen by his hand, one recognizes a spirit very different and far distant from that of other painters, and a certain subtlety in the investigation of some of the deepest and most subtle secrets of nature.'[36] What Piero did with those close observations matters: he painted animals, real and imagined, with an extraordinarily expressive range and depth – and the power to generate in spectators reflections about how different, if at all, humans are from them.[37]

This characterization represents not just Piero's personal sympathies but possibly the influence of engravings such as the *Satyr's Family* by Jacopo de' Barbari (*c.* 1503–4, illus. 19).[38] In that print, a satyr displays his refined sensitivities by playing a lira da braccio to bring pleasure to his nursing wife and infant. Both Piero and Jacopo also reflect important active philosophical debates dating back to antiquity about the nature of animals. These discussions regarding animal sensibilities must have been current in fifteenth-century Florence because they had been popular throughout antiquity and during the Christian medieval period. Piero's enthusiasm for studying animals may not be a personal idiosyncrasy but rather his response to this scientific-philosophical exploration of the world surrounding humans.

Aristotle (384–322 BCE), the most influential ancient writer on animals, divided living things into three orders: plants; animals, to which he attributed emotions; and humans, which he distinguished from animals by their rationality and volition. His writings provided the framework for an enduring Western philosophy that became known as theriophily, or the love of animals.[39] Although not entirely consistently, Aristotle outlined in his *Historia animalium* (History of Animals, IX, 1) the different emotional and mental reactions of the males and females of many animal species. He also differentiated among the intelligence of various species.

In his *De anima* (On the Soul), Aristotle argued that animals had a complete 'sensitive soul', although they lacked the 'intellective soul' of humans (II, 2–3). By a 'sensitive soul', Aristotle meant that animals had emotive and sensory capacities and employed their senses to gain knowledge and to assess how best to put this knowledge to use and to communicate their responses.[40] This process implies that they analysed the actions of other animals and humans and reacted to them.

Among the major Greek and Latin authors influenced by these theoretical notions were Homer (eighth century BCE), Lucretius and Plutarch (46–119 CE). The same ideas marked the writings of prominent theologians such as Thomas Aquinas (1225–1274) and widely read writers like Geoffrey Chaucer (*c.* 1340s–1400). There was even a debate about whether it was better to be a human or an animal. The pre-eminent humanist Leon Battista Alberti (1404–1472) wrote treatises such as *Theogenius* (Origin of the Gods, *c.* 1438–41), which described men envying the powers of animals or insects like the tiny poisonous fly that could kill a man.[41] The same writer's *Momus*, written about 1450, described men who chose to be transformed into animals. According to Alberti, Charon, after he had recounted an alternative theory of creation of human and animal forms, 'realized that some of the humans were unhappy with the form he had given them and granted them the freedom to change their shape into any of the animals they pleased'.[42] Animal emotions and agency were played out as well in the contemporary popular genre of bestiaries and in animal fables, such as those by Aesop (*c.* 620–564 BCE). Leonardo tried his hand at the type in his fables and prophecies.[43] Clearly, these issues were probably known to Piero's commissioners and their peers, who wanted to display their knowledgeable philosophical backgrounds. Piero's animals and half-animals, such as the emotionally responsive dogs, centaurs and satyrs, reflect not simply his independent empathy but contemporary debates on animals' sensibilities and their capacity to feel and emote. These two factors provide the basis for a significant distinguishing feature of Piero's art: he seems to have transmuted his ambivalence about humans into a hypersensitivity to the possible range of animal responses. He endowed animals with emotions usually associated with humans and then created an effective engagement of the human audience by using the animals, to which humans are sometimes more emotionally vulnerable, to express reactions to his paintings' drama.[44]

To return to the painting's details: behind this compelling scene of inadvertent murder stretches a grassy knoll that leads to a sandy beach. Shore birds and dogs go about their lives at the beach's edge. Their inclusion has further meanings. The pelican splashing in the water at the right is a symbol of self-sacrifice because the bird legendarily tore off its own flesh to feed its young. For that reason, it is often represented above the body of Christ on the cross. In Piero's painting it could be a sign that the dead woman, whether Procris or the nymph Callisto, made the choices that led to her death – Procris to disbelieve her husband or the nymph (compelled) to break her vow of chastity – and thus caused her own death. The triad of herons at the left is included because they were known for their expression of pain: according to Pliny, they shed blood from their eyes and screamed during sex and childbirth (*Natural History*, X, 164–5). Certainly, they make an appropriate chorus to the tragic death of the young woman in the foreground. More specifically, they lend weight to her identification as Callisto, since her tale revolves around her forced impregnation by Zeus, a story at which the herons might well shed tears of blood.

Piero mobilizes the landscape behind the death scene as a protagonist: its smooth, flat planes create a melancholic but beautiful and peaceful setting to calm the tragedy. The distant view in tones of blue and grey is capped by a sky full of subtle movement.

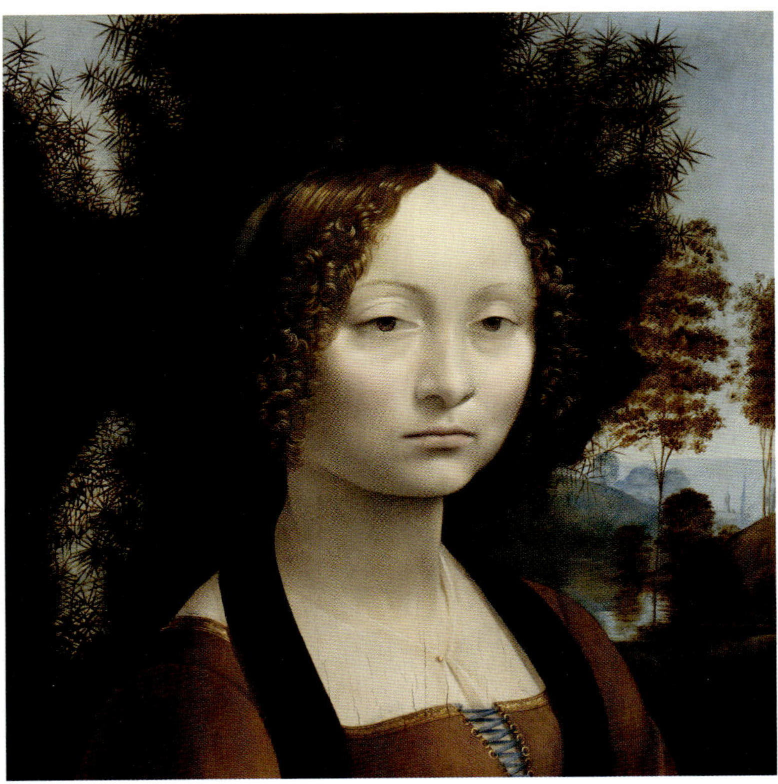

Luminous fingers of barely visible white clouds merge into the bluish sky and stretch horizontally across the panel, much in the style of the Netherlandish paintings being imported into Florence or Leonardo's own early work. The rough levels of the paint, which Piero applied in a revolutionary manner with his own fingers, move down through the sky and can be seen with the naked eye in close-up views of the painting.[45]

Especially relevant to Piero's resorting to painting with his fingers are the several examples by Leonardo that precede this panel. A much smaller but similar vignette of a landscape is found

20 Leonardo da Vinci, *Ginevra de' Benci*, c. 1474–8, oil on panel.

behind Leonardo's portrait of *Ginevra de' Benci* (*c.* 1474–8, illus. 20).
To vary the sense of light and air currents in the sky, Leonardo
laid in the oil paint with his fingers to gain surface texture. It is
one of the earliest paintings in which the artist's manipulation
of the paint with his own hands is visible. The technique of finger
painting is also obvious in his unfinished *St Jerome*. In the latter
painting the finger marks are faintly visible to the naked eye in
the background skyscape. An expert conservationist who has
studied Leonardo's paintings calls the phenomenon 'a distinctive
painting technique, not an occasional use of the fingers for cor-
rective measures'.[46] He traces the practice to Leonardo's invention
while he was in the workshop of Andrea del Verrocchio from
about 1466 to 1476, when Leonardo first experimented with oil
paint to shape forms through chiaroscuro effects.[47]

Such a manipulation of paint is most easily achieved in oil.
It seems likely that what Piero learned from Leonardo was not
how to paint in oil, as Vasari claimed, but instead finesse in oil
painting, particularly the device of finger painting in oil to give
texture to the paint and a spontaneity and subtlety to the forms
in his paintings.

Probably the most charming of Piero's mythological paintings
is his *Perseus Liberating Andromeda* (see illus. 6), which illustrates
Ovid's *Metamorphoses*. The painting was commissioned by Filippo
Strozzi the Younger, despite Vasari relating it to his father. Strozzi
paid Piero and a woodworker to initiate decoration of the master
bedroom of the family residence in 1510–11.[48] As Vasari describes:

> Piero painted, for the elder Filippo Strozzi, a picture with
> little figures of Perseus delivering Andromeda from the
> Monster, in which are some very beautiful things . . .
> Piero never made a more lovely or more highly finished
> picture than this one, seeing that it is not possible to find
> a more bizarre or more fantastic sea-monster than that

which Piero imagined and painted, or a fiercer attitude
than that of Perseus, who is raising his sword in the air
to smite the beast. In it, in trembling between fear and
hope, Andromeda is seen bound . . . The landscape is
very beautiful, and the colouring sweet and full of grace.[49]

It was possibly intended to honour the younger Strozzi's
marriage to Clarice de' Medici in 1508 and could have been part
of the couple's still surviving throne-bench, a prestigious gift to
them from the Medici family.[50] A telling marker of the high regard
in which the painting was held is that when it entered the Medici
collections in the late sixteenth century, it was displayed in the
Uffizi Tribuna, one of their most prestigious display sites, and
was called a collaboration between Leonardo and Piero, for which
Leonardo provided the compositional drawing and Piero the
painting.[51]

Piero presents the myth as a multi-scenic narrative, told
through dozens of tiny figures, of Perseus killing the supposedly
fearsome dragon in an expansive landscape whose shape is calculated to hold about ten equally emphasized episodes. Such a
sequence of clearly separate events in chronological order and
organized in a counter-clockwise direction is unusual in most
domestic paintings, including Piero's. As we have seen, his mythological compositions are often enacted by a few large figures in
the foreground. In the paintings with many figures and vignettes,
they were simultaneous vignettes relating to the central subject,
as in *The Battle of the Lapiths and Centaurs* (see illus. 8).

Like almost all his other domestic paintings, Piero's *Perseus
Liberating Andromeda* is a modestly sized oil on wood. He exploited
its probable position close to eye level, which allowed it to be seen
close up and be carefully studied. The panel unites a series of
episodes played out by small figures, which diffuses the narrative
focus. However, the numerous figures are all immersed organically

in the landscape that ties together the separate incidents. A surprisingly docile dragon at the centre dominates the scene. It seems transfixed, more like a fanciful child's toy than a fearsome monster. The small scale of the dragon and human figures minimizes any potential implication of menace to the much larger viewer. Painstaking detail throughout the painting rewards repeated study and ensures a decorative focus, which is reinforced by the soft colours that calm any potential sense of dread. It certainly relates to an image of a sea-monster given, according to Vasari, by Piero to Giuliano de' Medici, brother of Lorenzo the Magnificent, which was

> so extravagant, bizarre, and fantastic in its deformity, that it seems impossible that Nature could have produced anything so deformed and strange among her creations. This monster is now in the *guardaroba* of Duke Cosimo de' Medici, as is also a book, likewise by the hand of Piero, of animals of the same kind, most beautiful and bizarre, hatched very diligently with the pen, and finished with an incredible patience; which book was presented to him by M. Cosimo Bartoli, Provost of S. Giovanni, who is very much my friend.[52]

The sequential episodes that circle the dragon in a counter-clockwise movement — from scenes of dread and sadness to rejoicing — reveal Perseus in the upper right, clad in his magical winged sandals, flying to the rescue of Andromeda; in the centre, Perseus balanced atop the dragon, ready to swing his scimitar to kill it; the partly nude Andromeda at centre left, shrinking as far as possible from the dragon; and her relatives and friends bemoaning her fate in the lower left. Finally, looking ahead to the denouement at the lower right, we see the merriment of the group once Perseus has freed Andromeda, and the happy pair's approach to the king, who grants Perseus her hand in marriage. In a tiny vignette at the centre right, Perseus gives thanks to Jupiter, Mercury and Minerva, the three gods who helped him, by sacrificing to each a bull, a calf and a cow, respectively, on separate altars.

Ovid locates the myth in Ethiopia, but most of the figures in Piero's painting seem to be white. Only a single musician playing a fantastic instrument is depicted as Black. Ovid provided ambiguous information about whether Andromeda was Black. In the *Metamorphoses*, he describes her as like marble, which could be either light or dark coloured, though in several of his other poems he calls her Black. As a result, most artists and literary figures of the period represented her as white.[53]

Ovid offered no information about the other figures. One might have expected the members of the court and onlookers to be depicted as Black Africans, especially since Florentines in Piero's day considered the ownership of Black African slaves to be prestigious, and the Strozzi family had several slaves and was active in the slave trade from Africa.[54] In other paintings they commissioned, like Filippino Lippi's *Madonna Holding the Reading Baby Christ* (see illus. 48), which Piero virtually copied, there are three Black Africans in the background of the Strozzi property. This served as an assertion of the Strozzi family's wealth and status. In their family chapel in Santa Maria Novella, dedicated to Filippo Strozzi's namesake, St Philip, the Ethiopian eunuch baptized by Philip is included in a scene of his miracles. In that very different context, the Black Ethiopian eunuch stood as an indication of the global reach of Christianity and the Strozzis' proud claims of their connections to St Philip's missionary activity.[55]

Otherwise, in his visualization of the myth of Perseus and Andromeda, Piero seems to have scrupulously followed the tale in Ovid's *Metamorphoses*, but he has transmuted its near-tragic life-and-death drama into a charming fable interpreted whimsically.

Precisely these disjunctions between content and presentation caused the Surrealists to delight in Piero's pagan subjects, which they saw as a prelude to their own approach. In the 1930s, two articles were devoted to Piero in the Surrealist journals *Minotaure* and *Documents*. As Georges Pudelko, an author in *Minotaure*, explained, 'only the experience of Surrealism has given us the tools to appreciate the unique mentality behind Piero's grandiose view of the cosmos and the unconscious.'[56] Another Surrealist commentator, Georgette Camille, writing in *Documents*, claimed that Piero's paintings conveyed how 'he truly by misanthropy or a magical knowledge of nature, preferred the company of animals to that of humans'.[57] Although the Surrealists captured a valid aspect of Piero's fascination for viewing audiences in his milieu, they – Pudelko particularly – were short-sighted not to acknowledge the overwhelming popularity Piero's interpretation of secular subject-matter had already achieved among fifteenth-century patrons.

In *Perseus Liberating Andromeda*, Piero creates a fairy-tale cast and setting surrounding a supposedly threatening dragon. In a characteristic display of empathy for the wounded beast, he represents it exuding saliva from its mouth and nose as it sinks to the side and gradually bleeds to death. These details are intended to stir our sympathy for the creature's pain, despite its malevolent goal of eating Andromeda. As Vasari effused, no creature 'more bizarre or more fantastic' was to be found.[58] Or more pitiful!

Worthy of note is that Vasari applied virtually the same words to a fresco by Filippino Lippi (1457–1504) showing St Margaret with the dragon that had disgorged her, which he painted for the nuns of Santa Margherita in Prato. He described the dragon as 'so strange and horrible, that it is revealed to us as a true fount of venom, fire, and death'.[59] Several times the biographer applied such words of wonder to Filippino, who also worked on the city's pageants and for the same patrons as Piero, specifically the Strozzi and the del Pugliese families. Much like Piero's mythologies and legends, Vasari characterized Filippino's narratives as constructing 'scene[s] with little figures, executed with so much art and diligence that when another citizen besought him to make a second like it, he refused, saying it was not possible to do it'.[60] He praised him, 'so abundant his invention in painting and so bizarre and new were his ornaments'.[61] He described Filippino's Strozzi Chapel as 'executed so well, and with so much art and design, that it causes all who see it to marvel, by reason of the novelty and variety of the bizarre things that are seen therein'.[62] It is possible that Vasari was tiring of devising different vocabulary in his biographies, but more likely he saw similar characteristics in these two contemporary Florentines. Vasari appears to have found Filippino the most kindred spirit to Piero di Cosimo. One crucial distinction is indisputable: he lauded Filippino for his lifestyle and professional manner, and his description became almost a foil for his criticism of Piero's lack of social graces and discipline. Filippino was 'ever courteous, affable, and kindly, he was lamented by all those who had known him . . . so excellent in all his actions' and was praised for 'the modesty and regularity of his life'.[63] Nevertheless, despite Vasari's reservations about Piero's character and personality, he enthusiastically applauded the originality and charm of his interpretation of mythological subjects.

TWO

Legendary Subjects

Various scenes with little figures . . . [and] different fantastic
things he delighted to paint . . . and any other fanciful things
that came into his head.
GIORGIO VASARI, *Lives*

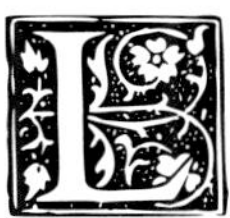ike Piero's mythological scenes, secular legendary
paintings decorated private residences and were com-
posed mainly of *spalliere*. The commissioner of the first
two legendary scenes considered here, the so-called *Hunting Scene*
(see illus. 7) and *The Return from the Hunt* (see illus. 9), is uncertain. What is undisputed is that they are two of the most inventive
and fascinating paintings produced during the Renaissance. More
accurately, their narratives concern the early history of man. That
they belong together is made clear by their related subject-matter
and nearly identical dimensions. They have been associated with
Francesco del Pugliese, a distinguished Florentine merchant and
civic figure. That hypothesis derives from Vasari's summary
description of paintings in the del Pugliese residence:

He [Piero] also executed round a chamber in the house
of Francesco del Pugliese various scenes with little figures;
nor is it possible to describe the different fantastic things
he delighted to paint in all those scenes what with the

buildings, the costumes, the various instruments, and any other fanciful things that came into his head, since the stories were drawn from fables.[1]

The paintings were clearly intended to enthral the viewer and to stimulate discussion. The lack of precise details about their themes stymies certainty as to which fables are represented, a perhaps deliberate ambiguity geared to contribute to the dialogue sparked in their viewers' reactions. The theory of Francesco del Pugliese's patronage is buttressed by his family's role as a loyal commissioner of Piero.[2]

Both *A Hunting Scene* and *The Return from the Hunt* are painted in oil and tempera on panel (although *A Hunting Scene* has been transferred to Masonite) and picture dozens of small figures in wild landscapes, in accord with Vasari's general description. Both scenes take place in a similar, but apparently different, wooded setting. Piero depicts a panorama of multiple slaughters with blood-curdling gusto. Only the repetition of colours and the vistas of two wide, partly cleared spaces opening diagonally from a pair of prominent trees in the foreground hold the *Hunting Scene*'s composition together. There is so much action that the viewer takes it in only after close, careful looking. Episodes seem to flicker in and out of focus because they are crowded so closely together and sometimes because they are so thinly painted. In *A Hunting Scene*, humans dressed in animal skins, animal hybrids (satyrs and centaurs) and animals compete to eat or be eaten. Occasionally satyrs and humans collaborate and gang up on an unfortunate beast, but such cooperation is opportunistic and fleeting. The group in the foreground draws our eye: a satyr is poised to club into insensibility a lion that is eating a bear while a man attempts to drag by its tail that same foraging lion off the bear. Another man struggles to pull a second bear away from the lion. Piero depicts him dressed in a lion's skin replete with tail and testicles, thus

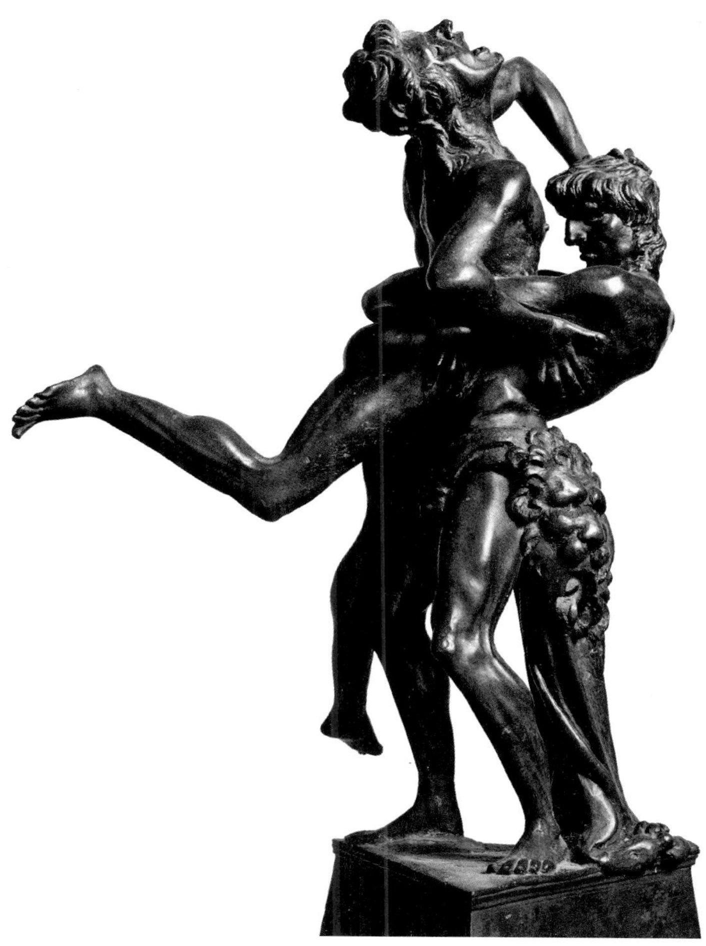

relieving the terrifying horrors of the scenes with his typical wit
and humour.³ The club-wielding satyr's sinewy nude body winding
into an impossible back bend recalls the figures of Piero's Florentine contemporary Antonio del Pollaiuolo (*c.* 1432–1498), for
example in his bronze statuette of Hercules and Antaeus (*c.* 1475,
illus. 21). To the right, a nude man sits on his heel atop a horse,

21 Antonio del Pollaiuolo, *Hercules and Antaeus, c.* 1475, bronze.

grabbing its neck and straining to flee the fire as fast as possible. Behind him on a tree is some sort of thinly painted cat that is difficult to identify because the trunks of trees show through it. The humans and hybrids do not attack each other but focus on the animals. They are all engaged in a combat of survival of the fittest. Dead beasts and humans lie on the ground in extreme foreshortening, demanding the viewer's attention and once again showing Piero's study of Uccello's frescoes (see illus. 18). A fire, probably set by lightning, races through the forest background and flushes out game to hunt. In this primitive stage of the earth's development, it is unlikely that humans have mastered fire.

As Piero's visualization makes clear, at this early point humans are clearly akin to animal hybrids and close to animals. The forest world is far from an anthropocentric, comfortable environment for humans; it is instead a threatening, horrible place.[4] Piero makes viewers imagine the grunts, groans and cries of pain of humans, animals and animal hybrids alike as they struggle for supremacy. Some of the animals, like the lions, show evidence that the artist studied them in real life. These beasts were the symbol of Florence and a number were kept in a cage in the city centre for all to watch and hear.[5] On a more temporary basis, staged animal combats in which the lions were primed to kill prey were planned to honour important guests, like that in 1459 for Pope Pius II and Galeazzo Maria Sforza, son of the Duke of Milan. For such events, wild boars, buffaloes, cows, horses, goats and bulls were brought in, providing an artist fascinated by animals like Piero the opportunity to study them.[6] The lions in that contest proved lethargic, but in other opportunities, and in Piero's imagination as we see it here, they certainly did not. The horrifying mayhem represented is relieved by a touch of Piero's typical whimsy: a monkey has climbed high in a foreground tree to escape and twists its head to confront the viewers as if to ask what they think of this spectacle – and of the viewers' own brutal human origins.

The companion panel, *The Return from the Hunt* (see illus. 9), represents the nascent effects of Venus putting an end to the violence by seducing Mars, which has led to a later stage of evolution. It also represents the development of the 'intellective soul' that Aristotle considered unique to humans. It is a peaceful scene where people work together towards a common good. Women are included, and several have already paired off with mates. One nude female in the right foreground rides bareback atop her chosen centaur partner, indicating the interbreeding of animal hybrids and humans. The men have already captured several animals to eat. One carries a boar while a cow lies on the ground nearby. There are three boats still being built at the edge of the bay nearby, even though men and women are aboard them. On the first, what seem to be two dead cattle have already been laid out. That boat and the two moored beside it appear to be built of woven reeds and bent branches. One boat's mast and an arch on another, decorated with the skulls of animals already eaten, provide the clearest indication that they have been snapped off, not cut, because their wood is made of untrimmed tree trunks. This suggests that Piero is painting a world before the discovery of metalworking, but humans do seem to have evolved to the point of using fire to hunt. They are taking advantage of a fire, probably caused by a spontaneous lightning flash, to hunt long-antlered deer fleeing the forest at the left and plunging into the adjacent bay to escape the flames. Deeper in the bay, men propel several boats towards them, hoping to trap the animals. Two male onlookers stand behind bushes at the left as though spying on the scene, the branches criss-crossing their faces. The head of a man swimming in the water before the boats looks out to confront our gaze, as if sharing an enigmatic commentary on all this activity. The detail seems added to delight the scrutiny of the patron or his guest who carefully studies the painting and perhaps to provoke reflection about human progress between the two scenes – and between life then and the fifteenth century.

The Forest Fire (see illus. 10) is a third painting often grouped with the two *Hunt* narratives. Unlike them, it is painted in oil, not oil and tempera, and it does not match them exactly in length. All three panels' height, however, is almost the same. The panels could have fit into differently shaped areas of the panelling, or the painting of *The Forest Fire* could have been commissioned by another patron who, impressed by the *Hunt* scenes, requested his own version. Its subject-matter would make it appropriate not just for a city residence, like the two paintings above, but for a villa where pastoral scenes were favoured.[7]

Like the two *Hunt* scenes, *The Forest Fire* abounds with small-scale figures such as Vasari described in the paintings in the residence of Francesco del Pugliese. All the scenes depict the consequences of forest fires, one of nature's most potent tools in reshaping the world. In *The Forest Fire*, however, most of the characters are animals or birds fleeing in terror from the flames. There are only a few humans. At the right, the most prominent of them herds his oxen home to his hut and seems unperturbed, although the oxen are running. The herdsman wears shoes and a tunic of woven cloth and carries a scythe. His animals' yoke is shaped from wood and some metal parts. Near the hut, tiny fig-ures stand near a barking dog, and women (judging from their long robes) draw water from a well. Thanks to the peaceful conditions for which Lucretius, in *De rerum natura*, credits Venus, humans have learned to make their own clothing and habita-tions. They have grasped how to use fire to shape metal and make tools. All mark a more advanced stage in human development. In addition to these momentous implications, this panel should be considered a landmark in the history of landscape painting because of its focus on the natural world. It is the first depiction in an independent painted panel of a carefully detailed vista of animals, birds and plants that allocates to humans only a very minor role.

Piero creates a stunning display of a forest fire and the many terrified birds and creatures that flee it by land or water. The fire breaks through trees in the background, causing cascades of sparks to burn brightly and outline their trunks. In the left foreground, far from the blazing foliage, a pile of embers glows next to what resembles scattered stones. They have been identified as hardened pieces of metal caused by the roaring fire's heat opening and melting underground veins of metal.[8] This accident of nature is considered to have allowed humans to learn how to shape metal.

Piero painstakingly painted the panicked reactions of dozens of animals and birds scared from their lairs in the forest by fire. His small-scale images are so exacting that each species can be identified. Infrared examination shows free drawings in thin black paint underneath the paint level and reveals that Piero captured the essence of each animal or bird almost intuitively.[9] The underdrawings are difficult to read, but a beautiful independent drawing, one of the few that survive of animals of the many Vasari said Piero made, gives an idea of his approach to recording different breeds. Rendered in pen and brown ink over traces of silverpoint on prepared pink paper (*c.* 1500–1505, illus. 22), it reveals Piero's careful analysis of a bear and her cub, two stags and an ox, all animals that appear in the painting. His gift for capturing their stances, movements and attitudes (the mother bear nursing her cub as she protects it with her body; the proud, erect pose of the stags) confirm Vasari's claim that Piero was fascinated by the natural world, studied it carefully and was deeply sensitive to animals' moods and reactions. Vasari had apparently seen many of Piero's drawings of animals, then housed in the collections of his patron, Duke Cosimo de' Medici. He described them as 'most beautiful and bizarre, hatched very diligently with the pen, and finished with an incredible patience'.[10] The many

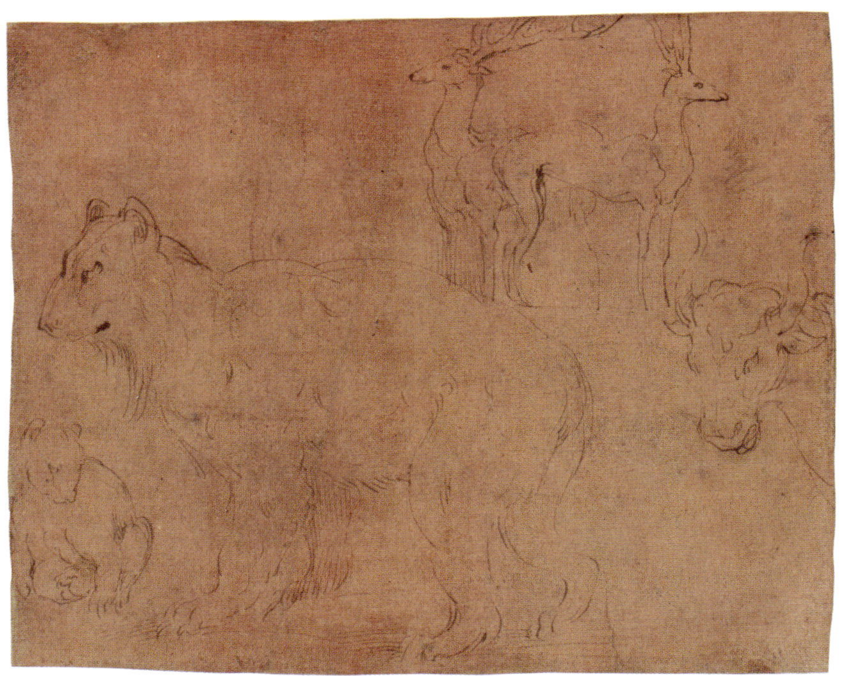

species of animals and birds were studied separately in individual drawings and the finished studies applied directly to the panel, which accounts for their contradictory spontaneity and fixed quality.

In telling fashion, Piero goes further than portraying the animals' positions and gaits: he depicts their distinctive responses of fear to the forest fire. At the centre foreground an ox furrows its brow, opens its mouth, bares its teeth and protrudes its tongue its entire length in an almost audible bellow. A lioness to its right strides off, tension visible in her lifted tail and the low growl that her open mouth seems to emit. The common crane at the far right is posed with its head arched vertically in the position of calling.[11] To the left of the ox, a mother bear roars

22 Piero di Cosimo, *A Bear and Her Cub, Two Deer and the Head of an Ox*, c. 1500–1505, pen and brown ink over traces of silverpoint on pink prepared paper.

orders to the three cubs behind her to follow as she struggles up a hill in flight.

These immediately recognizable creatures mingle with fantastic hybrids such as a human-faced pig, which turns to confront the viewer as he and his mate behind him move away from the fire. To their left is a pair of red deer. The stag in front resembles its counterpart in Piero's drawing, but its mate has the head of a human. Infrared images show that both these hybrids were originally planned to be ordinary animals. There is a pig's snout in profile underneath the human head turned in our direction. The deer originally had a typical stag's head in the position of its replacement. This proves that Piero altered them during painting of the panel. The original hybrid creatures may reflect the influence of the fifth-century BCE philosopher Empedokles, whose ideas about extinct 'man-faced ox creatures' were known in the Renaissance through the writings of Aristotle and Plutarch.[12] Several Greek and Latin authors engaged in the arguments about whether such creatures were fanciful or had gone extinct. As Lucretius wrote, 'In the beginning there were many freaks. Earth undertook/ Experiments – bizarrely put together, weird of look – ... many kinds of creatures must have vanished with no trace/ Because they could not reproduce or hammer out their race' (*De rerum natura*, V, 837–56). Lucretius specifically opposed belief in the existence at any point of 'monsters of twin natures', which he considered centaurs to be, and presumably man-headed deer and man-headed pigs too. His argument was that they had 'a twofold body joined together out of mismatched limbs' that could never be equal in their powers and growth (V, 878–81).

These controversies about the primitive evolution of animal and human life may have made their images desirable to Piero's patrons, who wanted to display their intellectual credentials – particularly their critical reading of ancient authors – and to parade their erudition in the paintings they commissioned. On a more basic level, the paintings provided reassuring evidence to their fifteenth-century audience of the superior status of educated humans in their day to primitive man. The violence and bestiality in Piero's paintings incongruously gave them pleasure because they confirmed the owners' and their privileged viewers' civility. Not just the references to Graeco-Roman literature but the quotations of earlier fifteenth-century art and the refinement of the paintings' facture contributed to this gratifying message.[13]

There is no precedent for this sort of subject-matter in Renaissance art — no scenes of the primordial history of the world, no representations focusing on fire or almost exclusively on the natural world, no hybrids other than the traditional Graeco-Roman mythological centaurs and satyrs, and no 'portraits' of animals' bodies, emotions and communication. Some artists, like Pisanello and Leonardo, carefully studied animals and sensitively portrayed them, but they did not focus on the animals' feelings and interactions to the extent Piero did. They certainly did not situate them in early scenes of creation. Some of Piero's individual pictorial details were inspired by other artists, but the narratives he depicted were not. In *The Forest Fire* he confronted boldly the challenges posed to the visual arts from the literary evidence of Greek painting. Pliny's *Natural History* had recorded the wonders of Apelles' unique ability to transcribe in visual terms the ineffable and evanescent, 'the things that cannot be represented in pictures' (XXXV, 96). Pliny specified that he meant thunder and lightning bolts, phenomena that can be seen and heard. In a bravura display surpassing that of any earlier Renaissance painter, and indeed Pliny's hero Apelles, Piero evoked powerfully a concatenation of transitory effects experienced by all the senses — sight, hearing, touch, taste and smell: the visual effects of the fire and fleeing mammals and birds, the changing lights and colours of a spreading fire, the crackling sounds of burning wood, the frightened cries of animals, the smell of smoke and charred wood, so sharp they could be tasted, and even the solidifying ores melted out of the earth by the terrible heat, which humans could touch and exploit when cooled. He so effectively conjured these effects that the viewer could imagine these sensory repercussions of the narrative.

Piero's scenes interrogate the origins of man, a subject addressed by several ancient authors. Vitruvius, a well-known authority, described primitive man in a brief passage that was popularized by Boccaccio's incorporation of it in *De genealogia deorum*. The depictions depend primarily upon the longer descriptions in the recently recovered Lucretius, prompting questions about how Piero became acquainted with such literary material. Ovid had been well known throughout the medieval period, and Pliny's *Natural History* began to circulate among literary figures, starting with Petrarch, in the mid-fourteenth century, but knowledge of Lucretius' *De rerum natura* dated only from the early fifteenth century.

Other than his paintings, no indication survives that Piero himself had a direct interest in such Greek and Latin authors, or that he could read the texts. His understanding of their ideas and stories must have derived from his patrons or their advisers, although no information survives about such consultations. Vincenzo Farinella made the most recent attempt to identify Piero's learned adviser. In his opinion, Michele Marullo Tarcaniota (1453–1500), a Greek scholar deeply versed in Lucretius who transferred to Florence in 1489, is the most likely candidate.[14] He cites Marullo's ties to the collateral branch of the Medici to support his claim, but there is no certain evidence that Marullo advised Piero. Other historians, such as Alison Brown, have taken the opposite tack and claimed that Piero could have known a great deal about Lucretius' ideas simply by existing in the highly 'vocal' society of Florence, 'where the cultural climate after 1494' encouraged the spread of Epicurean thought.[15] It seems clear that Piero's patrons turned to him to visualize the texts, however the artist was exposed to them, because of his uniquely imaginative abilities to transform them into pictorial interpretations.

Despite the indirect transmission through patrons and advisers, aspects of Piero's lifestyle suggest that he responded to various philosophical currents from the ancient world, which then informed his paintings. Already discussed is theriophily, or the love of animals and belief in their sensibilities. Vasari's remarks about Piero's fascination with nature and its creatures and his careful study of them explain such sympathetic depictions as the dog who sits at the feet of the dead nymph, palpably mourning and inspiring us to share its sorrow. Another philosophical current to which Piero was exposed indirectly was Epicureanism. In this case the transmission was probably through Lucretius, which seems to have influenced several features of Piero's lifestyle that Vasari considered weird, even bestial.

> . . . he would not let his garden be worked or his fruit-trees pruned . . . for it pleased him to see everything wild, like his own nature; and he declared that Nature's own things should be left to her to look after, without lifting a hand to them.[16]

Lucretius' poem was the earliest surviving text about ancient ideas on the history of the primitive world, and the most extensive.[17] He was a Roman follower of Epicurus and intended his verses to popularize Epicurus' philosophy. Although the number of available manuscripts was limited: about fifty, copied in the fifteenth century, survive to this day and three printed editions were produced in the second half of the fifteenth century.[18] We know that Filippo Strozzi the Younger, patron of the Triumph of Death masquerade and Piero's *Perseus Liberating Andromeda*, owned a copy of Lucretius.[19] His father had been a great patron of the arts and of ancient literature, so the younger Strozzi was continuing in his father's footsteps. The cultural interests of the elder Strozzi are epitomized by his role in producing a luxury edition of Pliny's *Natural History*. Along with Ferdinand I, king of Naples, he had sponsored a magnificently illustrated, luxury vernacular edition of Pliny's work while living in exile at the court of Naples. The edition became a best-seller. The Strozzi also seem to have had access to an edition of Pliny the Younger's *Letters* (first century CE) and so were well equipped with a basic roster of major ancient texts.[20]

By the end of the century, the Epicurean naturalism that Lucretius advocated had penetrated even the city's popular culture.[21] To measure Lucretius' effect more broadly, there were sixty printed editions of the *De rerum natura* and eight biographies of the philosopher produced by Renaissance humanists by about 1600.[22]

Of particular interest to Piero's paintings are the Roman philosopher's themes of an all-powerful nature that generated and destroyed, shaped human evolution through its changes and altered the relations of humans to animals that man first fought and then domesticated.[23] Lucretius described human origins, when 'primitive man lived the vagrant life of wild animals' (*De rerum natura*, V, 930). His theories must have seemed confirmed by the expeditions to other parts of the world such as Africa, the Americas and Asia by explorers like Christopher Columbus and Amerigo Vespucci. Vespucci's letters written to Lorenzo di Pierfrancesco de' Medici, who had been his fellow student at the Medici court under the humanists Marsilio Ficino and Angelo Poliziano, and to a member of the Ridolfi family made Florentines aware of fascinating peoples who behaved differently from Europeans and responded to other societal and cultural norms. They could relate Lucretius' discussions about the various stages of human and animal development to these phenomena.[24] Vespucci's lengthy missives repeatedly alluded to these far-off peoples' links to Epicurean ideas. In recounting his travels to Lorenzo in a letter published in 1503, he claimed that 'the inhabitants of the New World live naked in the wild . . . They live according to nature and might be called Epicureans rather than Stoics.'[25] Inhabitants of other areas, like the so-called torrid zone beyond the equator, were categorized in the same way. Letter IV Ridolfi Fragment, a partial copy of a letter by Vespucci about the torrid zone, reports that 'their life is rather more Epicurean than Stoic or Academic.'[26] In Letter VI to Piero Soderini, Vespucci discusses the 'Fortunate Islands' in the 'Ocean Sea'. Once again, he notes about the people there, 'I judge their life to be Epicurean.'[27]

Vespucci's accounts of the flora and fauna of the places he visited probably also inspired *The Forest Fire* and the two *Hunt* scenes. In a letter to Lorenzo, he exclaims about a site in the region of the Antipodes:

> I must be near the Earthly Paradise . . . What is there to say of the quantity of birds, and their plumes and colors and songs and how many kinds and how beautiful they are? . . . who could tell the infinite number of forest animals . . . And we saw so many other kinds that I think so many kinds could not have fit in Noah's Ark.[28]

Vespucci also comments of the Fortunate Islands that the

> animals they do have are so numerous, and all are wild, and they use none of them for work, that it would be impossible to enumerate them. What are we to say of birds, of . . . which there are so many and so many sorts and colors of plumage that it is a marvel to behold them?[29]

A final description by Vespucci that can be seen reflected in Piero's paintings may be found in his report of how the humans in the Antipodes were afraid to enter into the dense woods:

> When they can get it, they eat the meat of other animals and birds. But they do not catch many of them because they have no dogs, and the land is very dense with forests which are full of ferocious beasts, and for this reason they seldom venture into the woods.[30]

In each of Piero's *Hunt* paintings, humans and hybrids profit from fires accidentally or deliberately set that flush animals out of the dark, frightening woods and enable the beasts' capture. They take advantage of such occasions, when they occur, rather than risk entering the murky and threatening thickets in the animals' pursuit. Vespucci recounted repeatedly that the usual practice of peoples in all the places he visited was in fact to eat human flesh: as he says about people in the Antipodes, for example, 'they dismember and eat their dead enemies.'[31] In *The Forest Fire*, meanwhile, man has already domesticated animals and is not interested in trying to capture the wild beasts escaping the blaze.

Various passages in Lucretius' poem correspond closely to Piero's paintings. 'A Hunt' seems to visualize the world before Venus' intervention, specifically Lucretius' description of its brutal strife:

> They chased their quarry of forest animals, and felled
>   their prey
> With stones or cudgels. Many they slew – from some
>   they ran away
> By fleeing into their lairs. And like the wild and bristly
>   boar,

When night caught with them, they lay down on the
    forest floor
Rolling their naked, woodland-dwelling limbs up in a
    nest
Of foliage and the boughs of trees.
(De rerum natura, V, 968–73)

Back then the fate of an untimely death was no more
    rife
Than now, when men with moaning leave the sweet
    light of this life.
To be sure, each was more likely to be caught by some
    wild beast,
Gulped down in toothy jaws, supplying it a living
    feast,
Filling the groves, the hills and woods with groans,
    because he was
Buried alive, he saw, inside a living sarcophagus.
(V, 988–93)

The Forest Fire seems to derive in part from the following:

. . . once the scorching flame,
With an awful roar, had gobbled up the forest, down as
    deep
As the roots, and baked the earth to a crisp, the
    burning veins would seep,
And trickles of silver and gold, also copper and lead,
    would stream
And pool in the earth's hollows. When these cooled,
    men saw the gleam
Of their glinting colours in the soil, and drawn to what
    they'd found –

> The shiny smoothness of the nuggets – pried them
>   from the ground,
> And saw these bore the shapes of the depressions
>   where they lay.
> Then this drove home that they could shape the
>   nuggets in this way –
> Melting them down and pouring them into any mould
>   they made.
>
> (V, 1252–62)

It also seems to draw on Lucretius' understanding of animal communication:

> Why should it be so wonderful that the human race
>   expresses
> Different things and feelings with different sounds,
>   since it possesses
> Such marvellous instruments of tongue and voice,
>   when if you take
> Dumb flocks, and even all the creatures in the wild,
>   they make
> A range of sounds, and voices in a wide variety
> When they are terrified, or are in pain, or burst with
>   glee?
> This is quite obvious from observation, as you see.
>
> (V, 156–62)

The *De rerum natura* is not the source of all of Piero's inventions, however. Lucretius categorically denies the existence of the kinds of hybrid creatures that, as we have seen, populate all three of these scenes. Clearly, Piero's scenes draw on other authors, most obviously Ovid, who recounted tales of centaurs in several of his myths and often directly refuted Lucretius' assertions about them.[32]

Piero's renditions of the legends of humankind's origins are his most original and disquieting paintings. They find literary inspiration in Lucretius' verse epic *De rerum natura* and in Vespucci's letters about the far-off areas he explored beyond Europe. But neither of these sources had previously influenced the arts, with the limited exception of woodcut illustrations of Vespucci's texts. Piero's subjects are unprecedented in independent painting, but they are true to the grisly portrayal that Lucretius created of humankind's first impulses, which must have seemed validated by Vespucci's descriptions of humans living crudely in nature, outside the world Europeans had previously known. Piero's patrons must have asked for this content with the goal of showing off their awareness of the latest discoveries and intellectual fashions, as well as their high level of culture and their skill in comparing and analysing different authors' accounts. Despite the novelty of the commissions' learned themes, Piero adeptly translated them into paint.

THREE

Portraits

And since Piero drew most excellently from the life,
he made in Rome many portraits of distinguished persons.
GIORGIO VASARI, *Lives*

 asari enthusiastically commended the young Piero for his portraits and made clear contemporaries' recognition of his skills. He singled out for praise the likenesses of the noblemen Virginio Orsini and Roberto Sanseverino, as well as Valentino Borgia, writing: 'Afterwards, also, he made a portrait of Duke Valentino, the son of Pope Alexander VI.'[1] Unfortunately, none of these portraits can now be traced. Despite Vasari's later praise of Piero's early period in Rome, the young artist did not receive many portrait commissions. This chapter deals first with three paintings that are straightforward independent portraits, then proceeds to an idealized image of a deceased historical figure for whom Piero invented a visual rendering and ends with an example of a patron standing in for a saint.

The portraits of Francesco Giamberti (Sangallo) and Giuliano da Sangallo (*c.* 1485–90, illus. 23) are vivid likenesses. In this format they are an unusual pairing of father (Francesco Giamberti, on the right) and son (born Giuliano Giamberti). Equally unusual is the emphasis on both men's professions. Most double portraits and diptychs are of husband and wife, such as in the case of the

Portinari couple by Hans Memling (*c.* 1470, illus. 24), now reduced to a diptych of the pair, who originally prayed to a central panel of the Madonna and Child. A few depict friends, as in the case of Filippino Lippi's *Double Portrait of Piero del Pugliese and Filippino Lippi* (*c.* 1486, illus. 25), discussed below. Painted pairs such as these were meant to immortalize the figures' likenesses and the close emotional ties between them for the appreciation of their patrons' contemporaries and for posterity. They tended to omit career identifiers and focus on the figures' relationships. Such 'keepsake' double portraits were probably inspired by northern Italian models, specifically Andrea Mantegna's two lost paintings of friends, *Leonello d'Este and Folco da Villafora* (1449) and *Janus Pannonius and Galeotto Marzio da Narni* (1458). Unlike Piero's and Filippino's paintings, Mantegna's lost images seem to have had a friend

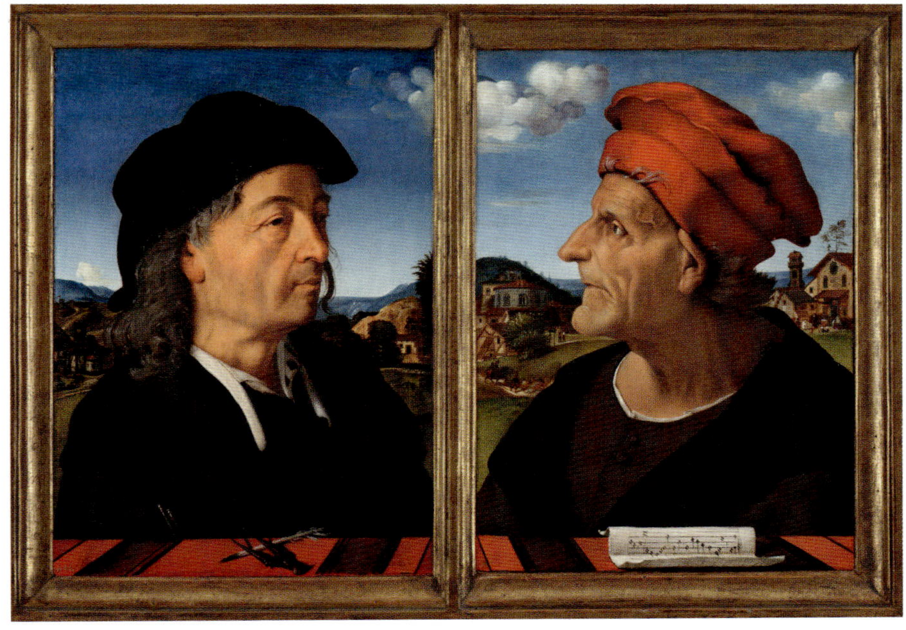

23 Piero di Cosimo, *Francesco Giamberti (Sangallo)* and *Giuliano da Sangallo*, *c.* 1485–90, oil on panel.

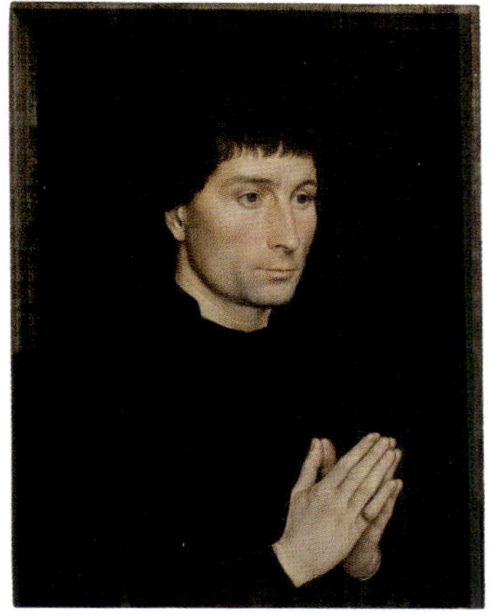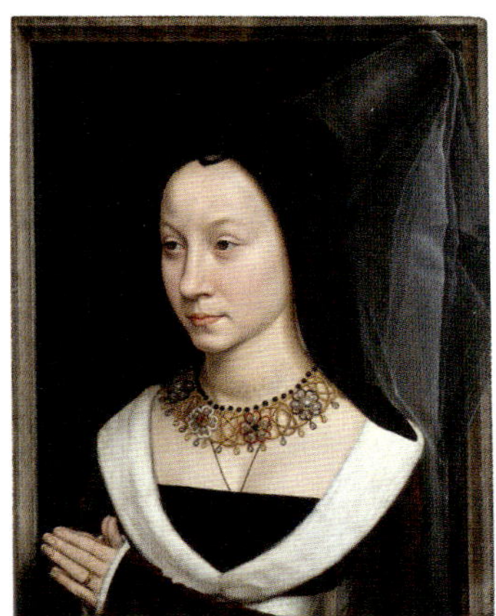

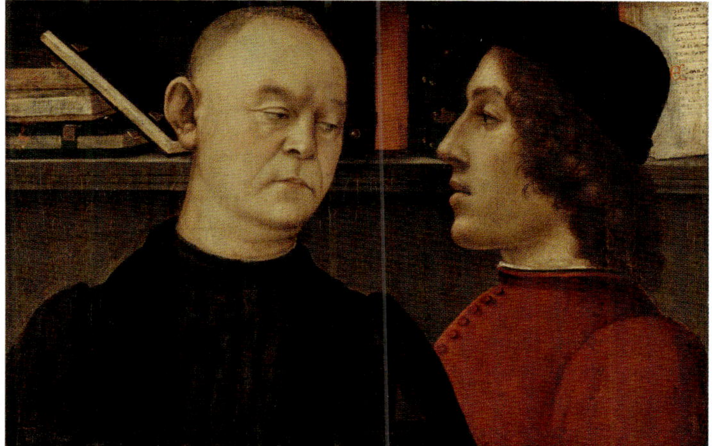

portrayed on the front and back of the panel, judging from the laudatory poem written by Janus Pannonius about Mantegna's likeness of his friend and him.[2]

The dates of Giuliano da Sangallo's life (1445–1516) mean that he probably commissioned Piero to paint the portrait of his father, Francesco Giamberti (1404–1483), several years after

24 Hans Memling, *Tommaso di Folco Portinari* and *Maria Portinari (Maria Maddalena Baroncelli)*, *c.* 1470, oil on wood.

25 Filippino Lippi, *Double Portrait of Piero del Pugliese and Filippino Lippi*, *c.* 1486, oil on panel.

the elder man's death, to create a pendant to Piero's already completed image of himself. Technical examination has revealed evidence of changes in the direction of recession in the stripes of cloth covering the parapet on the original image of Giuliano. Piero repainted them so that the new lines would recede towards the right to create a single unified perspective with the stripes in the cloth in the added image of Francesco. Careful study reveals that the original stripes are just visible to the naked eye. The quill and compass on the ledge before Giuliano were added after the repainting to match the sheet of music in the second image, a prop alluding to Francesco's profession.[3] In imitation of Netherlandish painting, Piero painted these likenesses on lime-wood, rather than the poplar panels usually used by Italian artists. The decision seems a nod to his rivals in northern Europe, who were famous for their portraiture.[4] Piero also created the works in oil, the favoured medium of northern Europeans, not in a tempera and oil mixture, which was his more common medium in his early painting. Piero imitated the northern Europeans' penchant for creating likenesses that seemed alive: Giuliano's hair looks tousled and uncombed, while his father's face is sunken, his oversize, flappy ear is bent out by his cap and his sheet of music is painstakingly folded and reveals carefully shaped, legible notes.

Vasari provides the important information that his friend Francesco da Sangallo (1494–1576), a sculptor and architect, had been a friend of Piero's and owned the diptych, which was probably bequeathed to him by his father. Vasari claimed that the portraits 'seem to be alive', which is an oft-repeated trope, but Vasari knew Francesco da Sangallo personally, noted his veneration of his ancestors and alluded admiringly to the paintings, which he may well have seen in person.[5] Just to apply to the portraits a variation on the humanist writer Bartolomeo Fazio's famous lines 'you would judge he lacked only a voice', was an honour.[6]

The portraits justify Vasari's praise, especially in their carefully modulated flesh, the ways in which individual strands of hair are picked out, and the animation provided by telling physical characteristics like the crow's feet at the corners of Giuliano's eyes, the prominent bulging vein on Francesco's temple and the dots of white paint around his mouth, suggesting stubble. Details such as Giuliano's grey-flecked hair, wayward brows and drooping eyelids are particularly convincing. We gain an even deeper appreciation of Piero's skill in verisimilitude when we understand that Francesco's face was probably brought to life from a death mask, which was often made in wax or plaster in Renaissance Florence to preserve the likeness of a recently deceased relative. The use of a death mask as the basis for the portrait of Francesco is suggested by his sunken eyes and cheeks, and retracted mouth,[7] which are typical facial transformations after death. Piero minimizes these signs of death's effects.

The panels are the same small size, and the two figures face each other. Giuliano is in a three-quarter pose while Francesco is in profile, perhaps to minimize the problems of enlivening his painted image from a death mask. Because of its roots in ancient Roman medallions, the profile pose suggested the past and conveyed remembrance. In Piero's portrait, the three-quarter Giuliano juxtaposed with the profile of his father imparts the son's memory of his deceased father.[8] They are each represented in bust length behind a parapet and in front of a receding landscape and blue sky with clouds, which continue unbroken across the two panels. People trudge and ride along a dirt trail that winds without interruption between the panels. These features, like the red cloth, serve to unite the portraits and suggest their familial bonds.

The portraits celebrate the different accomplishments of these two notables from different generations of the Sangallo family: on the ledge before the musician Francesco, Piero placed a folded sheet of legible musical notes; before Giuliano, the favourite architect of Lorenzo de' Medici and later an architect of the new St Peter's Basilica in Rome, he put a compass and a quill pen to symbolize his architectural drawings. Piero's portraits are among the earliest to celebrate their sitters' professions.[9] This innovation brings into the fixed recording of likenesses another way to allude to their past achievements and create their personas. Just as deliberately incidental or casual details such as dishevelled hair enliven the sitter's appearance, professional props conjure up memories about their lives.

Piero follows models by Netherlandish painters like Hans Memling, whose birth date is unknown but who was active by 1465 and died in 1494. His paintings were commissioned by Florentines like Tommaso di Folco Portinari, who became manager of the Medici Bank in Bruges, and others in Italy collected them eagerly (see illus. 24). Paula Nuttall provides inventories of numerous Netherlandish paintings in Florence in the collections of the Medici and other families.[10]

A comparison of Piero's paired paintings with the example of Memling's *Tommaso di Folco Portinari* and *Maria Portinari*, whose praying gestures indicate that they originally invoked the Madonna and Child in a now lost central panel, raises several compelling points. Unlike Memling's paired portraits, which were once part of a religious triptych, Piero's father and son celebrate their secular professions. Piero, like many other Italian painters, admired and imitated Netherlandish artists and used the oil painting they favoured to render different textures, capture light and shade as it models objects and reflects off them, and construct convincing landscapes that hold people and buildings within them.

Documents discovered in 2015 reveal why a sheet of music figures prominently in the portrait of Francesco Giamberti: he was an organist in his parish church of the Ospedale di San Gallo, which is invoked by the stucco and brick building with a bell tower in the right background of his image, before which an outdoor Mass is being celebrated. The organist to the church's right wears a new red cap like Francesco's. Further tiny details identify the church: most importantly, the cocks strung up by their heads from a tiled canopy before the church's entrance. They honour the church's name saint, the Irish monk St Gall, or Gallo in Italian (which translates to cock in English).[11] Francesco's son, Giuliano, constructed the church on the commission of Lorenzo de' Medici. It was later destroyed in the 1530 siege of Florence. According to Vasari, Lorenzo was so taken by the architect's designs that he started calling the architect 'San Gallo' and teased that Giuliano should drop the family name of Giamberti and rename himself and his relatives San Gallo or Sangallo, after the church. Giuliano did just that, and thus the amusing detail of hanging *galli*, so typical of Piero's inventiveness, plays to family pride and honours the talents of Francesco and his son as well.[12]

Rising in the left background of Francesco's likeness is an unidentified, grander church whose elegant limestone, domed, circular second storey is rimmed by *bifore* windows with tracery. The building recalls the avant-garde religious buildings with domed centralized plans initiated by Filippo Brunelleschi in Florence, such as the unfinished Santa Maria degli Angeli (1430s), and imitated by Giuliano da Sangallo's own Santa Maria delle Carceri in Prato (1484–95). It seems out of place behind Francesco Giamberti, rather than in the panel memorializing his son, the famous architect. Francesco is said by Vasari to have also been an architect, but no evidence has yet been found to support the claim.[13] The structures behind Giuliano, surprisingly, seem humbler: on the left, protective shelters for the nearby flock of sheep and an elevated loft with a ladder for access, and on the right a simple dwelling. They have not yet been identified as relating to a specific site.

Piero's double portrait of the Sangallo father and son may have inspired Filippino Lippi's single-panel double image of the painter himself with his patron and friend Piero del Pugliese (see illus. 25), which also presents the sitters in bust length. Like Piero, Filippino poses one figure in profile (in this case, his self-portrait) and the other, del Pugliese, in three-quarter view. The painting inspired poetic tributes to its lifelike representation of Piero del Pugliese and stands as an unusual double image of artist and patron as intimate friends whose social status differed but who possessed equal virtues.[14] Neither this portrait nor the Sangallo commission is securely dated, so one cannot be sure which way the influence flowed. Nevertheless, the relationship between them corroborates that the two artists or perhaps their patrons were aware of each other's inventions. Throughout their careers there are many instances of Piero and Filippino exchanging motifs and interpretations.[15]

So few independent portraits by Piero survive that a less elaborate single female likeness is also worthy of attention. The *Portrait of a Woman* (c. 1503, illus. 26) is a charming but conventional bust-length profile portrait of a young widow. She is positioned against a plain, dark background, as portraits of widows often were.[16] All categories of female portraits frequently presented a woman in profile because in that pose her gaze was averted from the audience (as it usually was in real life in public), thus connoting her modesty and chastity.

The portrait could be based on a much livelier drawing of what seems to be a charming young woman (c. 1495–1500, illus. 27). Piero, working in pen and brown ink with brown wash and white heightening on yellow-brown tinted paper, has captured the spontaneous appeal of the girl by emphasizing her open lips and large, upturned eyes. The fine strokes of white heightening trace the light glinting in her hair. If the drawing served as a study, almost all the vivacity of its sitter has been drained to correct it into a socially acceptable painted portrait. The drawing might have served equally well as a basis for the St Catherine discussed

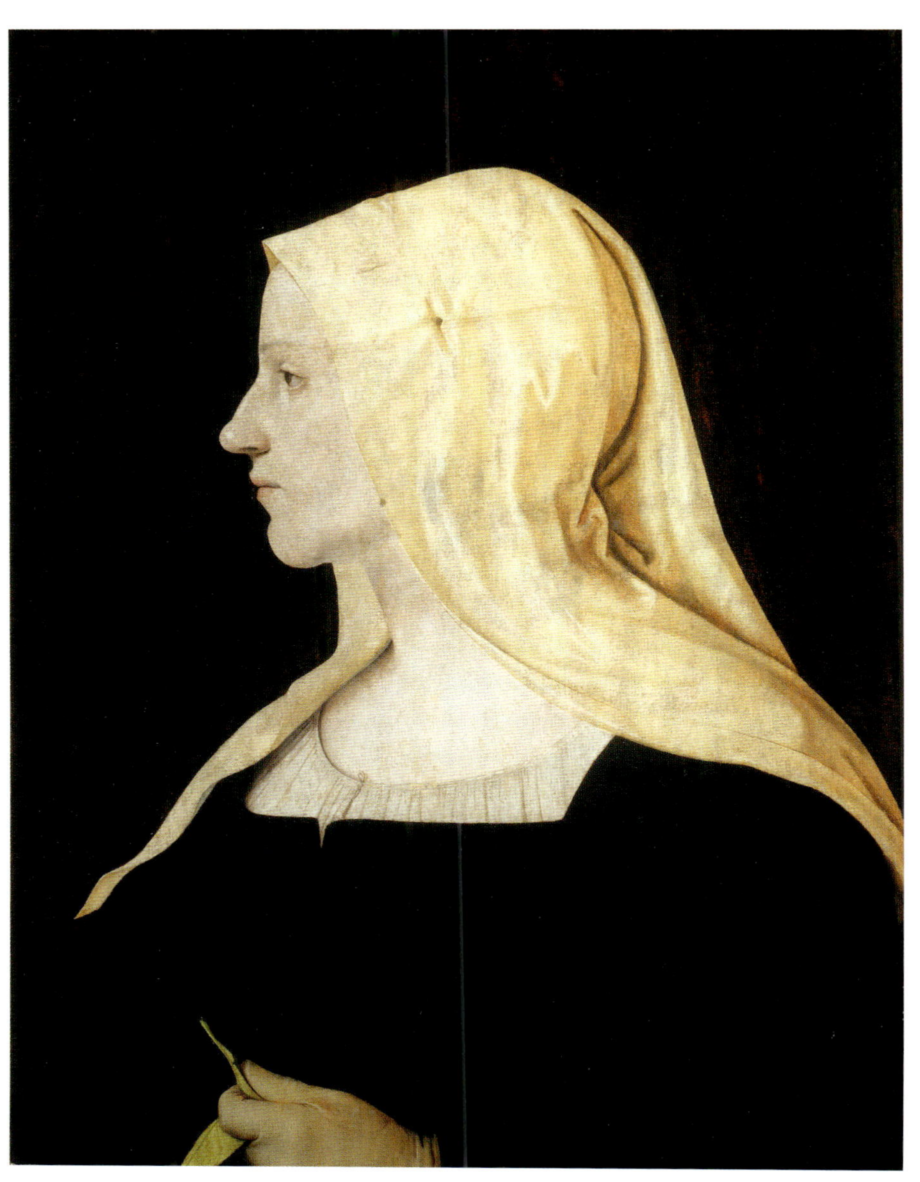

26 Piero di Cosimo, *Portrait of a Woman*, c. 1503, oil on panel.

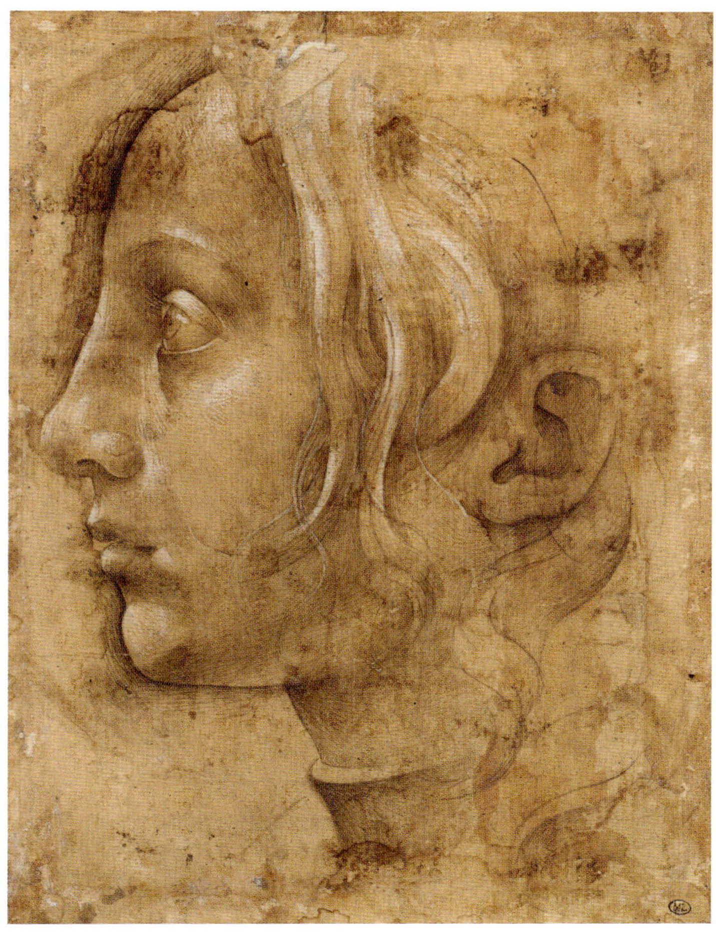

below, who is transformed in the painting to look appropriately saintly.

The widow is dressed in black, relieved only by the pleated, cream-coloured material of her *camicia* (shirt) at the bodice. The black background of the painting emphasizes her sombre dress. Her head and shoulders are covered by a cream-toned veil in a

27 Piero di Cosimo, *Head of a Youth (Young Woman in Profile)*, c. 1495–1500, pen and brown ink, brown wash and white heightening on paper.

heavier fabric that arches over her forehead, concealing her hair and trailing over her upper body. A small metal knob reveals that this fabric is pinned in place. She wears no jewellery. Clothing and pose close any window to her possible physical beauty. Although limited in palette and quite abraded, the image still shows Piero's ability to render details like the light-catching pin anchoring her veil and the veil's remnants of fold creases and volume. It also reveals his talent for making a sensitive likeness, but the viewer recognizes the resemblance to other heads by Piero, even those

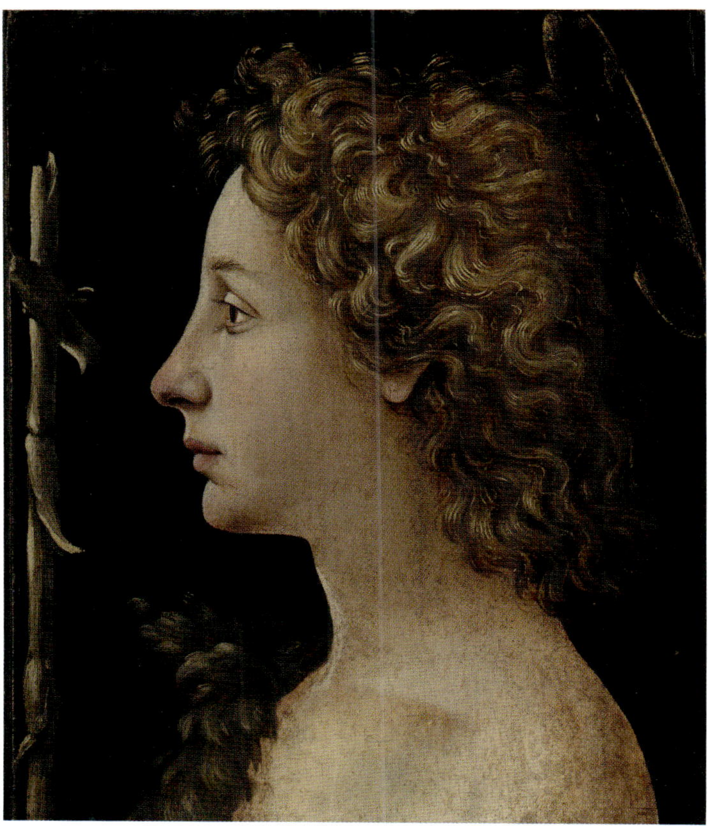

28 Piero di Cosimo, *The Young Saint John the Baptist*, c. 1480–85, tempera and oil on panel.

of males (illus. 28). The pale young woman has an idealized profile that nevertheless shows the facial contour and prominent nose found in other characters by the artist, for example the face of St Catherine in the del Pugliese altarpiece for the Ospedale degli Innocenti (Hospital of the Innocents, or foundling hospital) in Florence (*c.* 1493, illus. 46).

An atypical feature is the inclusion of one gloved hand that holds what looks like an orange leaf, a possible allusion to a lost love. While a widow usually holds some memento of her dead husband, it is more often a portrait of him. One hypothesis about the leaf's identity, based on the orange tree, which could specifically represent the Medici family, is that the painting depicts Semiramide Appiani, who married Lorenzo di Pierfrancesco de' Medici in 1482 and was widowed in 1503.[17] If that identification is correct, this would be the only painting that the Medici family commissioned from Piero di Cosimo. Even if not, the painting provides a valuable insight into period ideals. Sixteenth-century conduct books for widows make clear that images of females like this are meant to stand as exemplars of virtue for married and unmarried young women alike in their devotion to dead spouses or fiancés.[18] This portrait convincingly achieves that goal and demonstrates Piero's ability to fulfil the demands of period norms and conventions when necessary.

The next painting, a much less straightforward one, is an idealized female portrait and one of Piero's most famous paintings (early 1480s, illus. 29). In many ways, it is unique in fifteenth-century paintings: although it is in the standard pose of a bust-length profile image, the female sitter is bare-breasted, thereby apparently inverting the profile portrait format's customary intimations of modesty and chastity. Whereas most female images are posed within a window or door or on a balcony, Piero positions his sitter as though standing in front of a landscape. Meaningfully, she faces a setting sun, a dead tree and a dark storm cloud that

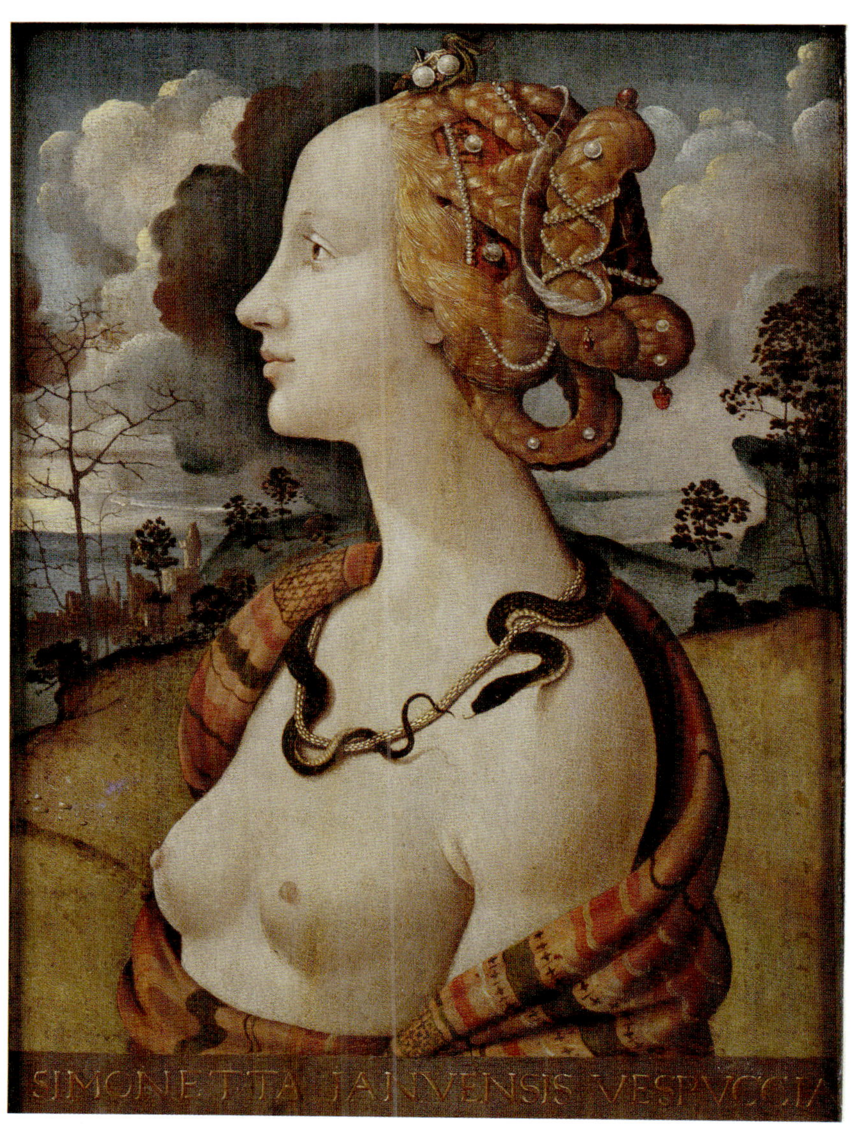

29 Piero di Cosimo, *Fantasy Portrait of Simonetta Vespucci*, early 1480s, tempera on poplar.

echoes the profile of her head. All portend a troubled fate for the young woman.

This is an ambiguous 'portrait' in both subject and type. The panel had traditionally been called *Cleopatra*, primarily because of the snake slithering around the woman's neck, the abundance of pearls bedecking her hair and Vasari's identification of the painting: 'Francesco still has a work by the hand of Piero that I must not pass by, a very beautiful head of Cleopatra, with an asp wound round her neck.'[19] He omitted mention of the inscription at the painting's base, which reads, 'Simonetta Januensis Vespuccia', or 'the Genoese Simonetta Vespucci'. Vasari's naming made the panel an imaginary portrait of the long-dead Egyptian queen who supposedly put a poisonous asp to her breast after Octavian's defeat of her native land. The pearls that wind through her hair were seen in connection with Cleopatra's famous huge pearl earrings, one of which she melted in vinegar and drank to win a bet with Marc Antony about her wealth (Pliny, *Natural History*, IX, 119–21). The anomalies of the contradictory inscription and of the snake entwined around the woman's gold chain, apparently chasing its tail and oblivious to the female who wears the necklace, remained. The legitimacy of the inscription was typically discounted as a later addition, and the snake's unthreatening pose was considered a decorative whimsy on Piero's part. New analysis, however, challenges the identification of the snake as a poisonous asp or cobra, instead naming it a harmless whipsnake, a breed very common in the Mediterranean area.[20] The reidentification further undermines claims that the female figure is Cleopatra. Both whipsnakes and asps were frequently found in Florence in the fifteenth century. Asps were hunted to concoct theriac, a cherished all-purpose remedy believed to be especially effective against the plague. Almost everyone would have known the difference, particularly an artist as interested in nature as Piero.[21]

In the case of this sitter's identity, substituting a whipsnake for an asp diminishes the possibility of her representing Cleopatra. As a common snake harmlessly encircling her neck and almost biting its tail, its symbolism could instead allude to the Greek and Egyptian ouroboros (literally, tail-swallower), a sign of perfection, eternity and immortality and an apt reference to Simonetta's ideal beauty and enduring reputation.[22] Its tail-biting circuit could mean immortality through allusion to the cycle of creation, continuity and perfection.[23] The more likely meaning, however, is to an uninterrupted cycle of life. Simonetta's earthly life and tragic early death are superseded by her everlasting fame.[24] The sitter's setting is charged with ominous change and suggests her doomed human existence: she is framed by dead trees, a setting sun and storm clouds that have gradually eclipsed the clouds lit by the sun, so portending her untimely end. She faces into the direction of this fate while behind her are trees in leaf and sunlit skies, suggesting bygone good weather and plenty.

The tail-biting serpent was also a specific emblem of Lorenzo di Pierfrancesco de' Medici, as seen on several of his medals.[25] Lorenzo di Pierfrancesco was married to Simonetta's step-niece, Semiramide Appiani. In that association and others, Lorenzo di Pierfrancesco is the member of the Medici family closest to Piero di Cosimo's ambient. Recall the letters written to him by Amerigo Vespucci about his discoveries, which seem reflected in several of Piero's paintings, and the possible identification of the *Portrait of a Woman* as his widow, Semiramide (see illus. 26). Lorenzo di Pierfrancesco also commissioned paintings – perhaps even Botticelli's *Primavera* (see illus. 14) – that deal with mythological subjects like those that Piero took on. In creating his image of Simonetta, Piero was directly competing with Botticelli's two ideal images of a clothed female lover, which Vasari identified as Simonetta (*c.* 1480–85, illus. 30).

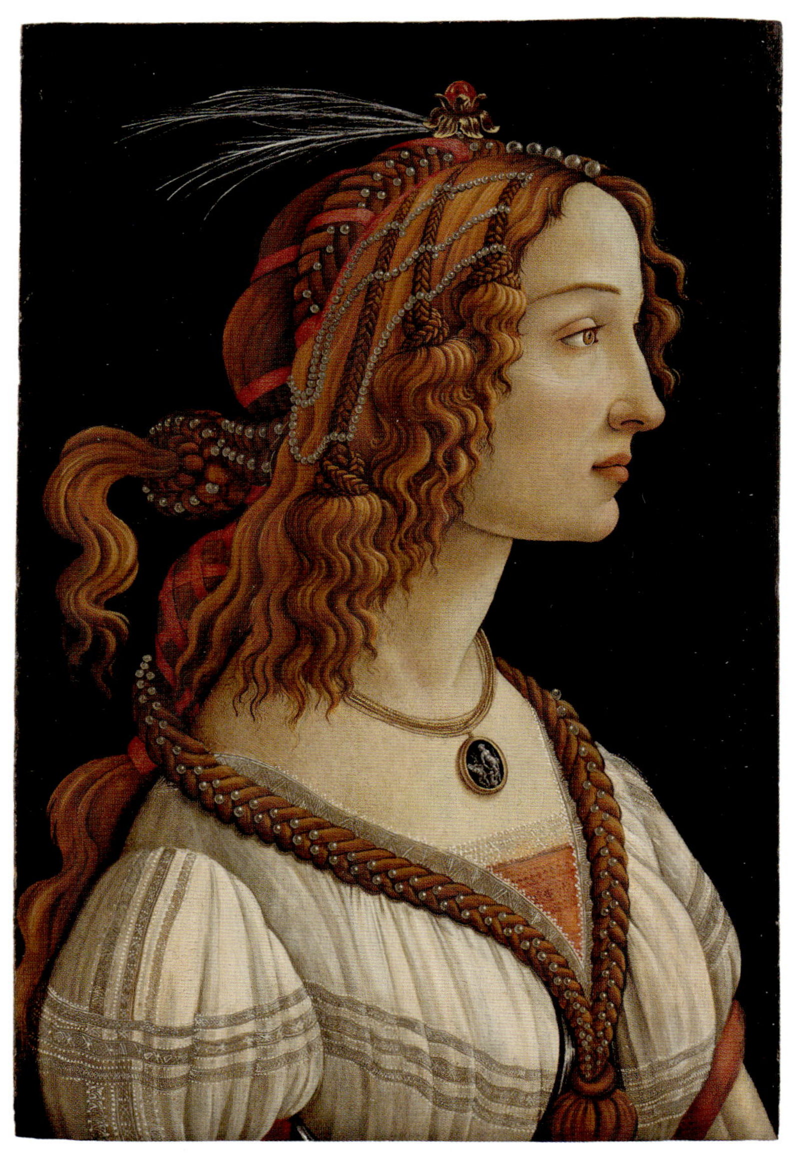

30 Sandro Botticelli, *Portrait of a Young Woman in Mythological Guise (Simonetta Vespucci?)*, *c.* 1480–85, oil and tempera on poplar.

More recently, the identification as a fantasy portrait of Simonetta Vespucci (1453–1476) has prevailed for additional reasons. Scientific tests have proved the inscription contemporaneous with the portrait, rather than a later addition: analysis revealed that there was nothing under the inscription, which means that it was not overpainted to conceal something else, such as a different inscription. The other option, that the painting originally had no inscription across its base, would have left an awkward, large blank space in a prominent area and seems unlikely. In addition, a note, hand-written in 1550–52 from the historian Paolo Giovio, was delivered by messenger to Francesco da Sangallo, the son of Giuliano da Sangallo, whose portrait was discussed earlier. It verifies Vasari's claim that Francesco was at that time the owner of the female portrait (although Vasari called it an image of Cleopatra).[26] Giovio, a collector himself, referred in the note to a portrait that the messenger should pick up, mentioning it by name as the depiction of Simonetta ('per la Simonetta'), so the identifying inscription was likely on the panel by then. Giovio is clearly specifying an inanimate object, given his request to Francesco to 'darla a questo messo', or 'give it to this messenger'.[27]

There is a possible argument that the inscription was added only in the late sixteenth century. This would accommodate Vasari's calling the painting a 'Cleopatra' and the imprecision of dating by scientific testing. According to this theory, the Vespucci family, which bought the painting in the late sixteenth century, could have added the inscription to a painting that had been identified as their ancestor for decades.[28]

Atop the woman's head sits a brooch with large pearls, an item of jewellery often associated with marriage.[29] In a secular context, the off-white colour, size, perfect shape and lustre of pearls suggest the wearer's beauty and purity but also stand for the material wealth of the gift-giving betrothed or husband. The woman wears a luxurious red brocade cap that is almost totally covered by her plaited hair (probably enhanced, especially at the back of her head, by the hair extensions popular at the time) and a pearl- and ruby-studded *vespaio*, or net, woven through it.[30] The net puns on her husband's name, Vespucci.[31] These factors consolidate the hypothesis that the portrait is an idealized image of Simonetta Vespucci and that Vasari misidentified her.

Simonetta was descended from the patrician Genoese Cattaneo family. She married Marco Vespucci, a distant cousin of Amerigo Vespucci. The Vespucci were political allies of the Medici. Lorenzo de' Medici lent the couple the Medici Palace for their wedding and the family villa at Careggi for the reception. Both he and his brother, Giuliano, were beguiled by her charms. She was Giuliano de' Medici's platonic lover. This designation should be understood in the context of courtly love and its lofty ideals of non-physical passion; there is no evidence that she was Giuliano's mistress.[32] At a jousting tournament in 1475, Giuliano carried a banner with Simonetta's image in the guise of the goddess Athena; it was painted by Botticelli and inscribed 'La Sans Pareille', or 'The Unparalleled One'. Upon winning the tournament, Giuliano named Simonetta the 'Queen of Beauty'. Many poems were written extolling her beauty. The painting can in many ways be seen as a form of visual poetry, paralleling the repeated references to Simonetta's otherworldly beauty in verse by Lorenzo de' Medici in his *Comento de' miei sonetti* (Commentary on My Sonnets) and also included in the *Raccolta aragonese*, a collection that he assembled of famous Tuscan poetry; in Poliziano's *Stanze per la giostra* (Stanzas on the Tournament); and in writings by Luigi Pulci and others.[33] Her good looks and grace made her the toast of Florence and supposedly the emblem of ideal beauty for artists like Botticelli. All Florence is said to have mourned her untimely death in 1476, at the age of 23, probably from tuberculosis. At the time, Piero was just fourteen or fifteen years old. The young woman's image would thus still be an imaginary and posthumous idealized type, although perhaps enhanced by descriptions of some of her actual features, like her hair and eye colour. As much as Simonetta epitomized female loveliness, comparison with another of Piero's idealized likenesses, *The Young Saint John the Baptist* (*c.* 1480–85), betrays the similarities in the artist's versions of the type, even across genders (see illus. 28).

Simonetta's fantasy portrait hews to the period's constant association in female images between beauty and virtue.[34] The depiction of Simonetta conforms to Petrarchan ideals of beauty, often adopted in female portraiture of the Renaissance: flawless pale skin, a rosebud mouth, golden hair, a plucked, high forehead and columnar neck, to name the most prominent. Her hair colour, strawberry blonde, was the most favoured colour of all.[35] There is a tension between the three-quarter position of her torso and her head's profile pose. She averts her eyes from viewers, suggesting the modesty expected in fifteenth-century well-born women, but turns her nude, upturned breasts towards them. Despite what may seem a frank sexual invitation, the uncovered breasts could allude to her purity. Of the many possible comparisons, we need only turn to the painting known as *Allegory*, which was probably paired with the *Simonetta*. It shows the allegory of virtue as a standing, bare-breasted female figure (*c.* 1500, illus. 31). In myriad ways, Simonetta 'teeters between the erotic and the pure'.[36]

A final comparison with a sculpted so-called *Double Portrait of Two Lovers* by the Venetian sculptor Tullio Lombardo shows the same slippery ambivalence between meanings (*c.* 1490–1510, illus. 32). Tullio's marble figures slide between looking like the stone from which they were crafted and human flesh. Piero's *Simonetta* similarly looks like both a two-dimensional likeness and a real woman. Simonetta's head in profile evades communication with us, whereas Tullio made his anonymous female confront us. The youthful bared breasts of both women are turned

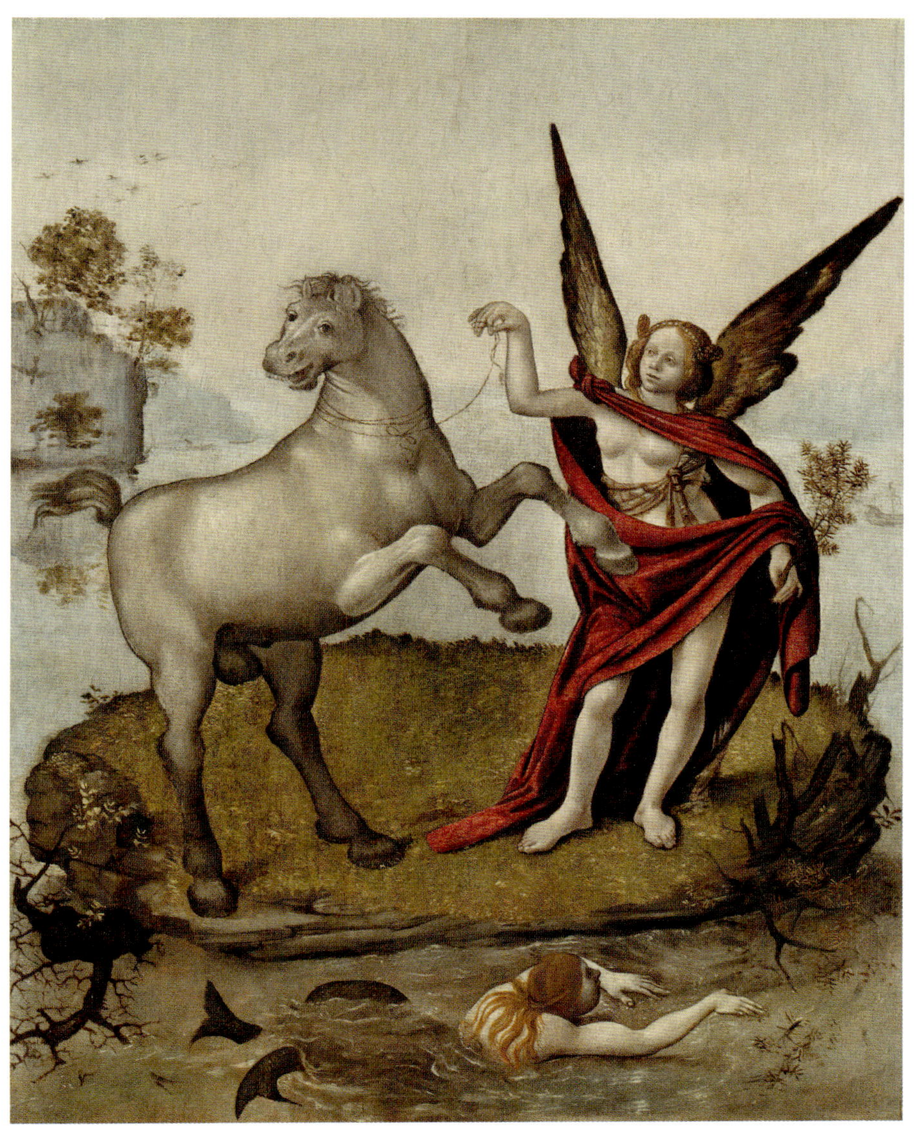

31 Piero di Cosimo, *Allegory*, *c.* 1500, oil on panel.

towards the viewer, and a fold of what seems to be human skin at the underarm invites our touch.

Simonetta's intricately plaited hair is wound through with strands, pins and brooches of pearls and rubies, precious jewels that are symbols of wealth and purity and of Venus, or love and marriage.[37] These multiple associations, above all to betrothal or marriage, reveal the image as a fantasy portrait, a conclusion corroborated by the snake encircling her neck and its connotation of ideal beauty and enduring reputation.

As suggested earlier, the *Fantasy Portrait of Simonetta* was likely paired with the *Allegory* (see illus. 31), which would move its date to the early 1480s, the probable date of the portrait. The size and proportions of the small, vertically orientated *Allegory* make clear that it was not a *spalliera* painting. It almost exactly matches the *Simonetta*. The *Allegory* most likely functioned as a cover or else a backing for the imaginary portrait. In 2014, technical analysis

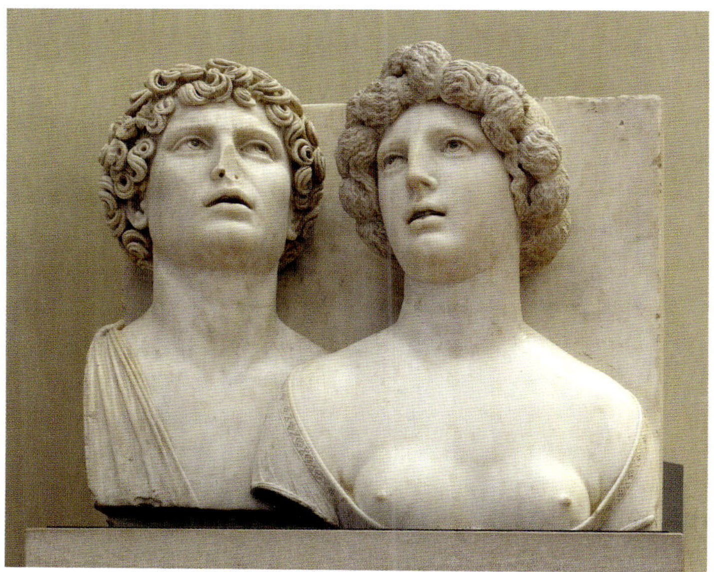

32 Tullio Lombardo, *Double Portrait of Two Lovers*, c. 1490–1510, marble.

revealed a barb, or unpainted edging, on the *Allegory* panel that indicates it once fit into a channel on the original frame, suggesting that the *Allegory* was a cover for the *Simonetta*. The barb and channel arrangement may have permitted the *Allegory* to be slid away to reveal the portrait. It makes it less likely that the *Allegory* was a backing for the *Simonetta* and faced in the opposite direction from it. In that arrangement the *Allegory* would not have shifted, and the barb would have served only for a permanent placement more easily achieved otherwise. Further laboratory analysis is necessary to validate this theory.[38] If accurate, this arrangement would have established a two-part reaction to the panels for the viewer – first the allegory, then the *Simonetta* portrait – stimulating a debate about the relation between the two panels and their different means of characterizing the erotic tension between lust and virtue.

The allegory of chastity and lust was frequently represented, but not like this. In the foreground, a double-tailed mermaid or siren, which can symbolize the dangers of lust, swims before an islet where a woman with a bare torso and wings (Virtue) holds in check a rearing stallion. The siren, which in Greek literature had been a bird-like monster, had become synonymous with the mermaid over the course of the medieval period.[39] She is nude, as her life in the sea requires. The nakedness and her long, wet, unbound hair sticking to her shoulders and back confirm that she represents lust because they were considered sexually charged female features.[40] The mighty stallion, another traditional symbol of lust, bares his teeth and seems as though he should overpower the woman, but she restrains him effortlessly with a thin cord loosely threaded between her fingers. She holds a branch of juniper, a symbol of chastity.[41] An alternative identification of the plant as yew would conjure the equally appropriate associations, for the accompanying *Fantasy Portrait of Simonetta*, of mourning and immortality.[42]

The stallion provides one of the few important clues to Piero's working procedure. A central enigma of his entire career is how a painter apparently unschooled in literature managed to create such multivalent, compelling and fanciful visual images of learned texts. Historians have found no better answer than the untestable hypothesis that advisers or patrons conveyed the gist of tales to him verbally and that Piero brilliantly, and with startling imagination, gave them visual form. We can prove that the rearing wild stallion derives from a drawing on parchment of about 1460 by the workshop of the Florentine painter Apollonio di Giovanni in a manuscript of Virgil's *Aeneid*. This correspondence suggests that Piero's clientele gave him access to their private libraries.[43] Other, yet untraced illustrations in the books in those libraries may have stimulated Piero's ideas as the image of the stallion seems to have done. If Piero himself worked as a miniaturist, as documents suggest, then his interest in these illuminated manuscripts and incunables of Graeco-Roman authors may have provided an important source for his own miniatures illustrating these writers' books. Patrons struck by his success in this medium could have encouraged him to transfer his narrative inventions to the different arena of larger-scale, more public painted panels. Regrettably, this enticing theory remains just that – until historians uncover illuminated manuscripts and books by Piero.

Thus far, we have been discussing independent portrait paintings, but Piero's patrons were interested in a second category of portraits: as stand-ins for saints in religious paintings. The most obvious example involves a portrait of Piero del Pugliese, one of Piero's most steadfast patrons, as the likeness of St Nicholas of Bari in an altarpiece called *Madonna and Child Enthroned with Sts Peter, Dominic, Nicholas of Bari and John the Baptist* (c. 1481–5), called the *Pala Pugliese* because it was commissioned by del Pugliese for Santa Maria a Lecceto, outside Florence (illus. 40). We can be sure of the identification because we have the *Double Portrait of*

Piero del Pugliese and Filippino Lippi with which to compare the patron's physiognomy (see illus. 25). Piero rendered the likeness of Piero del Pugliese in vivid detail and rich colour. He emphasized the stitching of his magnificent episcopal robes and the light-catching sheen of his golden dowry balls, the saint's most notable attributes. The altarpiece will be discussed in the next chapter, but here it is important to note that the portrait of a patron in the guise of a saint adoring the Virgin and Child flattered the secular figure's virtue and generosity in perpetuity and positioned an image of the patron very close to the sacramental rituals that took place at the altar. These advantages made the substitution of patrons' likenesses for saints a sought-after signal of a patron's eternal future placement in heaven.

FOUR

Altarpieces

Constant seeking after difficulties.
GIORGIO VASARI, *Lives*

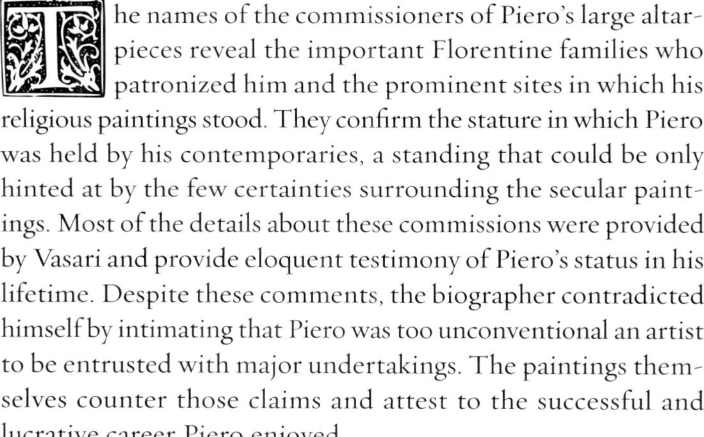he names of the commissioners of Piero's large altarpieces reveal the important Florentine families who patronized him and the prominent sites in which his religious paintings stood. They confirm the stature in which Piero was held by his contemporaries, a standing that could be only hinted at by the few certainties surrounding the secular paintings. Most of the details about these commissions were provided by Vasari and provide eloquent testimony of Piero's status in his lifetime. Despite these comments, the biographer contradicted himself by intimating that Piero was too unconventional an artist to be entrusted with major undertakings. The paintings themselves counter those claims and attest to the successful and lucrative career Piero enjoyed.

Altarpieces are important landmarks in Piero's career in another way: they are typically documented and dated. Most of his secular paintings are undated, leaving only the subjective criteria of stylistic analysis to arrange them chronologically. Not surprisingly, opinions diverge, making it impossible to arrive at any certain assessment of how Piero's career developed. The subject-matter and format of the altarpieces provide other important insights about Piero's career: they follow period norms, confirming that the artist adhered to the current sense of decorum. He distinguished between altarpieces created for public religious sites, with their attendant restrictions, and panels intended for private residences and limited viewing. Nevertheless, he still inserted hints of his humour and whimsy.

Three of the altarpieces in this chapter (see illus. 36, 40, 46) seem especially typical: they are in the Renaissance's standard *sacra conversazione* (sacred conversation) format of a lifelike yet impossible assembly of saints from different eras and parts of the world, who are envisioned in a unified space, surrounding and venerating the enthroned Madonna and Child. The assembly of saints usually includes the saint for whom the patron was named, the saints in whose chapel and church the altarpiece would stand and sometimes the saint who was the patron of the city where the church was located.

The other two altarpieces, the *Visitation with Sts Nicholas of Bari and Anthony Abbot* (*c.* 1489–90, illus. 33) and the *Incarnation with Sts Catherine of Alexandria, Margaret, John the Evangelist, Peter, Filippo Benizzi and Antoninus* (*c.* 1504–5, illus. 34), are arranged in a similar way. The principal figures (the Virgin Mary and her cousin St Elizabeth in the *Visitation*, the Virgin in the *Incarnation*) are interpreted as stationary actors who are surrounded by saints grouped as if writing commentaries on the scene or engaged in sacred conversation. Their patrons, the Capponi and the Tedaldi families, respectively, must have been supporters of the controversial new interpretation of the immaculately conceived Virgin (that is, that she was free of sin from the moment of her conception), as she is a principal protagonist in both paintings, and details associated with the doctrine appear in their paintings. The inclusion in this book of the del Pugliese sacred conversation altarpiece (see illus. 40) with its intact predella allows an analysis of the relation between its iconic central panel and the small

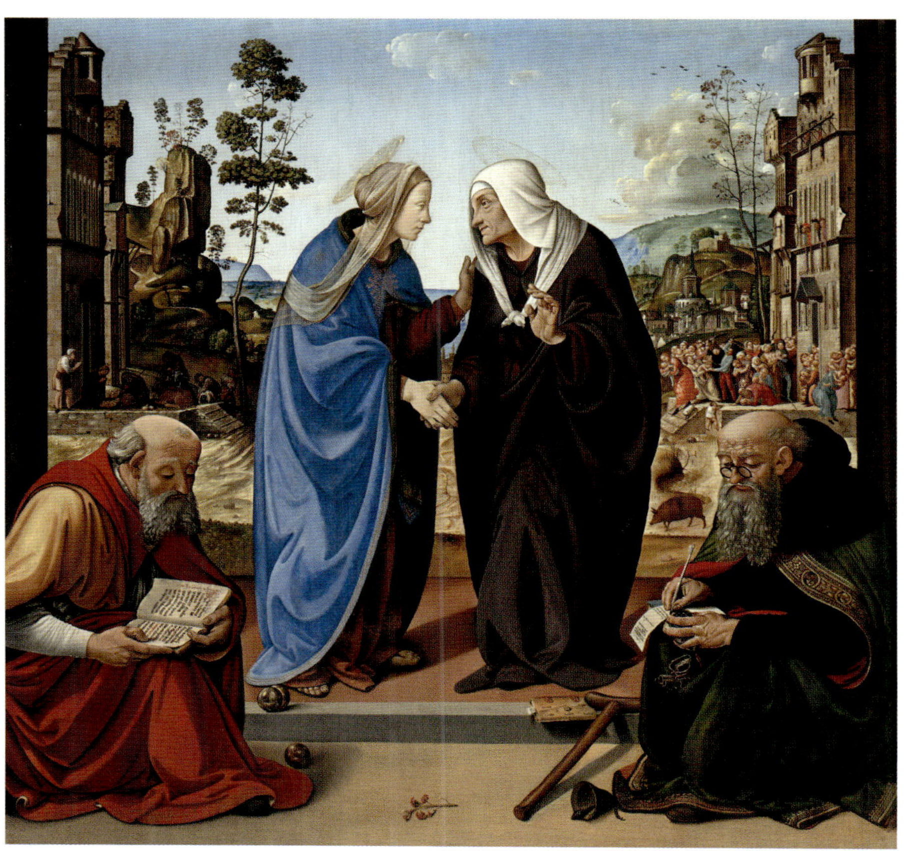

narrative scenes beneath. Although the predella was the standard place to illustrate the episodes associated with the altarpiece's main image, Piero sometimes juxtaposed lively narratives with the large figures of saints posed for our devotion in that panel. The *Visitation* is a good example: among much else, it contains a background scene of group infanticide (the Massacre of the Innocents); the Annunciation painted just below the cross on the upper storey of a religious building's facade; and a pig, which

33 Piero di Cosimo, *Visitation with Sts Nicholas of Bari and Anthony Abbot*, c. 1489–90, oil on panel.

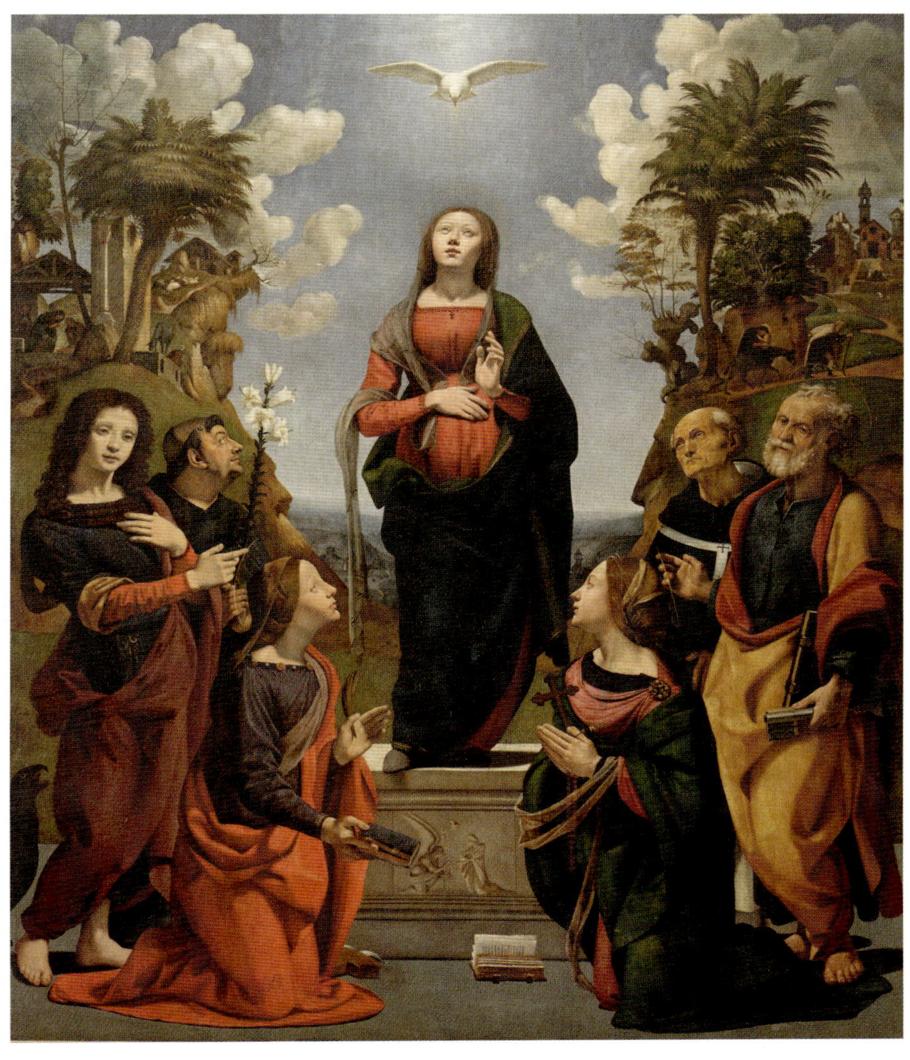

34 Piero di Cosimo, *Incarnation with Sts Catherine of Alexandria, Margaret, John the Evangelist, Peter, Filippo Benizzi and Antoninus, c.* 1504–5, oil on panel.

is Anthony Abbot's symbolic attribute, gambolling unfettered in the middle-ground (see illus. 45). The sacred conversation altarpiece commissioned by Piero del Pugliese for the Ospedale degli Innocenti (see illus. 46) is selected for discussion for two reasons: its sacred conversation is conjoined with an enactment of the mystical marriage of St Catherine and Christ, and it combines two media. The painting was originally surmounted by the *Annunciation* (illus. 35), a glazed terracotta relief sculpture by Andrea della Robbia (1435–1525).

Even in what is likely to be his earliest independent altarpiece, the *Madonna and Child with Sts Lazarus and Sebastian* (*c.* 1480–85, illus. 36), an undocumented painting for a small church in the countryside close to Florence, Piero displays his originality. The painting's likely date of about 1480–85 means he executed the panel when he was about twenty, so it is a sign of his precocious talent. Partly for this reason, the altarpiece was long considered the work of Piero's slightly older peer Filippino Lippi (illus. 37), so close in style were its thin, lanky and ascetic saints to figures in his paintings.[1] It stands as an important marker of how quickly Piero abandoned the ideas of his master, the old-fashioned Cosimo Rosselli, and began to study the innovations of his own contemporaries.

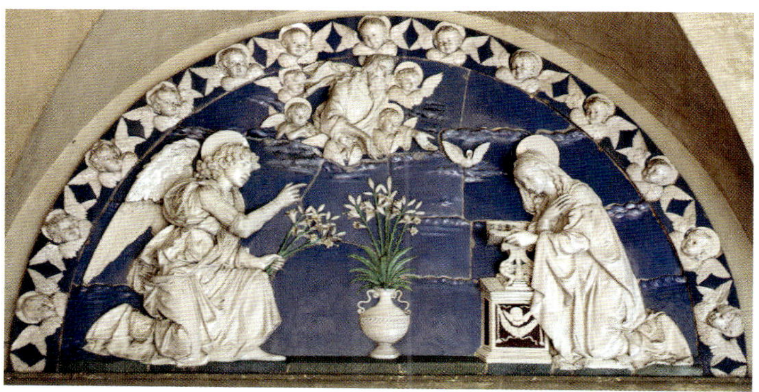

35 Andrea della Robbia, *Annunciation*, *c.* 1475, glazed terracotta relief.

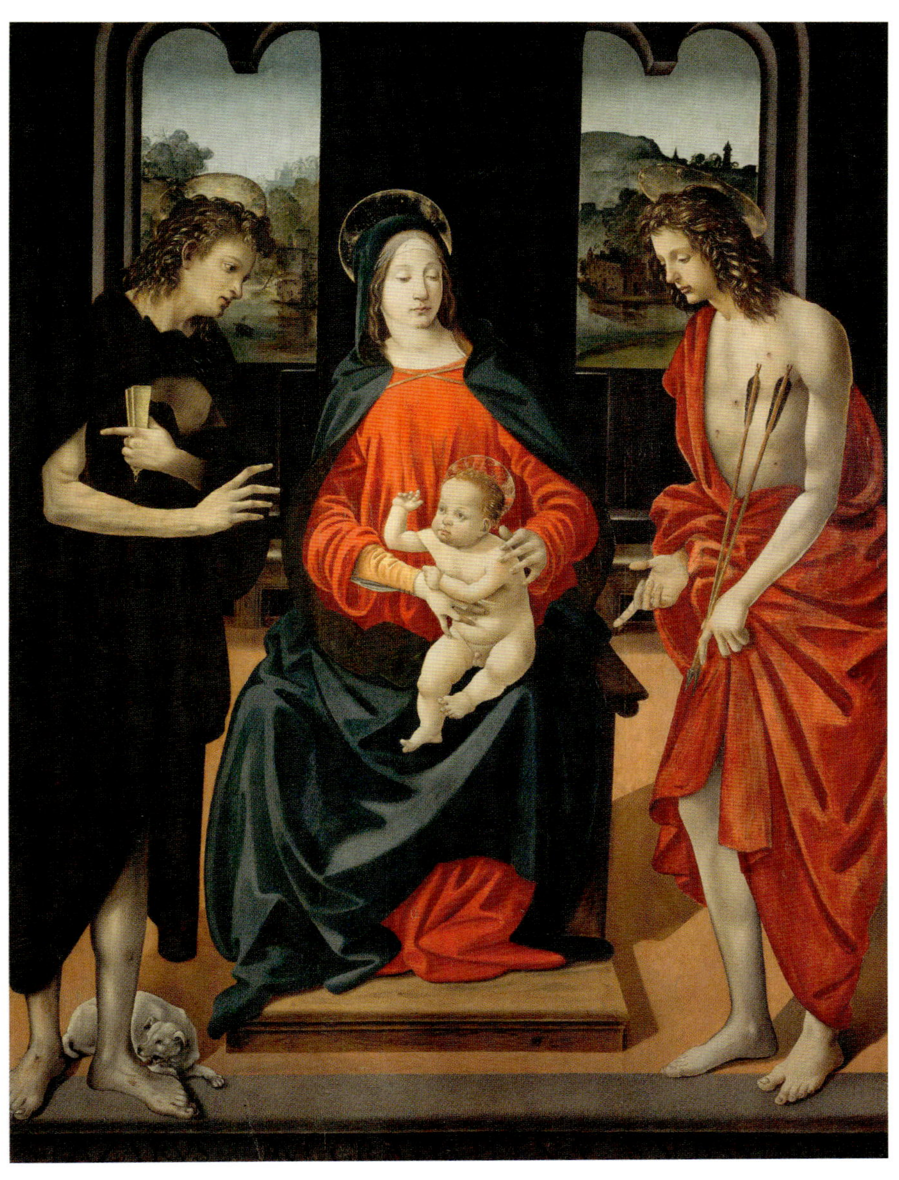

36 Piero di Cosimo, *Madonna and Child with Sts Lazarus and Sebastian* (*Montevettolini Altarpiece*), *c.* 1480–85, oil and tempera on panel.

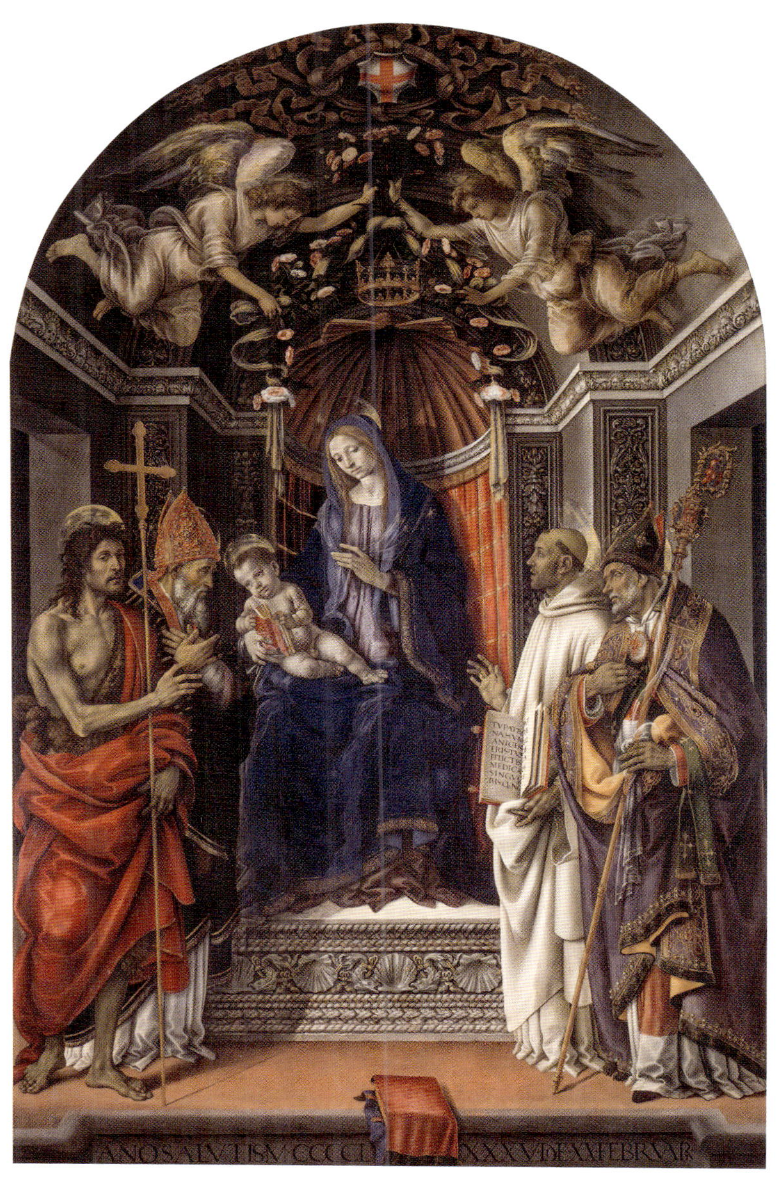

37 Filippino Lippi, *Virgin and Child with Sts John the Baptist, Victor, Bernard and Zenobius* (*Pala degli Otto*), 1486, oil and tempera on wood.

In this version of a sacred conversation, the seated Madonna and Child in the centre are flanked by two standing male saints, Lazarus on the left and Sebastian on the right. Both gesture towards Christ. Christ looks towards Lazarus and raises his hand in blessing. The saints' names are inscribed on the step riser beneath their feet, with three words abbreviating a common prayer to the Virgin, *Ave gratia plena*, or 'Hail, full of grace'. The words of a prayer were often included on the lower edge of a painting or frame so that the worshipper could read them and be prompted to prayer.

The painting's patron is unknown, but the inclusion of saints Lazarus and Sebastian suggests that the panel may have been commissioned in response to hoped-for deliverance from the recent outbreak of the plague (1479–80).[2] Lazarus holds the wooden clapper that a person with the plague or leprosy was required to shake vigorously if approached, so that his neighbour would hear the noise and move away to avoid contagion. A fly alights on the sore on the arch of his right foot to feed. Symbolically, it stands as an emblem of death, an appropriate reminder in a time of plague.[3] Piero certainly studied the realistic details of Netherlandish painting, but here he goes further, intending the gruesome and convincing close-up as a proof of his virtuosic painting skill. Artists as far back as ancient Greek painters sometimes aimed to prove their abilities by teasing the viewer with details like painted flies that at first seem real insects paused in flight on the actual surface of the painting. Renaissance artists picked up the *trompe-l'oeil* practice. A tiny white dog laps at the sores on Lazarus' other foot. With his sometimes macabre sense of humour, Piero pictured it licking the wounds with gusto, open-mouthed and tongue hanging out. Age-old belief held that a dog's saliva was an effective curative agent, and so the dog may be doing his best to heal his master. Modern science has validated this 'old-wives' tale'.[4]

Lazarus is described in Luke 16:19–21 as a man so poor that he hoped to catch crumbs falling from a rich man's table; while he lay on the ground, his sores were licked by dogs. Luke makes no mention of Lazarus having had the plague himself, but his sores led to his being associated with the plague. He is often depicted with the accessories appropriate to plague victims, as Piero has interpreted him here. What is more, hospices established for the quarantine and monitoring of plague victims all over Italy were called *lazzaretti*. One existed in Montevettolini, the town in Tuscany for which the altarpiece was commissioned.[5]

Sebastian holds two arrows, and his chest is punctured with bleeding wounds. He survived being shot by numerous arrows of the Roman Imperial Guard and is an obvious plague saint: since the time of Homer, the plague had been understood in terms of heaven-sent arrows intended to punish a sinful population. The *Golden Legend* (c. 1259–66), the book of hagiographies written by the Genoese friar Jacobus de Voragine, amplified his identity as a plague-deliverer by claiming that veneration of Sebastian had rescued the entire peninsula from plague in the time of the Lombards (sixth to eighth centuries).[6] After the outbreak of the Black Death in the mid-fourteenth century, Sebastian was frequently represented as a plague saint.

The figures seem fixed in their poses and somewhat stiff. The spatial recession of the room is unconvincing. It is unclear whether the saints are in front of the Madonna and Child, as the position of their feet on the foreground limestone ledge seems to indicate, or further back in the fictive space and much closer to them. Despite these awkward features, there is considerable evidence that Piero had been studying the paintings of his most famous contemporary, Leonardo da Vinci (1452–1519). Piero's close looking at the inventions of his most revolutionary colleague provides another indication of his ambition. Compositions by Leonardo like *The Benois Madonna*, painted in the late 1470s (illus. 38), provided a model for Piero's figures. Since that small devotional painting is a close-up view of the seated Madonna and Child, it offered no

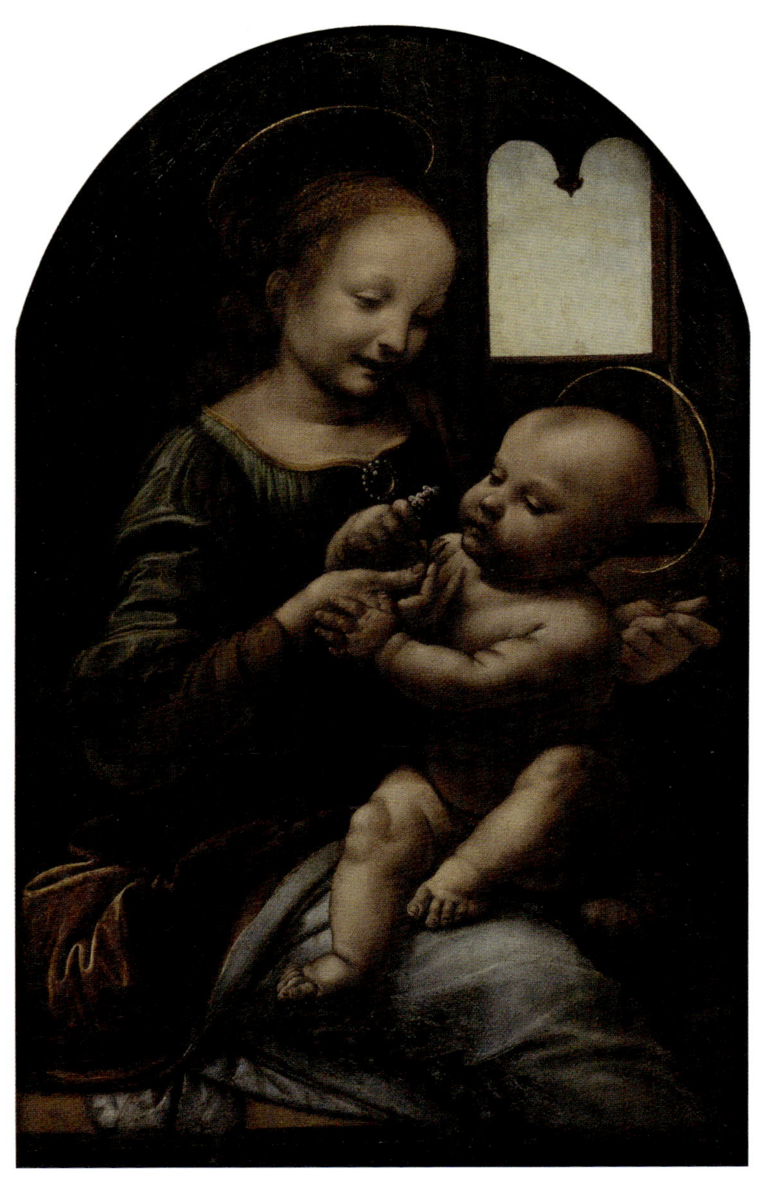

38 Leonardo da Vinci, *Madonna and the Child*, or *The Benois Madonna*, *c.* 1478, tempera and oil on wood.

help on secondary figures and spatial recession: exactly the areas
in which Piero ran into trouble. Piero seems to have imitated the
large head and lack of a neck of Leonardo's Christ Child. He also
was influenced by the way Leonardo emphasized the close positions of the Virgin's and the Christ Child's hands, although in his
more sombre painting, Piero transformed Leonardo's smiling
young mother, apparently playing with her child, into a serious,
stiff-backed, more mature woman. Piero has obviously adopted
the arched *bifore* window in Leonardo's painting, doubling it and
increasing its size to reveal a continuous landscape beyond the
dwelling. At the same time, the Virgin's face reflects study of
Botticelli in its shape and idealization.

The vista of a beautiful river valley where the water's surface
reflects both the adjacent buildings and the light of the surrounding atmosphere borrows directly from techniques and details
common in Netherlandish painting. The structure of Piero's
painting, as an interior room functioning like a plateau overlook-
ing the background landscape, does as well. Piero's choice to look
to the latest pictorial innovations confirms how daring he was —
and this during his opening years as an artist, when he was trying
to win patrons' attention. A telling comparison can be made with
Hans Memling's three-panelled painting created for the Dominican
bishop Benedetto Pagagnotti, which was in Florence by 1482–3
(illus. 39).[7] Pagagnotti was a major figure in Florence who was
behind Lorenzo de' Medici's son Giovanni securing a cardinal's
hat. He also officiated at the execution of the Medicis' enemy
Girolamo Savonarola in 1498. Both acts reveal his closeness to
the Medici family.[8] Piero's Montevettolini painting (see illus. 36)
makes it likely that he knew Memling's composition and simplified it by removing the two kneeling angels. That reduction leaves
a similar arrangement to Memling's two standing saints in the
wings either side of the Madonna and Child, who are enthroned
before a cloth of honour. Piero imitates Memling's two vistas

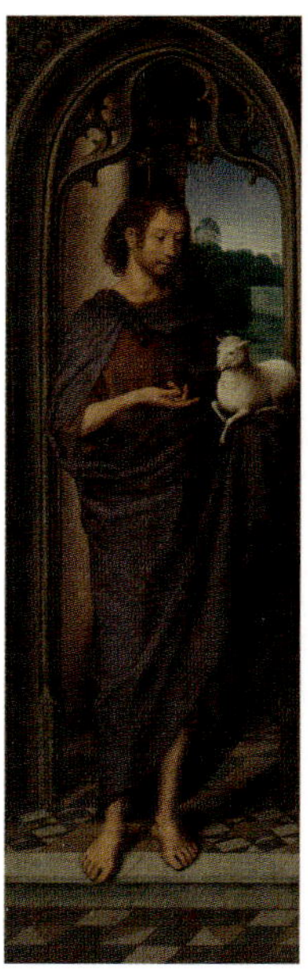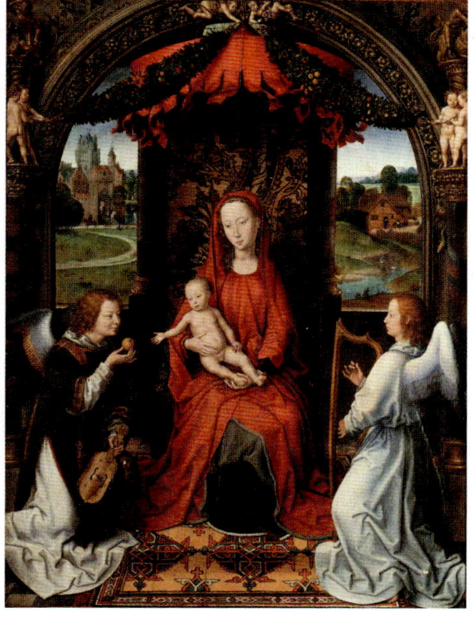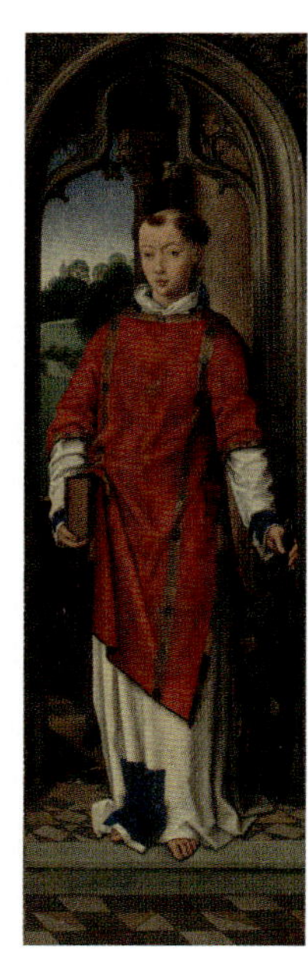

of a beautiful background landscape receding in atmospheric perspective on the far side of a river. As in the Netherlandish painting, minuscule figures and animals are at work on the river-banks, and its water surface reflects the surrounding light-filled sky and building profiles.

The following painting, another sacred conversation, this time an enthroned Madonna and Child flanked by saints Peter, Dominic, Nicholas of Bari and John the Baptist (see illus. 40), offers valuable evidence about Piero's reputation among his contemporaries. Unlike the *Madonna and Child with Sts Lazarus and Sebastian*, it was commissioned by a known patron, Piero del Pugliese. We have already encountered Piero del Pugliese and his nephew Francesco as fans of Piero. Vasari alluded briefly to them both as commissioners of Piero's secular paintings for their joint residence.[9] In this case, he commissioned the altarpiece for a private

39 Hans Memling, *Madonna and Child with Angels, Sts John the Baptist and Lawrence* (*Pagagnotti Altarpiece*), c. 1480, oil on panel triptych.

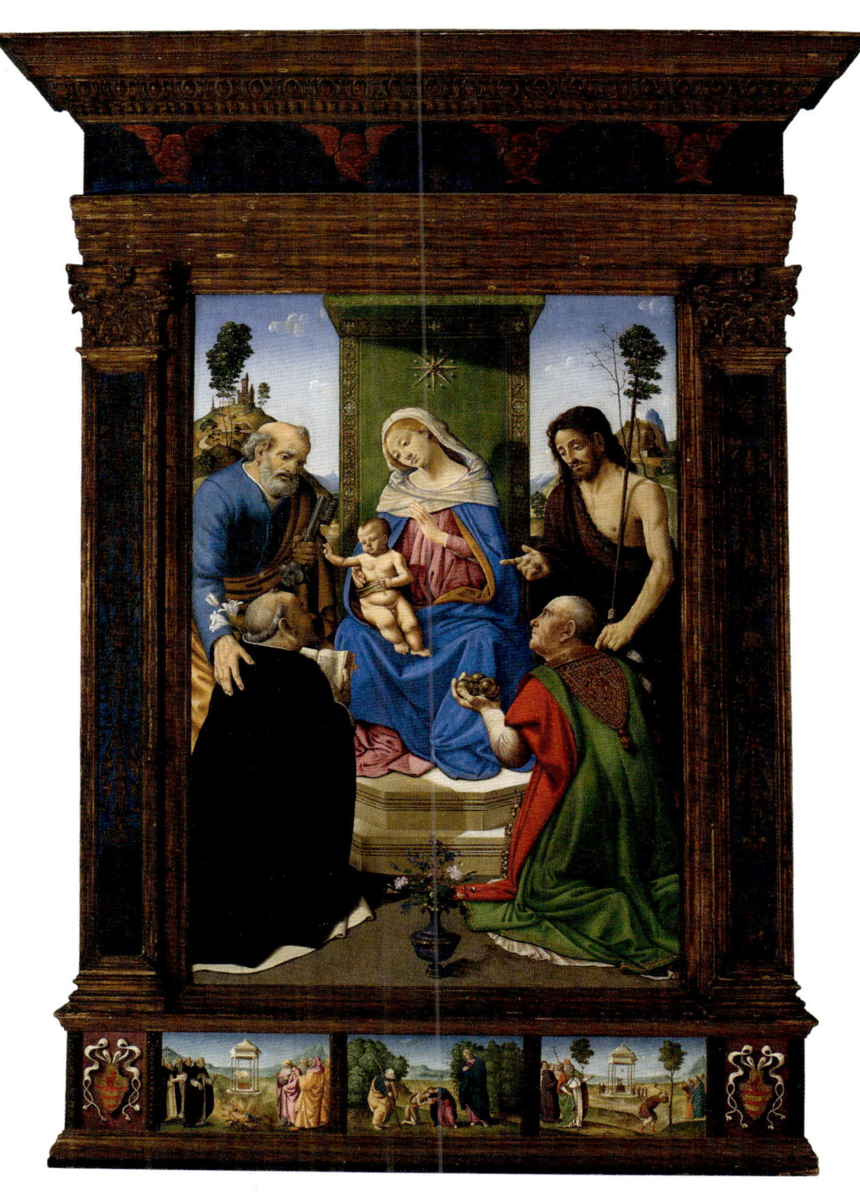

40 Piero di Cosimo, *Madonna and Child Enthroned with Sts Peter, Dominic, Nicholas of Bari and John the Baptist (Pala Pugliese)*, c. 1481–5, oil and tempera on panel.

family chapel in a Dominican institution, Santa Maria a Lecceto, outside Florence.[10]

Furthermore, the altarpiece's many levels of symbolism reveal how Piero di Cosimo could readily adapt to the demanding programmes his commissioners wanted visualized in their altarpieces and gain their satisfaction. To fit their needs, he created compositions with saintly protagonists and patrons who were readily recognized by worshippers and visually attractive. Many of the details of their lives, miracles, dress and identifying accessories were well known in the fifteenth century and did not need the interpretation provided below about the predella.

In the case of this altarpiece, we see the patron Piero del Pugliese in the guise of St Nicholas (270–343 CE).[11] As discussed earlier, his portrait is placed on the kneeling figure at bottom right holding the three golden balls, symbolizing the dowries of gold that the saint gave three poor young women, probably saving them from prostitution. The subtle variations of light, shade and reflected colour on the golden balls epitomize Vasari's observation that Piero sought out difficult things to paint. The correlation between St Nicholas and Piero del Pugliese flatters the Florentine patron's generosity in endowing the church. A sliver of Nicholas's jewel-encrusted mitre is visible on the ground before him. The gold-threaded embroidery on the plaque at the back of his green chasuble (a sleeveless liturgical garment) bears an image of St Paul (*c.* 5–64/5 CE) holding a sword, his typical accessory because it represents the weapon with which he was martyred. Paul may be included because he influenced St Nicholas's development as a Christian during his missionary work in Myra and Patara, communities where Nicholas lived.

John the Baptist (first century BCE–*c.* 30 CE; Florence's patron saint), on the right, points to the Christ Child, announcing Christ's mission of salvation and commending to him Piero del Pugliese in his guise as St Nicholas. St John almost touches Nicholas to convey these important messages. The Madonna and nearly nude Christ Child are the focus of the characters' (and the worshippers') devotion. The child's bared genitals and navel make clear the human aspect of his dual identity as God and man. The veil winding around him suggests the cloth that will be wrapped around his body after death and portends the end of his human life and his resurrection. Both are positioned before a green hanging drape emblazoned with symbols, which is called a cloth of honour because it hangs behind the throne on which divine figures sit. Above Mary is a gold- and pearl-embellished star, symbolizing her frequent epithet as the Star of the Sea. The pearls play a second role of suggesting her purity. As one medieval lapidary explained, 'The Margarita [pearl] is chief of all stones . . . it was gendered of the dew of heaven.'[12] The notion, without the Christian gloss, can be traced back to antiquity and Pliny's *Natural History* (IX, 107–9). Over the course of the medieval period, this Christian interpretation was expanded to emphasize the pearl as the result of the marriage of heaven and earth and the perfect symbol of the Virgin Mary.[13]

In the border of the fabric are symbols of the Holy Spirit (white dove), the third person of the Trinity and two symbols of Christ's Passion: the three nails that affixed him to the cross and the crown of thorns with which he was mocked as King of the Jews. On the left, opposite St John, stands St Peter holding the keys to heaven. Peter is the counterpart of Paul as a patron of Rome and of the Church. He introduces St Dominic, identifiable by the lilies symbolizing purity and the black and white habit of the Dominican Order he founded. The Madonna inclines her head and gaze towards St Dominic (in honour of his role as patron saint of the church) and the Christ Child raises his hand in a two-fingered blessing to the saint. There was a connection between St Nicholas and St Dominic: the first two chapters of the nascent Dominican Order met in the early thirteenth century at the church of San Nicolò delle Vigne in Bologna, and after Dominic's death he was buried in that church. Soon it was expanded and renamed in Dominic's honour, and his shrine was erected there.

In the front centre of the painting stands an eye-catching lapis lazuli vase trimmed with gold accessories. The choice of materials imparts manifold associations to the scene. Lapis lazuli is mined in the mountain peaks of desolate areas of Afghanistan; the stone has always been difficult to access and thus extremely expensive. Since ancient times, people related the rich blue colour of lapis to the heavens and considered it to convey divine power and the primordial force of life. Consequently, it was judged the most precious of all materials.[14] In the Old Testament, lapis lazuli (under the name *sappir*) took on further meanings. It was acknowledged as the stone that constituted the vault of heaven and the throne of God. It was perceived as one of the twelve stones engraved with the twelve tribes of Israel that adorned the pectoral of the High Priest, and then associated with other groups of twelve like the prophets and the apostles.[15]

Curiously, at the time Piero painted the del Pugliese altarpiece, there were no recorded objects in lapis lazuli on this scale in Florence. Documentary research reveals hardly any lapis lazuli objects were available in Italy. An inventory in 1457 of the collection of the avid connoisseur Pope Paul II indicates that he owned a vase in lapis lazuli; however, it did not pass into the collections of Lorenzo the Magnificent in Florence as much of his holdings did. In fact, there were no such impressive objects in lapis in Florence until 1534.[16] Thereafter, the Medici Dukes amassed them greedily, as the holdings of the Museo degli Argenti in the Palazzo Pitti in Florence make clear. As a painter, Piero would of course have been familiar with the ground pigment made from lapis and its rich blue colour. Think back to the tale of how the clueless Pope Sixtus IV chose Piero's teacher, Cosimo Rosselli, as the best artist in the team working on the Sistine Chapel walls (instead of

Botticelli!) because Rosselli bedazzled him with a calculated liberal dusting of gold and lapis on his paintings. We must hypothesize, until proved wrong, that Piero painted a lapis lazuli vase without ever having seen a hunk of the precious stone on this scale. However, he and his patrons would have been familiar with the collection of Judaeo-Christian associations it had acquired because they were already widely circulated by literary sources like the Old Testament. The lapis vase itself is interesting for a further reason: Piero painted such a vase, remarkably similar to vessels of this size and appearance crafted in lapis lazuli, decades before documents record they were produced in Florence or imported there.[17]

The vase holds flowers that enhance the religious meanings of the subject. They seem to be pink carnations, in Latin *Dianthus*, the flower of God, and blue larkspur, or *Delphinium*, a symbol of lament.[18] Both underscore the important role of the Christ Child as God's offering to humankind and Christ's ultimate sacrifice for human salvation. The flowers referring to the Virgin and Christ within a vase with associations to the Old Testament suggest the metaphor of how the Old Testament contained and led to the New Testament, which Christians view as its necessary sequel.

Various aspects of the painting betray how thoroughly Piero di Cosimo studied Netherlandish painting, a powerful influence on Florentine painting in the late fifteenth century. The rich and lustrous colours; the light and shade that models the flesh, giving volume to the figures' heads and bodies (note especially the chubby Christ Child); the shadow cast by St Dominic's body on the throne base of the Virgin; and the smaller but suggestive shadow of the vase on the floor: all show the facility of the painter with Netherlandish oil-paint techniques to enhance light, shade and colour. Also typical of Netherlandish painting is the way the landscape recedes convincingly in atmospheric perspective below a sunny blue sky with fluffy clouds. Piero's ability to capture textures shows further lessons learned from Netherlandish art: a few telling examples include the steely grey metal of St Peter's keys, the white-flecked strands of his grey hair and beard and the shiny balls of St Nicholas. The sketchy figures and light-filled window reflected in the golden balls held by Nicholas mimic a frequent Netherlandish pictorial feature. Mastery of these skills allowed Piero to create convincing likenesses of very different-looking people and settings.

Many Netherlandish paintings had been collected in Florence, but the lapis lazuli vase with blue larkspur (delphinium) and pink carnations (dianthus) in the centre base of the del Pugliese panel reveal that Piero had studied the most famous of all of them, for they play a similar symbolic role to the ceramic and crystal containers of flowers in Hugo van der Goes's *Portinari Altarpiece*, imported into Florence in 1483 at great expense (illus. 41). Sixteen porters had to move it overland to Florence after the ship docked at Pisa.[19] Portinari had the huge three-panelled painting hung over the main altar in the Church of Sant'Egidio in the hospital of Santa Maria Nuova, of which he was a patron.[20] Its scenes of the Nativity, the Journey to Bethlehem, the Adoration of the Shepherds and of the Magi completed the pre-existing mural cycle of the life of Mary by a group of esteemed Florentine artists.[21] The Florentine painters' Company of St Luke met in an oratory attached to the hospital complex, allowing the city's visual artists ample opportunity to study Van der Goes's masterpiece nearby and to compare it to Florentine paintings.[22]

Hugo's painting depicts the Christ Child lying naked on the ground outdoors with Mary kneeling in veneration before him. Surrounding the child are many angels flying or kneeling on the ground, the shepherds and Joseph, all of whom join Mary in praying to Christ. Many of the angels wear the liturgical robes associated with officiants of the Mass. Clearly, the painting does not represent a single episode from the Bible but is a symbolic assemblage. No surprise that the containers of flowers prominent in its foreground enhance these emblematic associations. The botanical specimens all announce the Passion of Christ and Mary's mourning of his future. A tall ceramic apothecary jar, which suggests the medicinal herbs and flowers such jars usually held, is positioned at the front of the painting's central panel, where those kneeling in devotion looked directly at it. Viewers would have been well acquainted with the healing associations of the contents of cylindrical jars through visits to apothecary shops, and with the symbolic meanings of the flowers in the containers through prayers, sermons and their frequent inclusion in other paintings. In this case, the jar holds orange-red lilies, a colour connoting the blood of the Passion, and white and blue-purple irises. The irises' long, narrow shape makes them like symbolic swords piercing the Virgin's heart and causing her sorrow. The white blooms symbolize Mary's purity, while the blue-purple blossoms allude to her melancholy at her son's foreordained death. The Venetian glass vase beside it contains blue columbines, which echo the irises' colour to suggest sorrow, and crimson carnations. Their deep red colour relates them to Christ's blood, and their number suggests the three nails that affixed Christ to the cross. On the ground around the vases are scattered many leafless purple violets (*Viola sororia*), which signify the Virgin's humility and suffering. Their leaflessness and

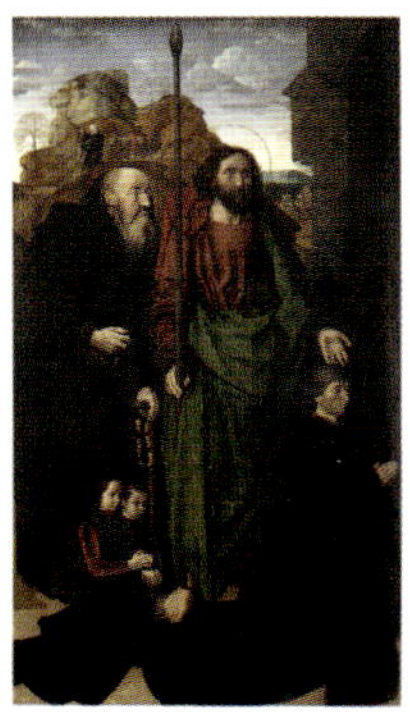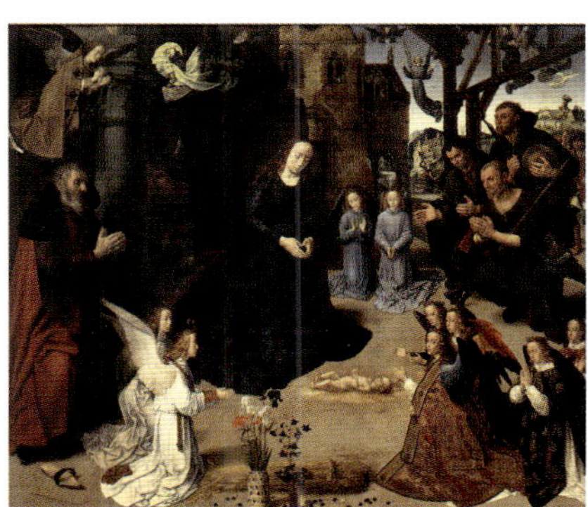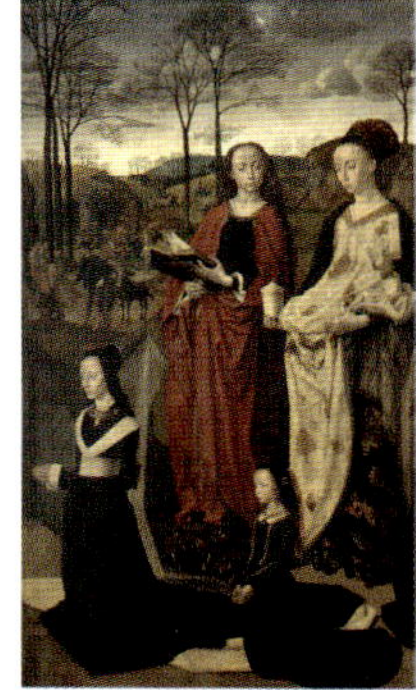

41 Hugo van der Goes, *Portinari Altarpiece, c.* 1477–8, oil on panel.

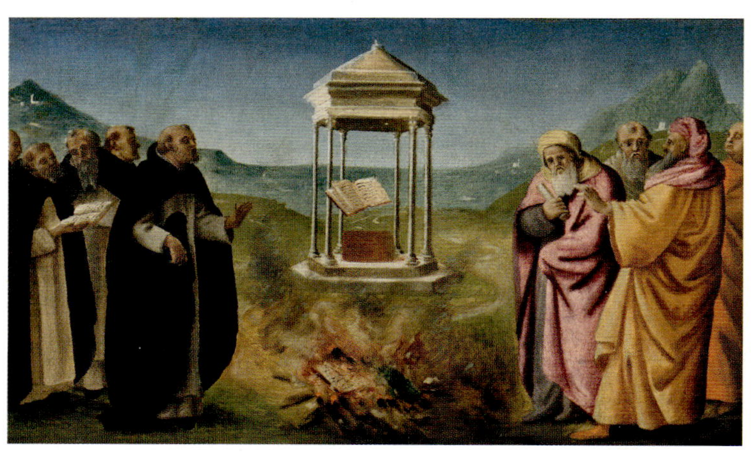

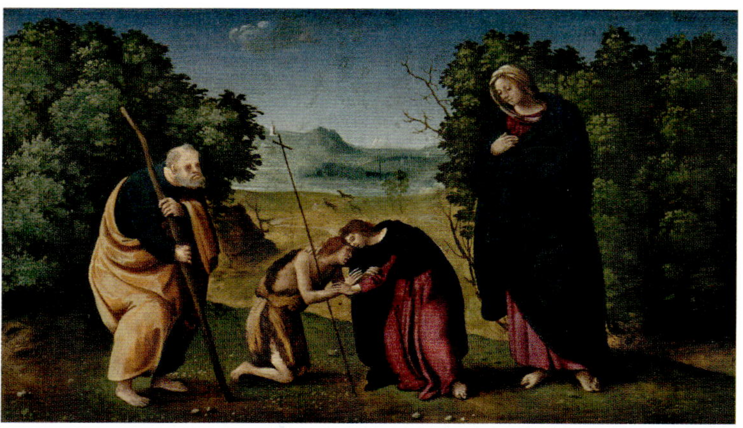

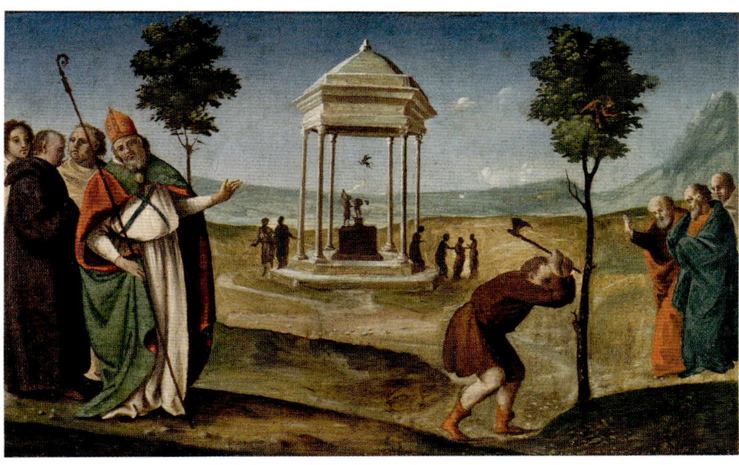

apparently random arrangement convey as well Christ's vulnerable nakedness.[23] Like the vessels in the *Portinari Altarpiece*, the vase in Piero's *Madonna and Child* sits at about the worshipper's eye level and is thus a main draw on the viewer's attention.

Piero's painting is often dated between 1481 and 1485 based on style, but the similarities with the *Portinari Altarpiece* suggest it dates after that painting's arrival in Florence in 1483. The altarpiece's frame, which is painted blue with a gold foliate pattern, is a nineteenth-century replacement but it preserves the original del Pugliese coat of arms on the lower supports of the frame contiguous to the predella.

The three smaller panels of the predella below the devotional image depict scenes from the lives of saints Dominic (1170–1221), John the Baptist and Nicholas of Bari. Expanding the representation of the saints in the main image vertically above the predella panels is typical of these scenes (illus. 42–4). From left to right, they first represent the well-known story of St Dominic's victory in a trial by fire. His Christian writings, when thrown into the flames, did not burn, whereas the books of the Albigensians, a heretical sect centred in southern France, went up in flames. This proved that the saint's texts represented the word of God, in contrast to the Albigensian books. The saint thereby successfully challenged and defeated the major opposition to Church doctrine in the thirteenth and fourteenth centuries.

Whereas the successful trial by fire of Dominic's texts is a standard theme associated with the saint, the second predella panel depicts the extremely unusual story of Christ consoling John the Baptist on his mother's death. The tale derives from several New Testament apocryphal books, including the *Life of John the Baptist*, which was allegedly written in Greek by the fourth-century CE theologian Serapion of Thmuis. The book provides the sole description of Elizabeth's death, although the predella painting does not follow all its details:

42–4 Scenes from the predella of Piero di Cosimo, *Madonna and Child Enthroned with Sts Peter, Dominic, Nicholas of Bari and John the Baptist* (*Pala Pugliese*) (illus. 40).

. . . when John is seven years and six months old, Elizabeth
dies, portentously on the same day as Herod the Great.
Jesus, 'whose eyes sees heaven and earth' [7:3], sees John
grieving and spirits himself and Mary to the desert on
a cloud. They bury Elizabeth and then Jesus and Mary
remain with John for seven days, teaching him how to
live in the desert.[24]

The scene depicts Christ hugging John the Baptist to solace him.
On the right stands the Virgin Mary, who accompanied Christ
to comfort John. Reasonably, the figure on the left leaning on
his walking stick is her aged husband, Joseph, but he is not included
in the text. The trees in leaf framing the scene and the green
grass in the foreground also do not correspond to the supposed
desert setting. The episode was included in the *Meditationes vitae
Christi* (Meditations on the Life of Christ) in the fourteenth century, through which it became better known.[25] In some versions, it
was also illustrated.[26] Nevertheless, it is surprising that the much
more common scene, John's baptism of Christ, is not included in
the predella instead.

The third predella panel is supposed to depict St Nicholas of
Bari cutting down a huge tree venerated by his fellow Lycians, who
had consecrated it to the pagan goddess Diana. According to the
saint's biography, he felled it himself, whereas the predella panel
shows St Nicholas on the left with his associates, watching a young
man doing the actual work. To the right of the young man are
figures who probably represent the pagan Lycians.

Overall, the small predella scenes with their few figures are
deceptively simple. Two of them are quite arcane narrative choices
among the many associated with the saints they honour. The altarpiece's main panel similarly betrays many levels of complex religious
meaning and suggests that Piero del Pugliese must have played a
role in its composition. Some features, like the characterizations

of the four saints venerating the Madonna and Child, follow standard formulas that would have been known to Piero di Cosimo, but St Nicholas of Bari's liturgical dress is complex and was especially important to the patron, as his portrait was used for the saint's head, which makes it likely he consulted with the artist on its details.

The Capponi altarpiece of the *Visitation with Sts Nicholas of Bari and Anthony Abbot* (see illus. 33) marks Piero's move into major metropolitan commissions. He was asked by the heirs of Gino Capponi, a major Florentine aristocratic family, to execute it for the long-standing family chapel dedicated to St Nicholas in the church of Santo Spirito, a major Florentine institution. The church was the home of the Augustinian Hermits and the only mendicant institution in Florence whose buildings belonged wholly to the Florentine republic.[27] This unusual circumstance meant that the artist and patron had to meet the requirements of several different overseers. The Capponi considered St Nicholas their protector, and the family chapel had been dedicated to him in the original church of Santo Spirito, which was replaced by Brunelleschi's fifteenth-century building.[28] The painting was executed probably in 1489–90, as the frame is documented to 1489.[29] Apparently not finished before 1493, it represents the meeting of the cousins Elizabeth and the Virgin Mary when both were pregnant, with John the Baptist and with Christ respectively.[30]

The oversight board, composed of friars and secular figures, probably controlled the uniform appearance of the chapels and their allocation to families. All the chapels follow the same model: they are niche-shaped and similarly sized, with altarpieces and altar frontals, a stained-glass window and usually a marble tomb slab right before the altar.[31] The altarpiece is one in a programme of five in the choir of Santo Spirito dedicated to devotion to the Virgin Mary. This coordination indicates the significant role that the Augustinian Hermits must have played in determining the theological subjects.[32] Standing at the painting's centre are the two women, who lean towards each other and clasp right hands in greeting. The *dextrarum iunctio*, or joining of right hands, meant more than just a casual greeting. It was a symbol of fidelity and harmony, often used in Roman funerary sculptures to connote marriage. It was also known through written history as a signal of accord on a treaty or other similar diplomatic exchange.[33] The gesture had been used in earlier Visitation scenes in northern European manuscripts and panels as a sign of the cousins' shared sense of intertwined, important destinies.[34] St Elizabeth is seen on the right, an old woman past childbearing age with a bony, lined visage. She raises her hand in respect to her younger cousin, who will become the mother of God. The Virgin, on the left, is ideally beautiful and young; she wears the more prominent halo. She comforts her cousin by momentarily grasping her shoulder.

The Visitation was a frequently represented scene because it underscored the miraculous nature of both women's pregnancies – possible only through divine intervention and their obedience to God's will – but, in the case of Piero's panel, excerpting the two women from a narrative setting and including two seated saints who read and write about their meeting is unusual. As recounted in Luke 1:41–5, when Elizabeth heard Mary's greeting, the baby leaped in her womb and Elizabeth was filled with the Holy Spirit:

> In a loud voice she exclaimed: 'Blessed are you among women and blessed is the child you will bear! But why am I so favoured, that the mother of my Lord should come to me? As soon as the sound of your greeting reached my ears, the baby in my womb leaped for joy. Blessed is she who has believed that the Lord would fulfil his promises to her!'

The apostle continues with Mary's famous verses, later called
the Magnificat, which begin (1:46–9):

> My soul glorifies the Lord, and my spirit rejoices in God
> my Saviour, for he has been mindful of the humble state
> of his servant. From now on all generations will call me
> blessed, for the Mighty One has done great things for me
> – holy is his name.

Some artists make the womb of Elizabeth visible and depict John
the Baptist in utero, excitedly moving and blessing Christ. Piero
leaves worshippers to imagine Elizabeth's stunned reaction to her
unexpected son's first kicks.

Flanking the two women are two informally seated, bearded
and balding male saints who are reading and writing texts. They
are not interacting with Mary and Elizabeth, and they are certainly not acting as intercessors for Capponi family members
to the Virgin and her cousin. They are clearly detached from
them: they sit on the step before the two standing women. Both
seem oblivious to the women and are engrossed in what they
read or write. They are reflecting on the meaning of the women's
encounter. Their introspection is intended as a cue to worshippers, especially the monastic community who frequented the
choir most often, to follow their lead and meditate on the consequences of Mary and Elizabeth's encounter. At the same time,
the figures' arrangement – the seated male saints in the foreground,
Mary and Elizabeth prominently behind them and yet separate
– recalls a theatrical staging of the Visitation such as might
have been seen in the enactments of religious texts popular in
the period.[35]

St Nicholas – again identified by his gold dowry balls, which
mirror the architecture and windows of Santo Spirito – is the
titular saint of the chapel. Although Nicholas was a bishop, he

lacks his distinguishing episcopal cope. The illuminated manuscript he is reading convinces the eye with its lettering style and curling old parchment. It is tilted towards the viewer and can be identified as opened to the first six lines of the Book of Wisdom, or Wisdom of Solomon.[36] The verses describe the qualities of righteousness, values associated by Christian theologians, notably saints Augustine and Anthony Abbot, with the Trinity, Christ and the Virgin Mary, all of whom figure in the scene of the Visitation.[37] Mary is visible, and Christ is already in her womb as she has been impregnated by the Holy Spirit at God's direction.

Anthony Abbot (251–356 CE), one of the fathers of monasticism, sits on the other side of the Virgin and Elizabeth, writing in an illegible scrawl with a quill pen. Despite having lived a millennium before the invention of the spectacles perched on his nose (late thirteenth century), Piero adds them to emphasize that the near-sighted old man needs them to write. The detail brings up important religious issues, intensified by the development of eyeglasses: the weakness of Anthony's physical vision must be corrected, as opposed to his perfect spiritual vision, which allows him to 'see' and write his divinely inspired text.[38]

The saint is identified by his most common accessories: the walking stick of a hermitic monk who traipses through the rough wilderness and the pig that connotes Anthony's background as a swineherd but which later became his protective constant companion. The pig is unusually independent of the saint. Instead of placing the pig docilely beside Anthony, Piero, in a typical twist, portrays it trotting unaccompanied in the middle landscape behind him. The third attribute, a small church bell that rings the hours of prayer, rests on the ground near the saint's feet. Anthony Abbot is dressed in the black habit of the Augustinians. Anthony Abbot was not a bishop, but his habit is covered by an episcopal robe. This suggests that the fourth-century hermit monk, a Desert Father widely considered the founder of Christian monasticism, may be deliberately conflated here with the bishop St Augustine (354–430 CE), since both were considered key figures in the creation of the Augustinian order associated with Santo Spirito.[39] The Augustinian Hermits pointed to Augustine's *Confessions* to support their contention that his conversion to Christianity had been influenced by the model of St Anthony Abbot.[40] In the fourteenth century they also claimed that Augustine had founded their order in the fifth century. This manoeuvre had many motives, not least of which was to gain them a more prestigious earlier date of establishment than their main rivals, the emergent Franciscan and the Dominican orders, whose beginnings dated to the thirteenth century.[41]

The seated saint is depicted writing, to underscore the claim made by the Augustinian Hermits that Augustine, the prolific Church Father, had established their order a millennium earlier and that they had inherited his blessing – and his writings.[42] To emphasize the conflated figure's writing, he is actively composing illegibly on a small piece of paper and carries a pouch of ink as well as a holder for additional quill pens and another ink pouch. Between the two seated male saints on the ground is a sprig with multiple pink and white blossoms. It seems to be *Lychnis* (or *Silene*) *chalcedonica* 'Carnea', whose flowers' cross shape and flesh colour evoke obvious links to the life and death of Christ.

Piero di Cosimo fills the painting with more scenes in an arid background area behind Nicholas and Anthony Abbot, of which they seem oblivious. He exploits the additional episodes to develop the meanings of the painting further. Behind St Nicholas, on the stepped terrace of a house, is a tiny scene of the Nativity, with Mary and Joseph kneeling to Christ, who lies on the ground. The Holy Family is approached on both sides by shepherds who come to pay him homage. In the distance, on a winding hill overhung by rocks, we see the Magi en route. These scenes about the birth of Christ are the sequels to the imminent birth of Christ implied in the meeting between Mary and Elizabeth and are distinguished by a green tree in full leaf, an auspicious omen. On the other side of the panel (illus. 45), the Annunciation, or the Archangel Gabriel's revelation to Mary that she will bear the son of God, is painted on a distant church facade like a decoration. The viewer must look closely and in a surprising place to find this visual clue. Its inconspicuous placement and small scale belie its importance in the narrative: the Annunciation presages the emphasized scene of Mary meeting Elizabeth. The Annunciation painting on the facade is a clever painting-within-a-painting; far more than a decoration, it is an essential element of the dramatic sequence. The last scene in this plot line is the first to catch the viewer's eye: a chaotic, horrifying narrative of infanticide, or the Massacre of the Innocents. Christ, the intended victim of Herod's decree to murder all first-born sons, has escaped, but dozens of other babies are killed by the swords of Herod's soldiers. Screaming mothers and children pour out of the house's door and drop from the terrace ledge while men and women watch the pandemonium from windows above. For some reason, what looks like a monkey moves without apprehension along an exterior beam at the building's roof. A dying tree overlooks the murders, symbolizing its horrors. Surprisingly, a black-robed Augustinian Hermit has a sword raised as though about to participate in the massacre. The faithful praying before the altarpiece, especially members of the Order of St Augustine, would have realized that the anachronistic inclusion of one of their confrères was meant to force their contemplation of their own potential sinfulness and to stoke their compassion for sinners.[43] What seems to be a solitary white lamb escapes. Could this be a clever allusion to Christ in his frequent guise as the Lamb of God, fleeing into Egypt to elude the slaughter?

There were precedents well known to Piero di Cosimo for enhancing the principal scene of an altarpiece with ancillary episodes. An obvious example is the *Portinari Altarpiece*, where the dominant episodes of the Nativity, the veneration of Christ and the Adoration of the Shepherds in the main panel are amplified by the vignette of the Annunciation to the Shepherds in the background. The left altarpiece wing with the male Portinari family members shows the flight to Bethlehem behind it, while the right altarpiece wing with the female Portinari reveals the approach of the Magi in the background. These secondary events are small in scale and fit into the landscape background, as in Piero's *Visitation with Sts Nicholas of Bari and Anthony Abbot*. There are two salient differences. In the *Portinari Altarpiece*, and most other paintings with secondary vignettes, the scenes are presented in chronological order from left to right, and all are enacted with

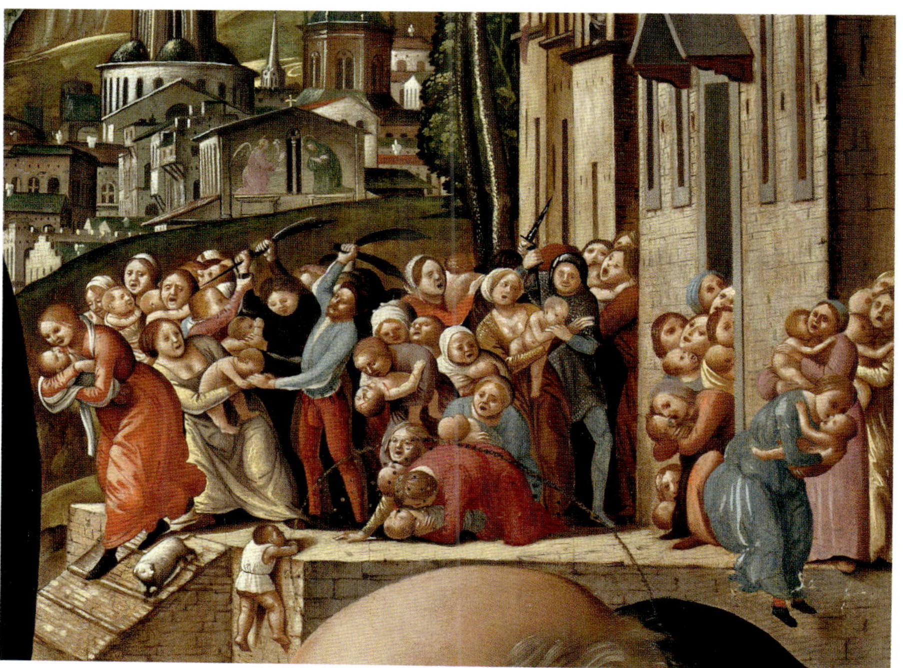

45 Massacre of the Innocents detail from Piero di Cosimo, *Visitation with Sts Nicholas of Bari and Anthony Abbot* (illus. 33).

human characters. Dealing with religious stories that were admittedly familiar to all believers, Piero makes his viewers figure out the enigma of the scenes' placement and put them in chronological order. The Annunciation is in the far right background, the Nativity and Adoration of the Shepherds is in the left background, with the Adoration of the Magi far behind them, and finally the Massacre of the Innocents is in the near right background. The second major point of difference is Piero's highly unusual construction of a narrative vignette as a painting on a church facade rather than acted out by human figures. The decision to set it behind an eye-catching massacre of children further obscures the scene. Piero forces the viewer to scrutinize the painting in search of the Annunciation, which is after all the necessary beginning of the Visitation's story. Piero defies the standard that altarpieces are intended to instruct ordinary viewers in the stories of their religion; instead, he confounds their expectations and presents a puzzle they must decode in order to follow its plot. Is this whimsy or a calculated demonstration of originality that he intends the viewer to admire? Both explanations may be viable, but probably only for a percentage of viewers. A third option presents another part of the answer: the altarpiece was in the church's choir, where most of its audience would have been the learned members of the Order of St Augustine. To the Hermits' initiated eyes, many of the altarpiece's peculiarities, such as the placement of the subsidiary narrative vignettes, could be understood through sophisticated biblical and extrabiblical exegesis, and so made sense.[44] In this altarpiece, Piero ingeniously took the subjects that needed to be included and spelled out different messages with them for the lay and religious groups who saw it. Vasari claimed that Piero was always 'seeking difficulties'.[45] This is usually understood in terms of pictorial and technical virtuosity – for example in the way Nicholas's gold balls reflect the church's choir in the actual physical space before the altarpiece, or in the convincingly deep landscape and cloudscape, bathed in light and shade. The structure of the landscape on both sides of the central scene mimics Netherlandish altarpieces like the *Portinari Altarpiece*. The view rolls back to the horizon in atmospheric perspective, winding trails along each side providing the path. Distant hills are coloured in blue-grey tones, establishing their distance from the foreground. Sunlight streams in from the left, creating light and shade contrasts on the craggy cliff on the left and the cluster of buildings on the right. The extraordinarily persuasive details of textures, colours and light and shade are all influenced by Netherlandish paintings. Piero used his technical ambition to intrigue the viewer into working out the deliberately idiosyncratic interpretations that he wove into his paintings. At the same time, he fulfilled the rigorous intellectual standards of the Augustinian Hermits and satisfied the difficulties of the multivalent meanings they demanded.

Another celebrated altarpiece by Piero (see illus. 46), commissioned for a type of setting very different from the rarefied, intellectual context of the church of the Augustinian Hermits, offers a chance to see how the painter reacted to a more popular situation. It is a sacred conversation for the Ospedale degli Innocenti in Florence, which was one of the first buildings designed by the great architect Brunelleschi. The site was an orphanage where babies and children whose families could not care for them, or who were abandoned, were raised and apprenticed in useful trades. Piero del Pugliese – who, as we have seen, hired Piero to paint another sacred conversation, as well as secular scenes – asked the painter to execute an image of the *Madonna and Child Enthroned with Sts Elizabeth of Hungary, Catherine of Alexandria, Peter and John the Evangelist* for his family chapel in the hospital church between 1491 and 1493. The altarpiece was installed in the chapel in late 1493, as documents prove.[46]

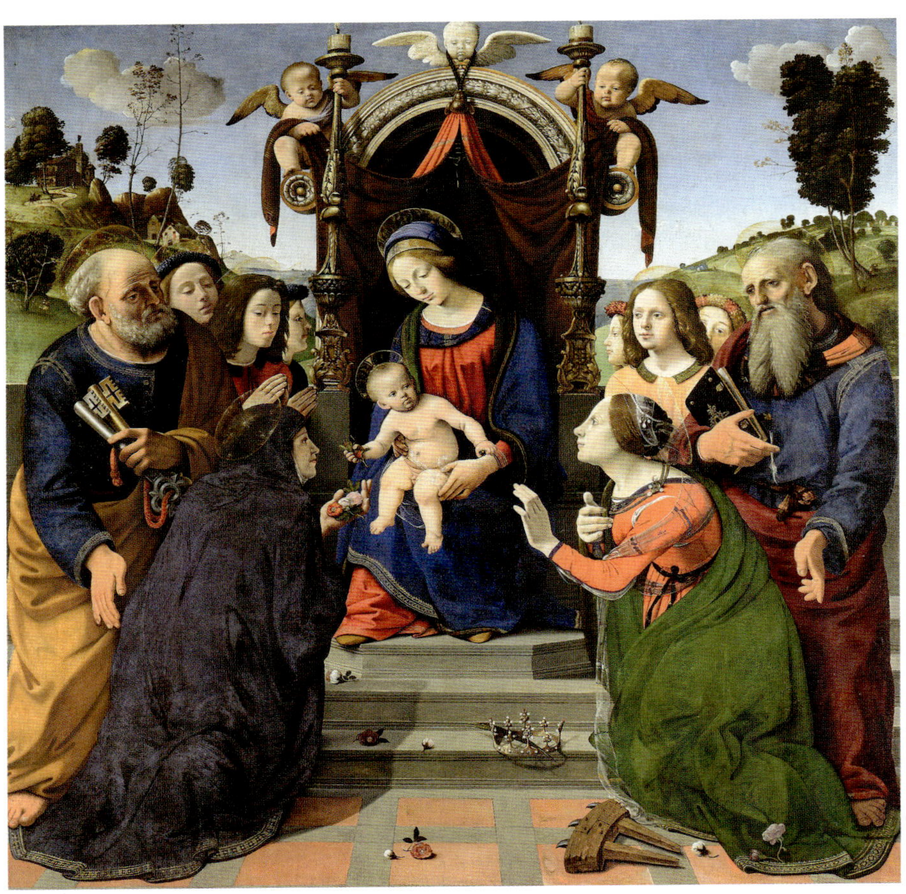

The new commission conforms to the taste for a grander scale, typical of late fifteenth-century Florence. The carefully coordinated combination of different media is also characteristic of altarpieces of this period.[47] The painted panel of a sacred conversation is surmounted by a glazed terracotta lunette of the *Annunciation* (see illus. 35) that further enhances its height. Brass candleholders once flanked the altarpiece, echoing the painted

46 Piero di Cosimo, *Madonna and Child Enthroned with Sts Elizabeth of Hungary, Catherine of Alexandria, Peter and John the Evangelist*, c. 1493, oil and tempera on panel.

ones on the Virgin's throne.[48] The Madonna and Child are seated within a complex canopied throne that overhangs their heads. Two chubby flesh-and-blood-coloured angels climb on the tall metal candlestands on each side while a white stone-coloured seraph (an order of angels without bodies) at the throne's arched apex supports a cloth canopy that hangs within the metal throne. On the left, a standing St Peter, the name saint of Piero del Pugliese, holds the silver and gold keys to heaven and earth and touches the kneeling St Elizabeth of Hungary's back, commending her to the baby Christ. In an unusual move, he steps on Elizabeth's robes. This strange saintly gesture is borrowed from Van der Goes's *Portinari Altarpiece*, where St Thomas indicates his endorsement of Tommaso Portinari to Mary and Christ by prominently placing his foot atop Portinari's robes.[49]

Elizabeth offers to Christ three roses in her hand. The Christ Child has already taken one stem of blooms, and several others lie on the ground. They allude to Elizabeth's miracle of the roses, in which the food she was carrying to the hungry transformed into roses. Food became flowers to conceal from her disapproving husband that she, a princess, was helping the poor. Elizabeth ultimately left him and joined a female order of Franciscans, hence her black veil and habit.

Christ's body inclines towards Elizabeth, and he turns his head to the kneeling St Catherine. John the Evangelist, identified by his book and quill as the author of a Gospel, presents St Catherine to him. He is included to honour by name the prior of the hospital, Francesco di Giovanni Tesori, and the Arte della Seta, the silk guild that oversaw the hospital, whose patron was John the Evangelist.[50] Behind the saints stand additional figures: two wear halos, the others ornate head garlands with flowers. Their lack of attributes makes them impossible to identify, although they may stand for the orphaned children for whom the hospital cared.[51] Ghirlandaio's high altarpiece of the *Adoration of the Magi*, dated circa 1488–9 and situated nearby in the hospital, includes in the foreground two much younger orphans with divine rays emanating from their heads; like Ghirlandaio, Piero may have been alluding to the hospital's mission.[52]

The selection of saints was motivated by the hospital's mission of caring for orphaned or abandoned children. St Catherine of Alexandria was the protector of unmarried women; her presence alludes to many of the mothers who gave up their children. Elizabeth was a founder of hospitals and a patron of charity, nurses and young widows. She is also associated with healing, the care of children dying young, the poor and the sick. All these connections justify her representation in a foundling hospital altarpiece. A final clue to St Elizabeth's identity is that a del Pugliese descendant in an early sixteenth-century bequest specified that the chapel was associated with her.[53] Confirming Catherine's presence are the fragment of the wheel on which she was martyred and the gold and pearl crown, an allusion to her royal background, which lies on the ground before her. Atop it is the palm, the common symbol of a martyr saint. She kneels before Christ, dressed as a bride in a pearl-adorned headdress with a pearl head brooch and wearing a pearl brooch on her shoulder.[54]

St Catherine raises her hand so that Christ can put a ring on her finger, making St Catherine his mystical bride. This frequently represented scene of Catherine's betrothal to Christ symbolized the saint's consecration of her virginity to Christ. As we have seen, the luminescent white of her pearls was traditionally associated with chastity and emphasized Catherine's virginal status. Their round shape and opalescent lustre evoked the moon, and thereby Diana, goddess of chastity, reinforcing the association.[55] In the context of the Ospedale degli Innocenti, the mystical marriage also alludes to the foundling girls, who, after being cared for at the hospital until a marriageable age, were wed so that the future wellbeing of these orphans could be safeguarded by their husbands.

If not wed, they became nuns, or brides of Christ, like Catherine. The Ospedale functioned as their 'institutional father', a role it could play only if the Florentine citizenry were generous in their charitable donations. Piero's altarpiece provides proof of past support and was meant to encourage more.[56]

The painted altarpiece was unusual in that it once was surmounted by a blue and white tin-glazed terracotta relief that functioned as its lunette and is now in a courtyard of the Ospedale. The play on materials in the Virgin and Child's throne below it – the metal throne, the lifelike angels, the white stone seraph at the throne's apex – prepare the viewer for the coloured sculptural lunette above the sacred conversation. At each end of the lunette may have been white glazed sculptures of angels.[57]

The sculpture, by Andrea della Robbia (1435–1525), the foremost practitioner in coloured glazed terracotta after his uncle Luca's death, created a multimedia ensemble surmounting the painted altarpiece that was unusual in Florence at the time. The blue and white colours of the lunette and its border of double-winged seraphim deliberately recalled the appearance of the swaddled infants that Andrea had created to mark the upper border of the exterior arcade of the hospital. The repetition of little angels inside and outside the hospital reminded all viewers of the institution's mission to care for their young charges. Even the foundlings could relate easily to this imagery from an early age. In addition, they must have learned to identify saints and other more complex aspects of their religion from the characters and details of this altarpiece and others in the complex, like that by Ghirlandaio. The bright colours and intricate details of accessories must have drawn their attention and been effective teaching tools. Visual and oral learning were the most important methods of training in popular culture.

The innovative combination of a glazed terracotta lunette atop a painted altarpiece in the del Pugliese commission was considered so successful that Andrea repeated it in several other Florentine churches.[58] The altarpiece's lunette relief represented the Annunciation. In the context of a hospital where newborns and babies were cared for, the *Annunciation* lunette proclaimed God's protective role in the birth of newborns and his care for innocent babies. In relation to the painted scene below it, the lunette showed the announcement of Christ's birth and the altarpiece the recognition of his divinity and spread of his veneration.[59]

Piero painted another major altarpiece, but of a very dissimilar subject, in the church of Santissima Annunziata, for the religious order known as the Servites. Their church is adjacent to the Ospedale. Its main panel, the *Incarnation* (see illus. 34), represents the word (Christ) made flesh in Mary's womb, attended by saints Catherine of Alexandria, Margaret, John the Evangelist, Filippo Benizzi and Antoninus.

Vasari recorded that this painting was commissioned for the Tedaldi Chapel in Santissima Annunziata, which is corroborated by a link to a bequest by the prominent Florentine Pierozzo Tedaldi, in 1505, for the altar in that church dedicated to St John the Evangelist and, jointly until at least 1515, Filippo Benizzi.[60] Tedaldi's bequest may have come at the end of Piero's work on the painting, so historians usually date it to a range of years prior to 1505.[61]

Filippo Benizzi, one of the seven founders of the Servite Order, a religious order devoted to the Virgin Mary, is the figure in a black habit whose hair is tonsured and who holds a lily, symbolizing purity. He stands on the left, closest to the Virgin. Although Filippo Benizzi was not canonized until 1671, he was greatly venerated in Tuscany, the region where the Servites originated.[62] Santissima Annunziata, founded in the mid-thirteenth century, is the mother church of the Servite Order and the site of a miraculous image of the Virgin said to have been painted by an angel. The painting was credited with working miracles, and pilgrims flocked to the church, which became a major site of devotion. When Piero painted this altarpiece for the Annunziata, the church was full of wax ex-voto portraits – which were sometimes life-size images – of the faithful, left in thankful testimony of the Virgin's miracles. These ex-votos themselves soon became a major attraction to visitors.

The Tedaldi altarpiece is organized like a sacred conversation but replaces the standard enthroned Virgin and Child at the centre with a standing pregnant Virgin. Mary touches her abdomen and looks up to the Holy Spirit (in its usual form of a white dove) and radiance of light above her. Around her neck and shoulders she wears a long, fringed white shawl with dark stripes, a Jewish prayer shawl. It conveys the meaning to Christians that the Incarnation of Christ marks the end of the Old Covenant and the beginning of the New.[63] Mary stands atop a stone base decorated with a low relief sculpture of the Annunciation: an angel holds a long stem of lilies, symbols of Mary's purity, while just above the angel is the dove of the Holy Spirit, which flies towards Mary. According to Luke (1:34–5), the Virgin, who interrupted her reading of the holy book in her hand, responded to the surprising apparition of the angel:

> Mary said to the angel, 'How can this be, since I am a Virgin?' The angel said to her, 'The Holy Spirit will come upon you, and the power of the Most High will overshadow you; therefore the child to be born will be holy; he will be called the Son of God.'

The painting visualizes both parts of Luke's testimony in an inventive way that is nevertheless true to the biblical verses: the angel's kneeling declaration to Mary on the marble base is the foundation of the narrative. That scene anticipates what is

pictured above: the standing impregnated Virgin and the dove
of the Holy Spirit and divine radiance, which have appeared,
'overshadowing her', and enacted the miracle. The emphasis on
Mary in the visualization of Christ's Incarnation may be the result
of a change in theological emphasis at this time. The meaning of
the Incarnation shifted from being a premise of redemption to
becoming the exact moment when humanity was saved. Another
theological argument centred on the Virgin's immaculacy, that
is, her sinless state when she was conceived by her mother, St
Anne.[64] This interpretation was controversial but was ardently
supported by the Servites. The solitary standing figure of the
miraculously impregnated Mary commanding the saints' and
worshippers' attention seems an apt articulation of these vibrant
contemporaneous explanations about humanity's redemption.

The striking image of the Virgin is venerated by St John the
Evangelist, the chapel's dedicatee, identified by an eagle, his traditional symbol, which stands on the ground behind him. John
is placed in front of Filippo Benizzi, the Servite founder who is
the chapel's other dedicatee. Kneeling to their right is St Catherine
of Alexandria, identified by a palm frond signifying her martyrdom and a fragment of the wheel on which she was tortured, as
we have seen before. On the right side stands Antoninus Pierozzi,
the venerable Archbishop of Florence, whose similar name
Pierozzo Tedaldi may have wanted to emphasize.[65] Antoninus
served as archbishop from 1446 until his death in 1459 and was
canonized in 1523. Before Antoninus is St Peter, identified by
the grey metal key he holds. Peter is the name saint of Pierozzo
Tedaldi, and so the proximity of the two figures consolidates the
connection to the altarpiece's patron. Peter stands on the robe
of a woman kneeling before him who holds a small cross and
says the Rosary. Their relationship is emphasized by the stance
borrowed from the *Portinari Altarpiece* discussed earlier. Vasari
identifies her as St Margaret, although she lacks her usual

accessory of a dragon, or Satan in disguise: the monster swallowed her, but she made the sign of the cross, which forced the beast to spit her out. The dragon was included in a preliminary drawing but omitted in the final painting.[66] According to Vasari, the scene was moved to the now lost predella:

> [Piero] painted some little scenes, very well executed; and, among others, there is one of S. Margaret issuing from the belly of the Dragon, wherein he made that animal so monstrous and hideous, that I do not think that there is anything better of that kind to be seen, for with its eyes it reveals venom, fire, and death, in an aspect truly terrifying … as for such things, I do not believe that any one ever did them better than he did, or came near him in imagining them.[67]

St Margaret may have been included because she was the name saint of Pierozzo Tedaldi's sister.[68] The female martyr, Catherine of Alexandria, may honour another female relative, but such a connection is not yet established.

The hillock behind John the Evangelist and Filippo Benizzi provides the stage for a scene of the Nativity and the Annunciation to the Shepherds. The closer vignette depicts Mary and Joseph venerating Christ in the shade of a thatched canopy built on a cut stone substructure. An unidentified figure dressed in secular clothing kneels in adoration behind the Virgin. It has been suggested that this is a self-portrait of the artist.[69] There are no contemporary portraits of Piero, so this remains an unprovable notion.

The humble shelter is contrasted with the remains of a once grand pagan building. Only a single column, fragmentary wall and substructure remain to mark the fallen civilization that the Christian era will supersede. With his typical tongue-in-cheek humour, Piero underscored the transition by placing animals always associated with Christ: the reclining ox on the substructure and the donkey eating the grass that overgrows it. Further back on the hillock is a perilously narrow and high cliff where sheep rest and shepherds have foolishly located their ramshackle buildings. A single shepherd stands with a hand raised to screen his eyes as he looks up at a dark area in the clouds, and presumably at the angel who announces the birth of Christ. The emphasis on the shepherds' dwellings and the landscape around them, combined with the minimalization of the watching shepherd, the core of the narrative, undermine the scene's meaning as an Annunciation to the Shepherds.

On the right side of the painting is another improbably steep and narrow cliff. On a small path that comes out of nowhere, Joseph leans on his walking stick while leading Mary and Christ, who ride a donkey behind. The scene represents the Flight into Egypt, where Christ's parents take him to escape Herod, who has vowed to kill all first-born sons lest one of them overthrow his rule. Their destination is atop a promontory. With a conspicuous church and belfry and secular buildings with lookout towers, overhanging eaves and thick walls, the settlement resembles a European mountain village more than Egypt. Most artists focused on the family's flight and omitted their destination, avoiding the problem of lack of knowledge about Egypt. This may be a conscious flash of humour, or it may represent a site important to the Servite Order and so serve as a symbolic respite for the family.

Characteristic of Piero, the vegetation seems a dynamic actor in the scene. Species unlikely to grow side by side are densely juxtaposed. To the left of the travelling family is a thick trunk with multiple burls that hangs unstably into the void. On its top are thin new shoots. It could be another metaphor of the old order, or pagan world, dying and yielding to the fresh growth of the Christian world. It could also suggest the pagan idols of Egypt that fell at Christ's approach, as it looks as if it is about to topple over the cliff. Just behind the donkey is a palm tree that bends over the Virgin and Child, as if in homage. The tree's leaning pose also conjures up the date palm that bowed to the family as they passed and offered them food and water. Two important points can be made here: the first is that Piero was a master of energizing nature imaginatively to his purpose. Vasari characterized him as a passionate student of nature, and it shows in his skilful differentiation of species and their growth to tell his story. At the same time, these anecdotes about the trees that helped Christ, and Mary and Joseph on their way to Egypt derive directly from apocryphal writings about Christ's infancy and demonstrate Piero's detailed knowledge of this literary source.[70]

The altarpiece may have had special meaning for Piero: he belonged to a confraternity attached to the church and planned to be buried there. However, other than the adherence to orthodox Christian imagery leavened by a subtle and meaningful play with natural details that is Piero's signature in religious painting, there is no clear sign of his presence. Historians have claimed that he included himself as a standing figure behind Mary in the Nativity scene in the left background. That figure, however, is in shadow and so small and distant that it is almost invisible. The typical inserted portrait serves the role of promoting the figure represented, so it seems unlikely that Piero would have commemorated himself in such an understated way.

Whether or not Piero inserted an image of himself into this altarpiece, his individual spirit lies behind all these large-scale religious productions for public settings. They show his wry sensibility, which nevertheless always remains within the bounds of religious propriety, and his love of the natural world. From the visual and documentary evidence, he unfailingly met the requirements of his exacting, wealthy Florentine private patrons and the various religious orders with their diverse agendas. These paintings would have constituted the impression of Piero's art that most of his contemporaries and succeeding generations would have known. The secular subjects, portraits and images for private devotion (to be discussed next), and even Vasari's biography, would have been familiar to only a few.

Private Devotional Paintings

He set himself often to observe such animals, plants, or other things as Nature at times creates out of caprice, or by chance; in which he found a pleasure and satisfaction that drove him quite out of his mind with delight; and he spoke of them so often in his discourse that at times . . . although he found pleasure in them, it became wearisome to others.

GIORGIO VASARI, *Lives*

rivate devotional paintings, a type of religious painting generally of much smaller dimensions than altarpieces, hung in residences. The images were intended to stimulate prayer and often were displayed in an alcove of a private family room. Prayer stools would be positioned before them and they were frequently flanked by candle sconces to illuminate the paintings and enhance the atmosphere of the believer's meditation.

Piero's interpretations of devotional paintings for private worship are generally in line with period norms, although they are enlivened by his characteristic flourishes. They typically depict just a few figures, usually the Madonna and Child in the close-up view suitable to spurring prayer in private devotion. All combine an awareness of his contemporaries' innovations, which he matches and extends. His panel *Madonna Holding the Reading Baby Christ*

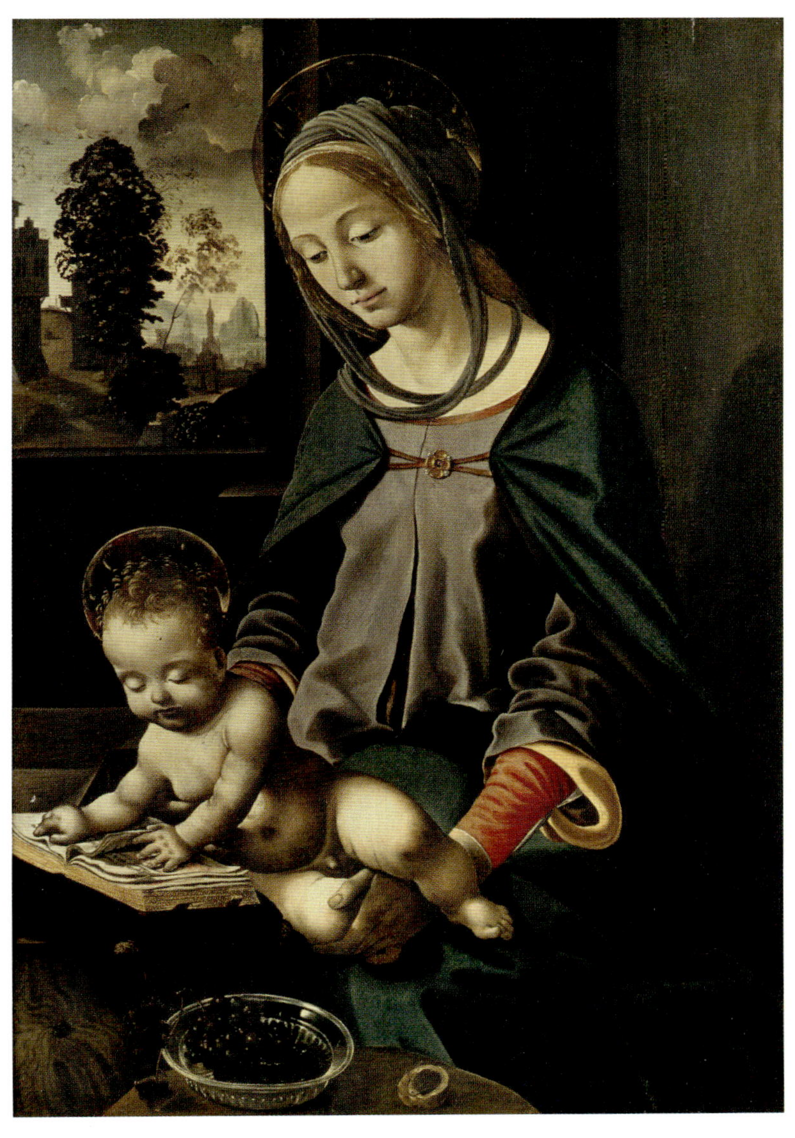

47 Piero di Cosimo, *Madonna Holding the Reading Baby Christ*, c. 1487–90, oil on panel.

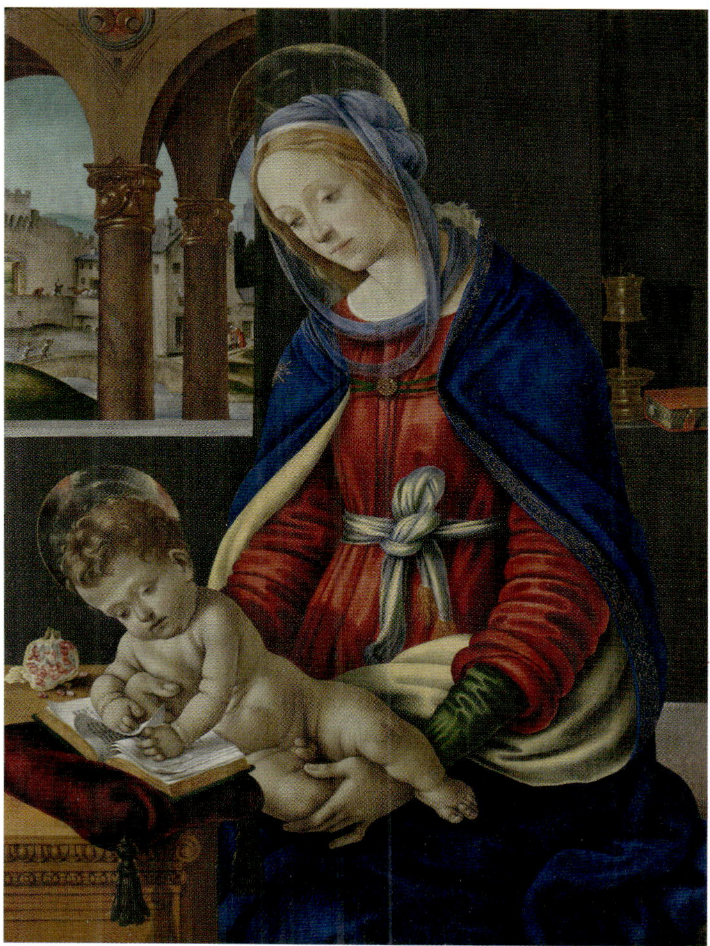

(illus. 47) is a virtual copy of Filippino Lippi's slightly earlier depiction of the same subject (illus. 48). Piero picked up Filippino's sensitive, meditative interpretation of his subjects, in this case Mary's sad recognition that her baby attentively riffles through the pages of an illuminated manuscript that foretells his death.

48 Filippino Lippi, *Madonna Holding the Reading Baby Christ*, c. 1485–7, oil and tempera on panel.

The child leans over the book and lifts pages of the text so that he can read them carefully. Piero's diffused light and shade modelling emphasizes the baby Christ's soft human flesh and mortality. Even the Madonna's unusually sombre grey dress, covered by a blue-green cloak, seems to reflect the funereal nuances of the painting. Piero's choice of muted palette is deliberately unlike Filippino's use of magnificent lapis lazuli for the blue robes of the Virgin.

Filippino was a student of his father, the wayward monk Filippo Lippi, and of Botticelli. Piero's dependence on Filippino is not surprising: as we have seen, the paintings of Filippino's master Botticelli frequently influenced Piero, most notably in *The Finding of Vulcan on Lemnos* (see illus. 12), the *Venus, Mars and Cupid* (see illus. 15) and the idealized female head of the *Fantasy Portrait of Simonetta Vespucci* (see illus. 29). His attentiveness to Filippino began with his earliest paintings, like the *Madonna and Child with Sts Lazarus and Sebastian* (see illus. 36). In addition, Piero and Filippino were sometimes in competition, as, for example, when both painted *spalliere* and altarpieces for Piero del Pugliese or private devotional panels for Filippo Strozzi, and they looked to each other for ideas.[1]

Piero is painting wholly in oil in the *Madonna Holding the Reading Baby Christ*, and the medium augments the effects of his muted palette. He very often painted in a mixture of tempera and oil. He likely did not learn oil painting directly from Leonardo as Vasari claimed: other Italian artists were using the technique exclusively in the last quarter of the fifteenth century. Many only sometimes used it, and in other cases — for example Filippino in his *Madonna Holding the Reading Baby Christ* — turned to a tempera and oil mixture. There were many Netherlandish and German painters resident in Florence and active in their own confraternities. The best example that has been documented was named after St Barbara and located at Santissima Annunziata, a church

Piero knew well. To really learn how to paint in oil required teaching by a skilled practitioner. By the last third of the fifteenth century, such northern experts were available in Florence.[2]

Like Filippino (and other contemporary Italian painters), Piero shows a fascination with the Netherlandish interest in textures, genre details and landscape. For example, the gleaming metal bowl full of dark grapes on the foreground table bespeaks this fascination with textures and light and shade. More than just a demonstration of virtuosity, the grapes allude to the wine that transubstantiates into the blood of Christ during the liturgy of the Mass, and thus to Christ's death on the cross and his redemption of humanity. The grapes reinforce the sentiment of the future events about which the infant Christ reads as he fingers the manuscript's pages. The worshipper praying before the image is intended to reflect on Christ's life from when he was a baby until his bloody torture and death. Next to the bowl of grapes is a peach cut in half, which is another allusion to Christ's Passion.[3]

The vista of a natural landscape seen outside a window is a motif found in many Netherlandish paintings, notably in the portraits by Hans Memling, and had already been assimilated into Italian portraiture and devotional painting, as discussed earlier. Memling's portraits reached Italy by the early 1470s, and several Florentine artists imitated their details. Memling turned often to versions of a landscape background in a hazy, atmospheric perspective, but his arrangement of nature is always orderly, unlike what we have come to expect of Piero: he substituted wild plant growth, multiple plateaus, obscuring shadows and storm clouds. While typical of the artist's originality, the turbulence is suitable as a portent of the painting's meaning.

Another devotional painting, the *Adoration of the Child* (illus. 49), dates probably to 1490–1500. Its round shape and impressive size introduce us to the *tondo*, or circular format, that became very popular in private religious paintings in the final third of the

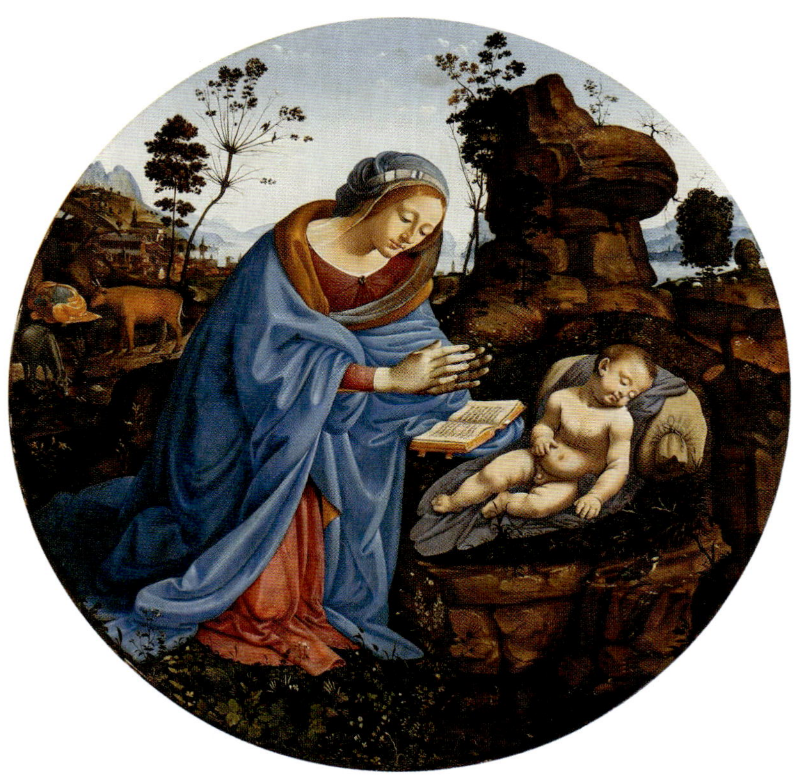

fifteenth century.[4] The circular shape was a recognized sign of divinity and eternity and so was deemed ideal for religious paintings. The most frequent subjects of *tondi* were close-up views of the Holy Family, that is, the Madonna and Child, Joseph and John the Baptist, although other saints could be included. Piero did not invent the *tondo*, but he used it often after its introduction early in the fifteenth century. There are twelve surviving paintings by Piero in this format, which represents about 20 per cent of his extant production.[5] Piero's versions of *tondi* were frequently copied and became the most influential category of his production. Dennis

49 Piero di Cosimo, *Adoration of the Child*, c. 1490–1500, oil on panel.

Geronimus compiled a listing of copies after Piero's paintings, many of which were *tondi*.[6]

Although the *tondo* format was a very popular type and was often produced in artists' workshops on speculation, the *tondo* of the *Adoration of the Child* was probably specially ordered. The subject of the Virgin kneeling in veneration to her child on the ground derives from an influential vision of St Bridget of Sweden much in vogue in the fifteenth century and imitated, for example, in the *Portinari Altarpiece* (see illus. 41). Bridget, on a pilgrimage to Jerusalem in the late fourteenth century, imagined Mary kneeling on the ground and giving birth painlessly to Christ and then worshipping her baby.[7] Despite the theme's popularity, the significant size of this *tondo*, its carefully structured and painted execution and its multiple complex symbolic details point to a specific commissioner who stipulated what he wanted.

The outdoor setting and landscape crowded with plants, animals and insects offer hints that the patron chose Piero di Cosimo because of his well-deserved reputation for a sensitivity to nature. Remember Vasari's words: 'one recognizes a spirit very different and far distant from that of other painters, and a certain subtlety in the investigation of some of the deepest and most subtle secrets of nature.'[8]

The painting depicts the Virgin, who, having read the Bible, kneels on a carpet of plants and flowers and humbly venerates the sleeping Christ. She prompts the believer before the painting to kneel in worship of the biblical verses and the Christ Child, as she does. The verses read by the Virgin have been deciphered: they derive from Paul's Epistle to the Hebrews, which is read during the most important Mass on Christmas Day: 'And thou, Lord, hast laid the foundation of the earth; and the heavens are the works of thine hands. They shall perish but thou shall remainest' (1:10–11).[9] The legibility of the script is planned to provide further food for thought to the individual privately praying to the image.

Just as the infant Christ Child read the pages describing his fate in the *Madonna Holding the Reading Baby Christ*, this is another type of proleptic image: Mary knows the contents and context of the text, and she imagines the sleeping Christ as an augur of the dead Christ. This conjures up her (and the worshipper's) reflection on Christ's entire life and death. Piero places the sleeping Christ atop a stony ledge that stands for both Peter, the rock on whom he will later found the Church, and the stone altar on which Christ will be ritually sacrificed in the Mass. The sleeping Joseph, ox and ass to the left are separated from Mary's intense devotion but are probably intended to recall when an angel's vision to Joseph led to the family's flight into Egypt to save Christ. Their distance and self-absorption in sleeping or drinking distinguish them from the Virgin and Child. The prescience of the Virgin about her son's fate is a standard theme.

The pool seems to spring from water that cascades from a rock, recalling Moses striking a rock in the desert to miraculously offer water to the thirsty Jews. The pool also alludes to baptism and entry into the faith. The dandelion clock, which emerges after the bloom dies, has all its seeds on grey filaments intact. It stands prominently before the pool and connotes through its bitter taste Christ's Passion. The white-and-black cormorants high above in the trees on the left allude to Christ's death and resurrection, whereas the small sparrow (perhaps a coal tit) at the edge of the water flowing down from the rock on which Christ lies stands as an example of God's care for even the lowliest creatures.[10] Such multivalent symbols abound in the painting and are calculated to provoke separate focuses for meditation on various aspects of the meaning of Christ's life, death and resurrection. They are intended to pique reflection in someone who looked at the painting day after day and prompt them to find new things to ponder. Those noted so far are standard, if unusual for their number.

Piero, perhaps advised by a theological expert, crowded the landscape further with other arcane symbols about Christ. Tadpoles teem in the small pool before the child; their metamorphosis into frogs can be viewed as an analogy of the word of God made flesh via Christ's virgin birth, conceived in Mary's womb without intercourse, because they reproduce without direct physical contact between male and female.[11] Reinforcing this theological premise through the phenomena of nature, the aforementioned dandelion clock symbolizes another type of indirect generation: the plant propagates through the wind blowing its seeds far and wide.[12] Piero may have himself made the connection between natural and divine generation; more likely he ingeniously created the symbolic landscape and creatures on a consultant's advice as to what to include. The water scorpion, or water stick insect, skating on the water's surface probably alludes to the biblical verses that explain that God's wisdom is displayed in his tiniest creations (Proverbs 30:24–8).[13]

Piero's use of nature's creatures in this unprecedented symbolic language is a highly unusual analogy of the many premonitions of Christ's crucifixion and death seen in scenes of his infancy. Multiple examples of this more standard foreshadowing are found in his *tondo* the *Madonna, Christ Child and John the Baptist with Sts Jerome and Bernard of Clairvaux* (c. 1495, illus. 50). On a foreground ledge, the toddler John the Baptist kneels in veneration to a Christ Child of similar age. Their embrace foretells their adult roles when John announces the coming of Christ. Leonardo seems to have invented this adumbration of their later history. Piero took from Leonardo's *Virgin of the Rocks* (c. 1483–91, illus. 51) the details of the very young John the Baptist kneeling and praying towards the Christ Child, who acknowledges his adulation; the large form of the Virgin, which unites the two babies; and the placement of the group in a landscape setting. Early in Piero's career, about 1481, Leonardo left Florence for Milan. As the many reflections of Leonardo's

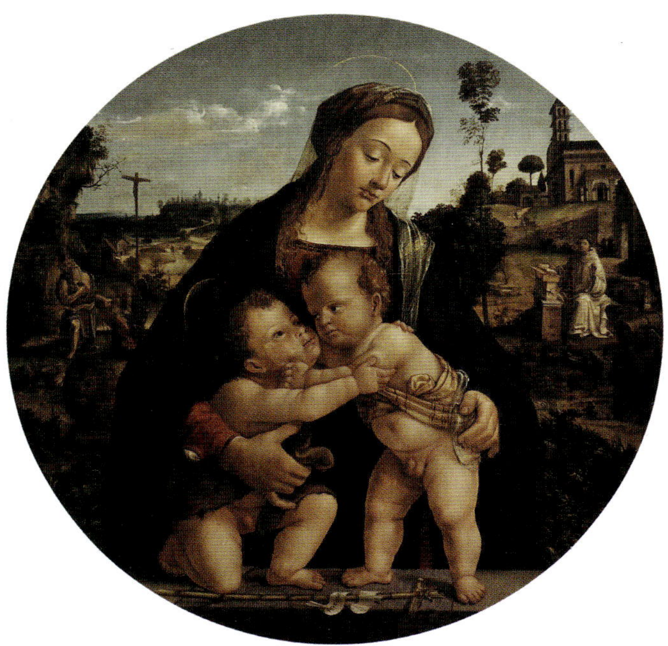

influence on Piero suggest, his drawings or those of his students
must have circulated in his native city.

In the landscape behind the Virgin, Christ Child and John,
two saints display their piety. On the left, St Jerome beats his
chest with a stone in penitence, while on the right, Bernard of
Clairvaux interrupts his prayers to look towards the group in the
foreground. Their role may be to encourage prayer directed
towards these holy figures. They may also provide clues, now
indecipherable, about the painting's patron.

Piero adds further standard symbolic language to this *tondo*.
Wrapped around Christ's upper torso, but baring his navel and
genitals (the signs of his humanity), is a striped gauze band,
which alludes to a Jewish prayer shawl and hence the end of the
Old Covenant and its replacement by the New in the person of

50 Piero di Cosimo, *Madonna, Christ Child and John the Baptist with Sts Jerome and Bernard
of Clairvaux, c.* 1495, oil on panel.

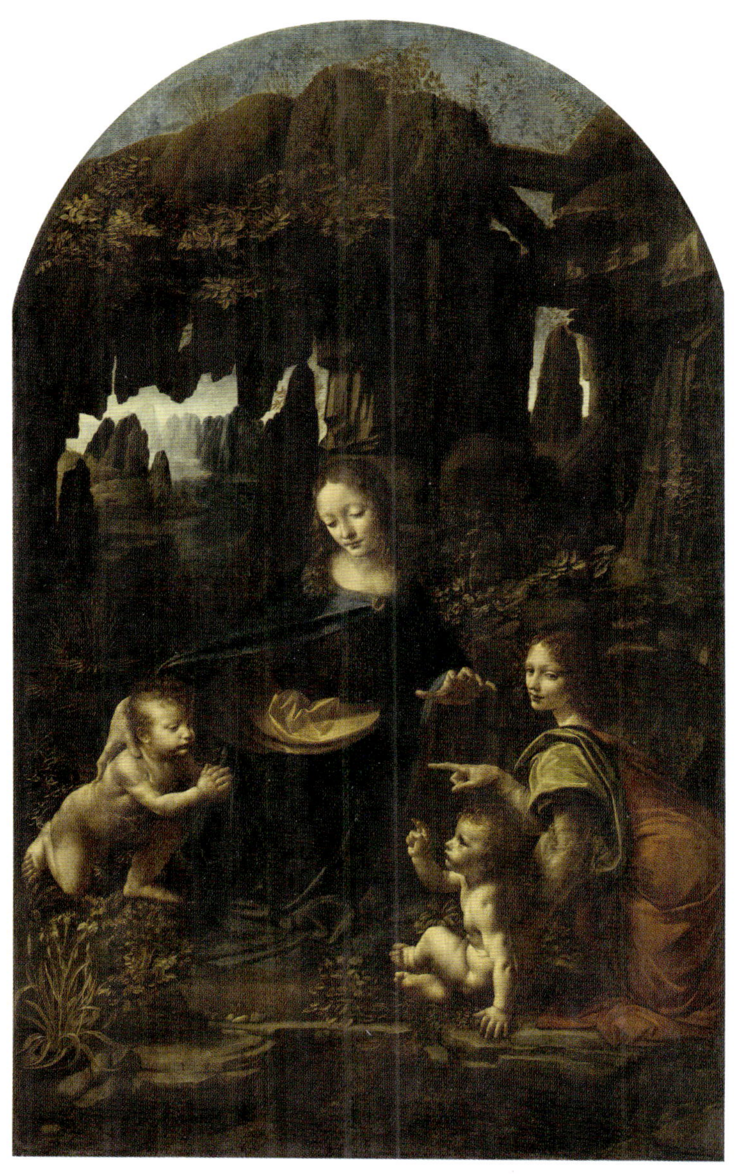

51 Leonardo da Vinci, *Virgin of the Rocks*, c. 1483–91, oil on canvas, transferred from panel.

Christ.[14] Simultaneously, the cloth suggests the burial shroud in which Christ's dead body was wrapped after the Crucifixion. The head of the Virgin is also idealized – the typical way many artists used to show her divinity.

Artists often enriched the nuances of meaning with standard Christian symbolism, as Piero did with Christ, but they rarely turned to nature's creatures and processes for this purpose. Piero is among the very few artists to use the species and habits of animals, birds and insects to explain Christian mysteries. One can imagine Piero studying natural wonders in his outdoor investigations. Vasari's emphasis on his delight at the oddities of nature he discovered seems justified. What Vasari omitted is that Piero also put those treasured natural phenomena to meaningful use in his paintings.

A very different type of image is the painting of a half-length St John the Evangelist as a young man (*c.* 1500–1505, illus. 52). Not circular in form, it is instead a small rectangular panel of the Evangelist within a window embrasure. Scholars have proposed that it was once part of a series of saints in this format, a theory for which there is no proof. Another hypothesis is that it was a pendant to the similar panel of Mary Magdalen, of roughly the same size.[15] The parallels in format and composition seem to validate the latter proposition.

St John is posed, as in a portrait, within a window and cut off at the hip. Following one of his legends, John blesses a chalice of wine that has already killed two men, flushing out a snake. In Piero's interpretation, the snake curls tightly into a decorative arabesque atop the chalice. Piero's *St John the Evangelist* is independent of Italian models. Its rare characterization of the snake's elegant, tightly coiled pose above the chalice follows a widely circulated engraving of about 1480 by the German Martin Schongauer (*c.* 1450–1491) (illus. 53).[16] But Piero's painting is otherwise unlike the print's full-length portrayal of John the Evangelist in a landscape.

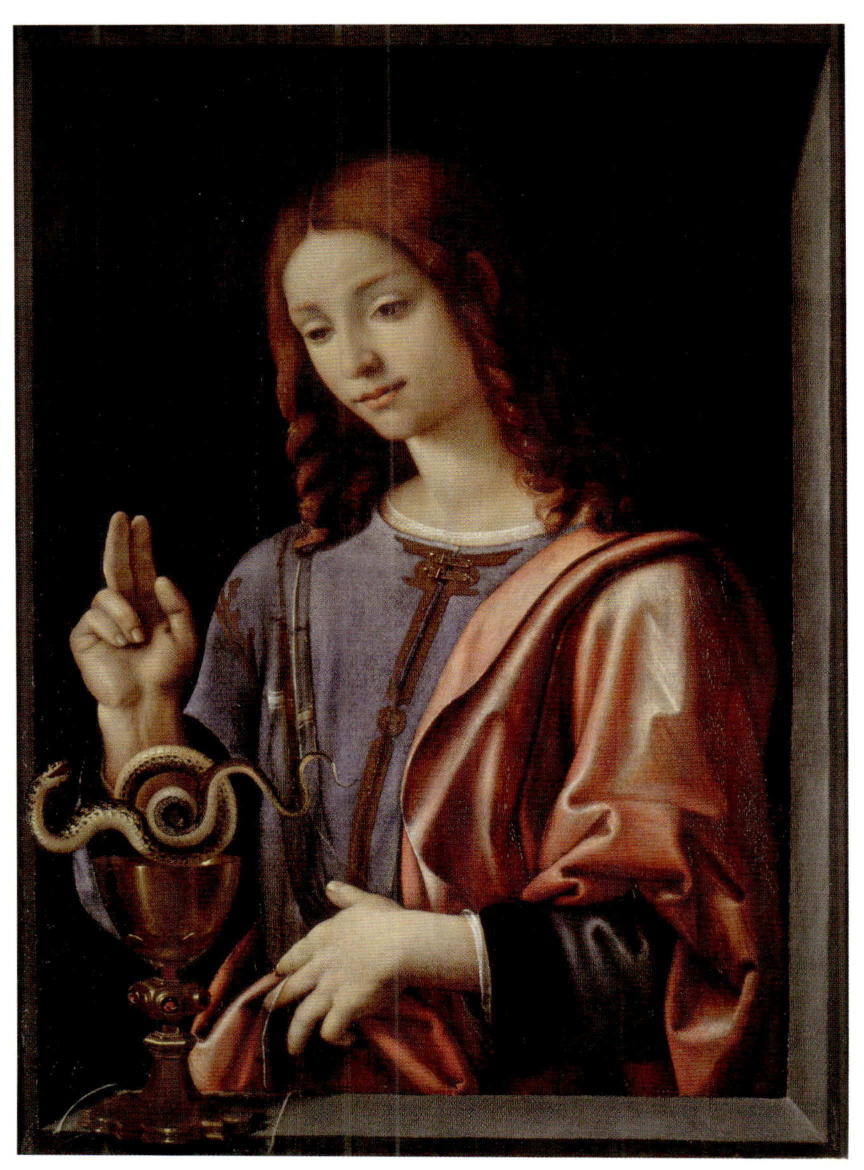

52 Piero di Cosimo, *St John the Evangelist*, c. 1500–1505, oil and tempera on panel.

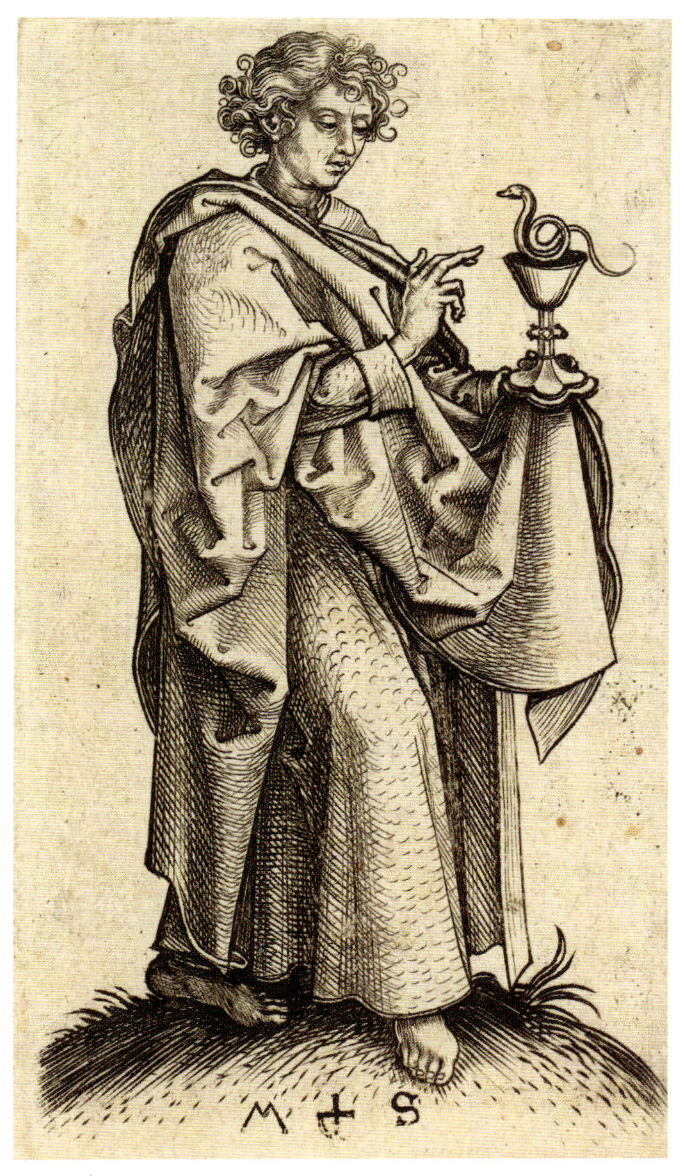

53 Martin Schongauer, *St John the Evangelist with Poisoned Chalice,*
c. 1480, engraving.

Protruding into the viewer's space on the windowsill before John is the gleaming golden chalice, which features raised enamelled images of saints on its stem's circular centre, or knop. The saint raises his hand in a two-fingered blessing, which causes a poisonous snake with open mouth to appear, coiling out from inside the chalice, whose contents the Evangelist was prepared to drink. The snake is fleeing from the vessel in the face of the saint's blessing. A surprising twist is that Piero, apparently knowingly, represented a harmless whipsnake as the villain, the same snake that he had used in the *Fantasy Portrait of Simonetta Vespucci* (see illus. 29).[17] Both whipsnakes and asps were common in Florence in the fifteenth century. Piero may have exchanged a poisonous asp for a benign whipsnake to indicate that after the saint's blessing, the snake itself was transformed.

The scene depicted follows one of the legends collected in the most famous compendium of holy stories, the aforementioned *Golden Legend*, written in the mid-thirteenth century by the Dominican friar Jacobus de Voragine. Jacobus recounts John's proof of the strength of his Christian faith by drinking a chalice full of poison given to him by a pagan priest trying to debunk Christian beliefs. John took this bold move even after two others drank the liquid and died. The Evangelist 'armed himself with the sign of the cross', downed the liquid, remained unscathed, brought the two who had died back to life and swayed the crowd to the Christian God.[18] The poison-filled chalice has further connotations, since it very much resembles the typical highly polished metal chalice used at communion. The liturgical vessel links John, Christ's favourite disciple and to whom he entrusted the care of his mother, directly to Christ: John is fulfilling Christ's command to his disciples at the Last Supper to drink the wine, which has been transubstantiated into his blood from the chalice he offered them. In the *Golden Legend*, the poisonous contents were neutralized after John invoked Christ through the sign of the cross, and the snake containing that poison left the chalice. The symbolism further connects the act of every communicant who drinks the blood of Christ from such a chalice, where the wine has been miraculously transubstantiated during the Mass, to the act of St John attesting Christ's powers, and to Christ's command.

The poisoned chalice of St John the Evangelist as an independent rendering is not frequent in Italian art but is found in Netherlandish painting. The vessel is intricately tooled, bejewelled and shining in the light, in literal reflection of Netherlandish examples, particularly one by Hans Memling (c. 1470–75, illus. 54). A painting by Memling of the chalice within a wall niche forms the reverse of a depiction of St Veronica, who holds up the cloth on which Christ's face was imprinted when she wiped it as he struggled up the hill of Calvary. This means that the front side of the joined paintings also had curative powers. Veronica explained that whoever looked upon her cloth's miraculous imprint of Christ's face, provided they had sincere piety, would immediately be cured. Memling coupled two emblematic episodes of the lives of John the Evangelist and Christ that he painted separately. Piero seems to have grafted them together, so he must have known this painting or something very like it. He imitates the chalice's shape and polished, light-reflecting metal, highlighted in a soft light. Also similar is the way the chalice's foot overlaps the ledge, breaking the picture plane and protruding into the viewer's space. As much as he borrowed from Netherlandish examples of the chalice of St John, it is entirely Piero's caprice to depict the curlicue of the snake transfixed about the chalice; in Memling's painting, the snake is posed undramatically, ready to slither away. However, Piero might have taken that detail from the Schongauer print.

Piero's half-length depiction of St John blessing the chalice is in an unusual format, for saints are rarely posed in close-up against a neutral background. Paula Nuttall, an authority on Netherlandish painting, claimed to have never seen that format used for a saint

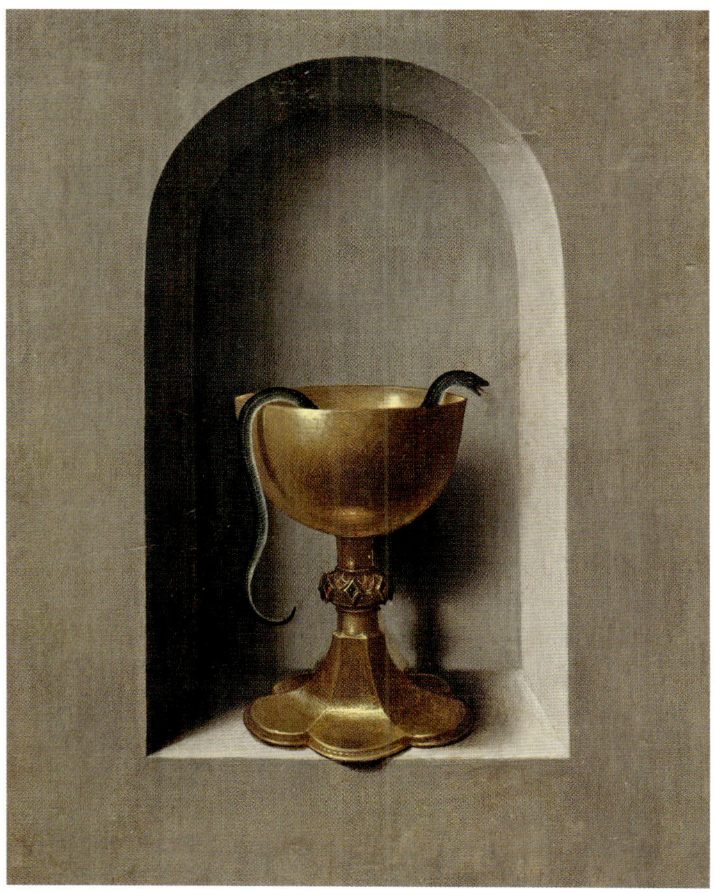

in that region other than the Virgin and Child.[19] I do not recognize it as an Italian invention. Piero's painting has been called 'the climax of Florentine Leonardism'.[20] The soft gradations of colour and light, so typical of Leonardo, and the unusual composition suggest that Piero may have adapted one of the standard image types of the Salvator Mundi, or Christ as Saviour of the World, in which Christ is viewed frontally and cut off at the waist by a

54 Hans Memling, *Chalice of Saint John the Evangelist*, c. 1470–75, oil on panel.

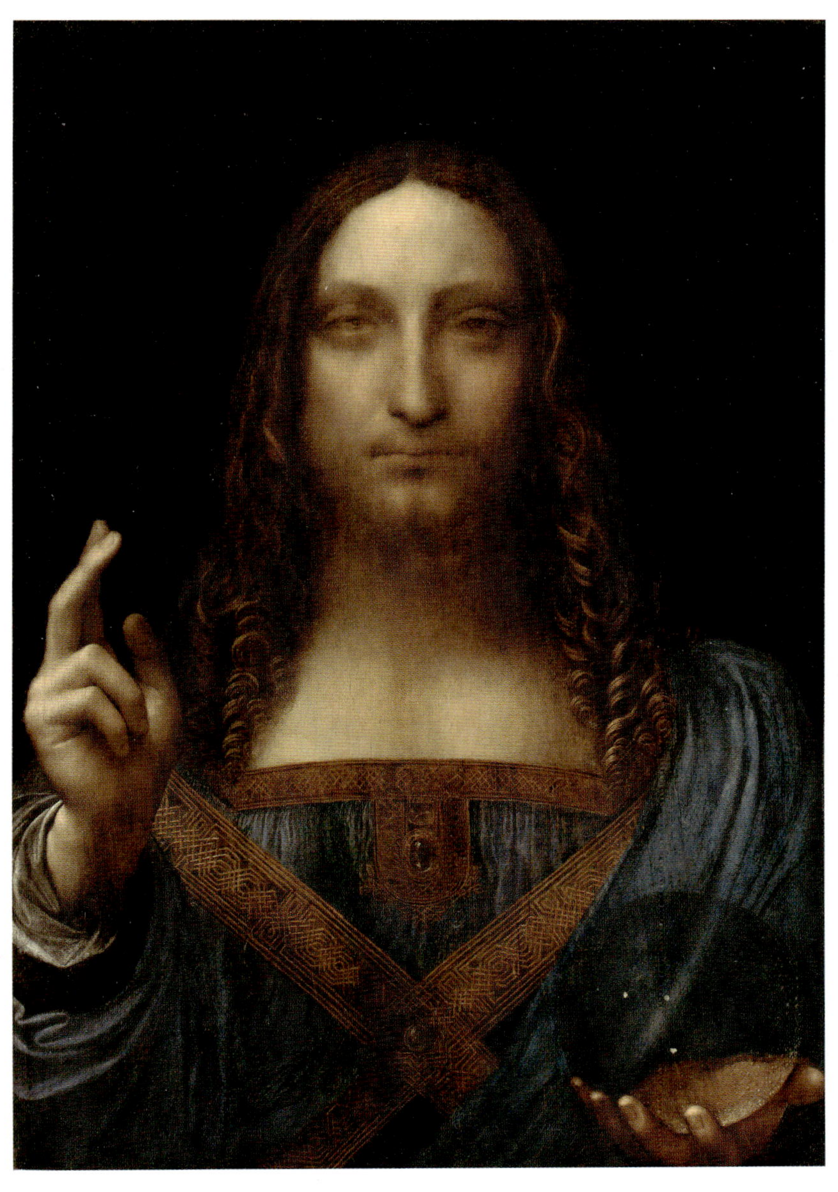

55 Leonardo da Vinci (attrib.), *Salvator Mundi, c.* 1499–1510, oil on panel.

ledge in front of him. His right hand is raised in a characteristic two-fingered blessing while his left hand holds a translucent crystal globe, which represents his dominion over the earth. The globe often has a cross atop it to convey his rule. In this variant of the Salvator Mundi, Christ is usually presented before an abstract background. These images of Christ were a variant of the 'vera icon' type, the legendary images of Christ copied over the centuries from the just discussed original portrait of Christ imprinted miraculously on the cloth with which Veronica wiped his face. This specific iconography became popular in the fifteenth century, decades before Piero painted the *St John*, and appeared in manuscript prayerbooks, prints and paintings.

One of the most famous examples of the type is the panel painting recently conserved and reattributed to Leonardo (illus. 55). It was often replicated by his followers, and Piero may have known one of the copies. Leonardo's painting of Christ and Piero's of St John the Evangelist are both dated to about 1500, based on style, which makes assessing their relationship tricky. Piero could have also been aware of earlier versions of the subject, such as that painted in Memling's workshop (illus. 56), but the physical presence of Leonardo's Christ, his gold-fringed garment and the pose of the blessing hand are closer to Piero's image of St John. To use a 'portrait' of Christ as a model for St John is not surprising, because it underscores the devoted relationship between Christ and his closest disciple. Piero depicts John like Christ, with long curly hair. Piero adapted the saint to a different focus: unlike Christ, who confronts the onlooker, John's attention is turned towards the chalice and the snake transfixed decoratively above it. In the light burnishing the poisoned chalice, Piero may be imitating the extraordinary transparency and reflections of the crystal orb held by Christ. Piero's soft modelling of John's skin suggests that he looked at a Salvator Mundi by Leonardo or one of his followers and applied its lessons about delicate shading, but the surface of the

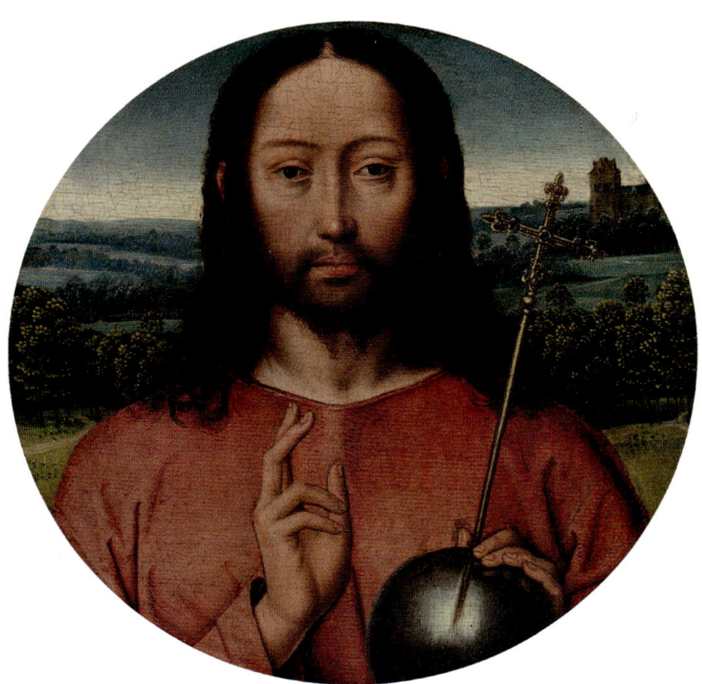

Salvator Mundi is too damaged to reveal many effects of Leonardo's usual technique accurately.[21]

Piero's *Madonna and Child with Two Musician Angels* (*c*. 1505–7, illus. 57) confirms the impact of Leonardo on Piero's career. Like the *St John the Evangelist*, it uses a rectangular, rather than *tondo*, format. The Madonna, Child and two angels sit in a unified group in an ill-defined outdoor setting that is nevertheless striking because of its deep blue sky in atmospheric perspective. The light from their open-air location models the figures three-dimensionally and highlights the rich colours of their garments, accessories and setting. Christ seems about to grab the bow of the music-making angel and puts his arm around his companion. The angel is radiant with happiness as he strums his exotic instrument (a cross between

56 Workshop of Hans Memling, *Salvator Mundi*, *c*. 1480–85, oil on wood.

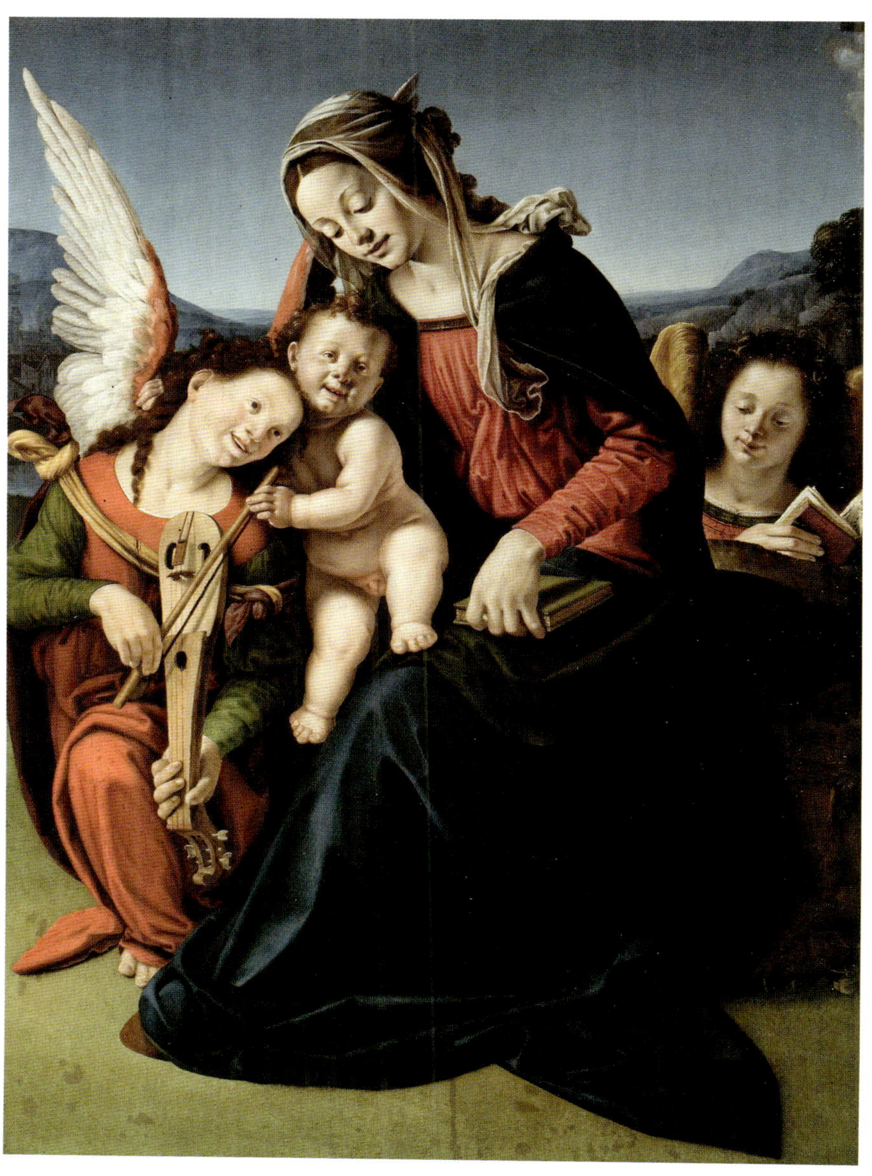

57 Piero di Cosimo, *Madonna and Child with Two Musician Angels*, c. 1505–7, oil on panel.

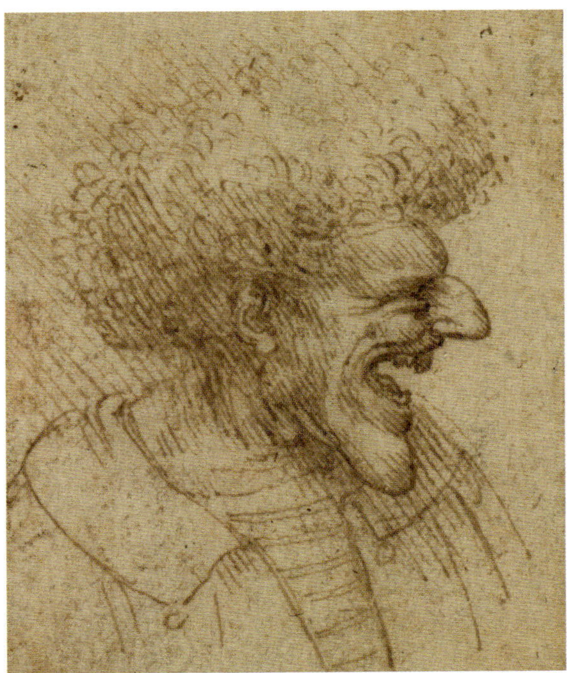

an Arabian rebec and a sitar-like citole), which was often used by troubadours and appropriated here for the music-making angels.[22] It and the other figures sport overexcited grins, which is unusual in scenes involving Mary and Christ because of Christ's tragic fate, which both knew in advance: note the books held by Mary and one of the angels, which allude to their having read of his future. Christ himself is surprisingly unidealized. Most striking is his gap-toothed grin, but he also has a cleft chin, a snub nose with wide nostrils and a broad head. His disconcertingly ugly appearance cannot help but puzzle the viewer used to the idealized likenesses of Christ, the Virgin and angels throughout Italian Renaissance art. Such disquieting portrayals of the holy figures account for much of Piero's 'offbeat' reputation.

58 Leonardo da Vinci, *Caricature of a Man with Bushy Hair, c.* 1495, pen and brown ink.

The painting provides the clearest indication of Piero's study of Leonardo's innovations. Leonardo does not take ugliness to the same unsettling end in painting, but Piero's exploration of emotions relates to Leonardo's famous experiments with facial expressions and body positions to convey feelings, particularly in his drawings of the late fifteenth and early sixteenth centuries. The tiny drawing of a laughing man suggests Leonardo's probing interest in how the 'motions of the parts of the face' betray these emotions (illus. 58).[23] Leonardo's investigations into the representations of human feelings changed Italian, and eventually European, art, and Piero's response is one of the earliest. Leonardo himself applied his theories about expression to the subject of the Madonna and Child, as the open-mouthed, laughing expression of *The Benois Madonna* indicates (see illus. 38). A small terracotta sculpture, dated to the second half of the fifteenth century, represents the smiling Madonna looking down affectionately at the laughing Christ Child, whom she holds in her lap (illus. 59). Christ is chuckling delightedly. Both figures' reactions are rendered convincingly, despite their inappropriateness to the situation they face. When first uncovered, the terracotta was attributed to Leonardo, but was subsequently ascribed to other fifteenth-century sculptors such as Antonio Rossellino, Desiderio da Settignano or Verrocchio. Only since 2019 has it been reassigned to Leonardo, based on its persuasive, lively humanity.[24] A happy characterization of Mary and Christ is startling and one reason to provoke an attribution to the inventive Leonardo (and Piero). There are two (partial) precedents: the dimpled and smiling standing Christ Child in a half-length terracotta sculpture of the Virgin and Child attributed to Donatello and dating to circa 1415, and Uccello's smiling Christ Child of circa 1435–40, who lunges away from his mother as though to welcome the worshipper or perhaps his own destiny.[25]

Leonardo seems to have influenced Piero's painting in another way. Piero apparently knew one of Leonardo's drawings (illus. 60)

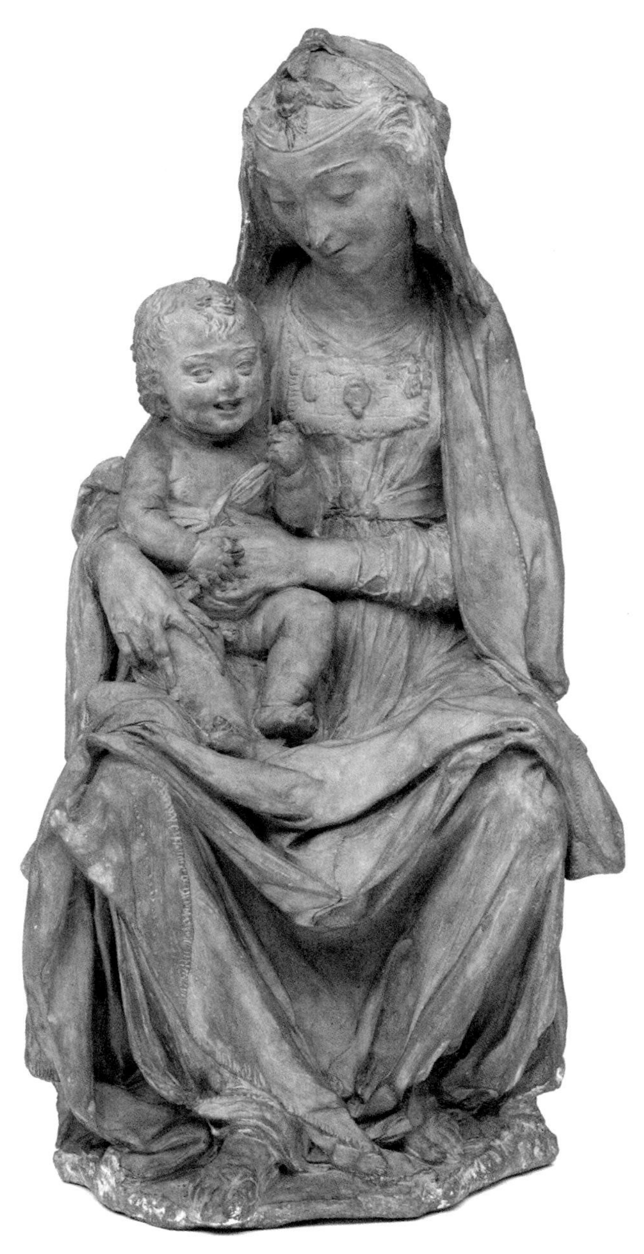

59 Leonardo da Vinci (attrib.), *The Virgin with the Laughing Child*, c. 1472, terracotta.

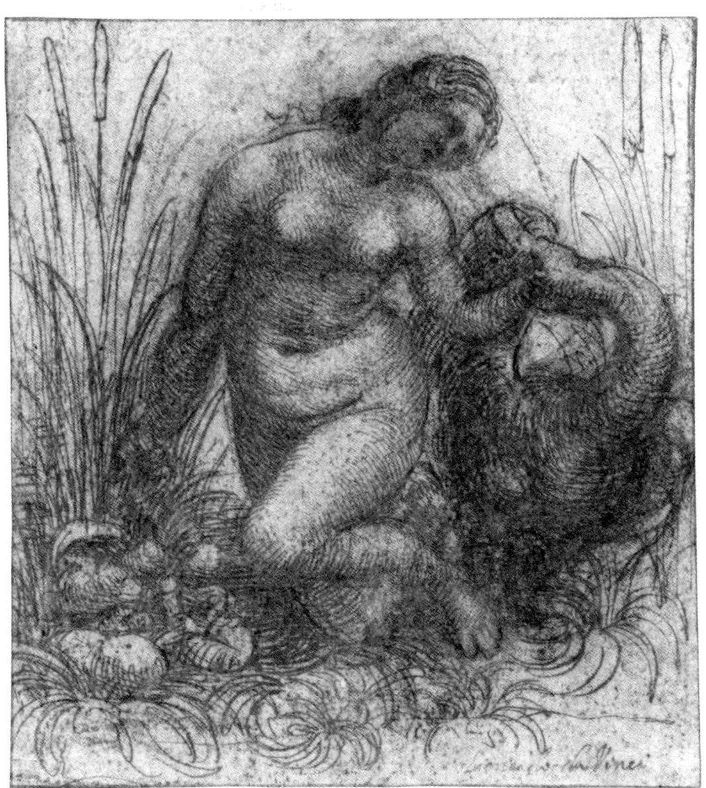

for his kneeling *Leda and the Swan* and transposed the cuddling position of the pagan Spartan queen and her ravisher Zeus, the king
of the gods disguised as a swan, to the asexual positions of Christ
and the music-making angel beside him. Quite an unorthodox
transformation! Leonardo and his followers made numerous
drawings and paintings of the pagan pair. They were remarkable
for the choreography of Leda's and Zeus' yearning bodies as they
bend and turn, almost rubber-like, towards each other. Leonardo's
own drawing is closest to Piero's figural arrangement, but many
of the versions of the pair of lovers anticipate the twisting of the

60 Leonardo da Vinci, *Study for Kneeling Leda and the Swan*, 1504–8, pen and brown
ink, black chalk.

angel's body and head as he leans towards Christ, and Christ's response of touching the angel's shoulder and resting his head atop the angel's.

According to Vasari, Piero's colour was 'very harmonious, for it is certain that Piero was a great master of colouring in oils'.[26] The historian attributed that accomplishment to Leonardo:

> He [Piero] gave his attention to colouring in oils, having seen some works of Leonardo's, executed with that gradation of colour, and finished with that extraordinary diligence, which Leonardo used to employ when he wished to display his art. And so Piero, being pleased with his method, sought to imitate it, although he was afterwards very distant from Leonardo, and worlds away from any other manner.[27]

This painting exemplifies Piero's mastery of 'colouring in oils', but, as already argued, many Italian painters were by this time using oil, or tempera mixed with oil, and so despite Vasari's belief, such a development did not result from Leonardo's influence. It is more likely that Piero learned the skilful use of oil paint from the Netherlandish and German artists living in Florence. Their presence in the city and the importation of northern paintings that occurred with increasing frequency in the last quarter of the fifteenth century advertised the virtues of the medium. Piero's mastery of oil may have been refined by studying Leonardo, but it was the result of diverse inspirations; it certainly became a key feature of his signature style and drew patrons to him.[28]

A final painting for private devotion epitomizes Piero's disconcerting reworking of time-honoured religious themes. It is a grouping of Mary and Joseph with the standing, nude, blessing Christ in a landscape titled *Holy Family with Young Saint John the Baptist* (illus. 61). Mary holds a prayerbook before her son, evoking

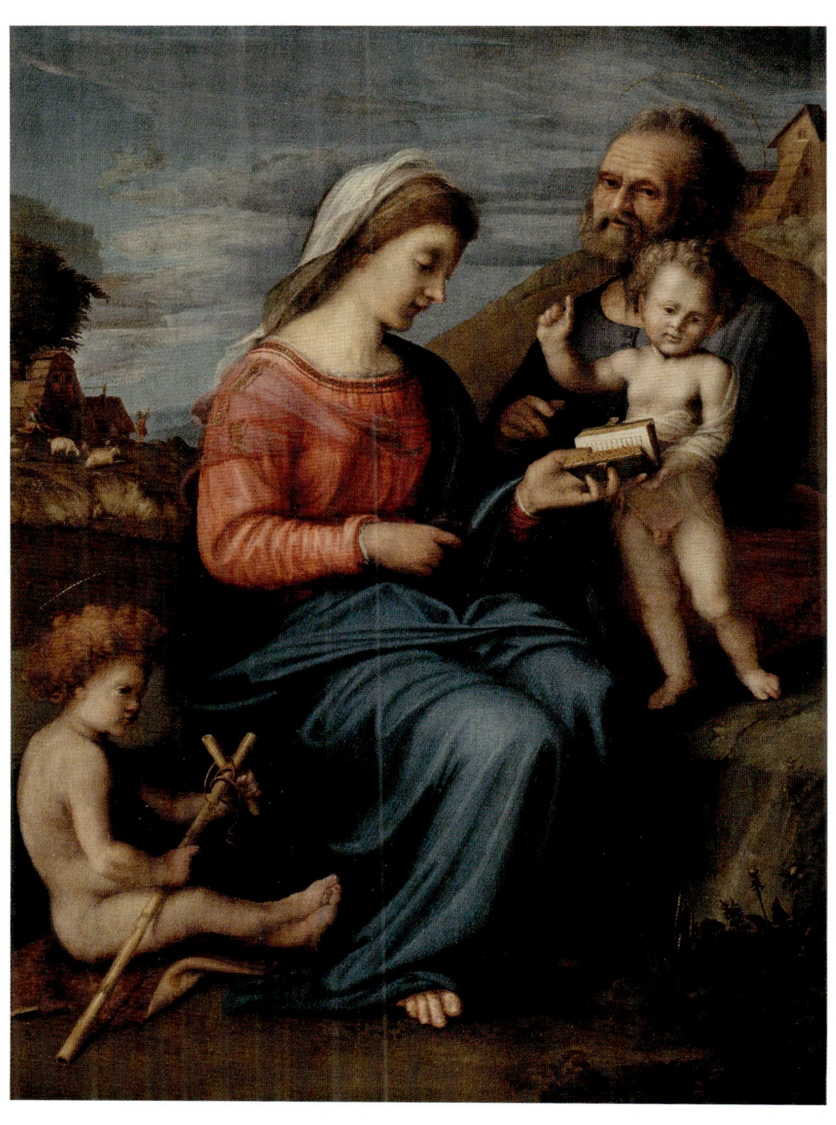

61 Piero di Cosimo, *Holy Family with Young St John the Baptist*, c. 1510–18, oil and tempera (?) on panel.

his fate. St John the Baptist sits on the ground beside them, tying together his reed cross with a leather thong. The depiction of the Baptist's pose – his legs stretched out laterally with his ankles crossed – is a rare one. The crossed ankles identify him as a prophet. He was the last prophet because he directly foretold Christ's coming.[29] His crossed ankles also allude to Christ's position on the cross, reinforcing the meaning of the cross he holds and his prophecy. In the left background, shepherds tend their sheep while one of them looks skyward as though he sights the angel who will announce Christ's birth to them. Several of these features Piero had already borrowed from Leonardo's *Virgin of the Rocks* (see illus. 51) for his *tondo* the *Madonna, Christ Child and John the Baptist with Sts Jerome and Bernard of Clairvaux* (see illus. 50). What is new and startling here is that John the Baptist sports a long, tightly waved mop of red hair that stands inches away from his head. This is an unprecedented hairstyle for any holy figure in the Renaissance. It seems an eye-catching, provocative detail without religious meaning – and in its expression of artistic independence, typical of Piero.

This detail demonstrates Piero's increased freedom in religious paintings for private residences. He did not have to consider the demands of religious orders in control of the sites of his paintings or the possible reactions of public audiences. He may have done such paintings on spec, but the examples considered here look too expensive and special in their size, details and careful facture not to have been commissioned. In this category of images, Piero still needed to suit his patron, so he painted standard religious subjects. With his distinctive artistic flair, Piero enlivened them with unusual details that presumably met the commissioner's taste but which surprise and even unsettle a modern viewer who has never seen anything like them.

SIX

Piero's Artistic Legacy

Tuscany, on her part, was not wanting in men of beautiful
intellect; among whom, not one of the least was Piero.
GIORGIO VASARI, *Lives*

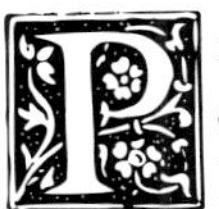iero di Cosimo lived until 1522, well into the sixteenth
century. He survived most notable contemporary
Florentine artists known for their painting, such as
Verrocchio (d. 1488), Ghirlandaio (d. 1494), Pollaiuolo (d. 1498),
Filippino Lippi (d. 1504), Botticelli (d. 1510), Mariotto Albertinelli (d. 1515), Fra Bartolomeo (d. 1517) and Leonardo (d. 1519).
An exception is Lorenzo di Credi, who was born around 1459
and lived until 1537. When one considers the earlier death dates
of painters active during Piero's lifetime and that even Leonardo,
who lived almost as long as Piero, spent most of his career outside Florence and produced little painting, the gap in artistic
leadership in Florence left open to Piero is clear.

As we have seen, Piero and Filippino mutually influenced
each other, and Piero studied the techniques and compositions
of Botticelli, Van der Goes, Memling and Leonardo. Piero's inter-
pretive and stylistic ideas made an impact on transitional artists
of the early sixteenth century in Florence. The first group, like Fra
Bartolomeo and Albertinelli, were trained alongside him in
Cosimo Rosselli's studio. Although Piero did not consistently

run a workshop for apprentices himself, major Florentine artists of the next generation, such as Andrea del Sarto (1486–1530) and Pontormo (1494–1557), trained for a while in his studio and took ideas from him. Several other painters not directly in Piero's orbit imitated various pictorial or technical features of his paintings and spread his influence. After Botticelli's involvement with Savonarola in the 1490s, when he became less active as a painter, and after Filippino's death in 1504, Piero was the only member of the older generation left in Florence to teach younger artists.

Piero's key role in early sixteenth-century Florence led to Vasari dedicating a biography to him and placing it so that Piero followed Leonardo as the second great Florentine artist of the new High Renaissance style in the sequence of his collected biographies. Vasari's decision seems justified, given the vacuum of active painters in the city, but he had an ulterior motive. He wanted to reinforce the supremacy of his native Florence in the development of the new High Renaissance style, which he judged as the perfection of Renaissance art. Leonardo spent most of his career outside Florence and so was a vulnerable standard-bearer for the city's primacy. Vasari's other obvious choice could have been Michelangelo (1475–1564), who spent more time in Florence than Leonardo, but still he was outside the city for about half of his artistic career. He spent these years mainly in Rome, prestigiously employed by a succession of cardinals and popes (1492–9; 1505–12; 1534–64). Despite this disadvantage from the viewpoint of Florentine promotion, Vasari positioned Michelangelo's biography as the culmination of his collection and judged him the greatest artist of all time. That placement was more significant than Michelangelo's contribution to the development of the High Renaissance style in Florence, especially as his patronage by various cardinals and popes could be viewed as a judgement of the superiority of the arts in Florence. Furthermore, Piero was an artistic ancestor of Vasari's own career. As the biographer tells us, Andrea del Sarto was Piero's student. Vasari, like several other artists, passed through Sarto's workshop. Prominent examples of Sarto's students include Pontormo and Rosso Fiorentino (1495–1540), who trained artists of the next generation who further shaped Vasari's art world through their influence on artists like Bronzino (1503–1572). Given this intertwined artistic genealogy, Vasari had a personal stake in promoting Piero di Cosimo.

For these reasons, Vasari bolstered his case for Florentine pre-eminence by touting Piero. As we have seen, he wrote that 'Tuscany, on her part, was not wanting in men of beautiful intellect; among whom, not one of the least was Piero.'[1] In another passage, he was more specific about Piero's unique abilities: 'And in truth, in all that there is to be seen by his hand, one recognizes a spirit very different and far distant from that of other painters.'[2] Given the talents that Vasari ascribed to Piero, his conclusion about the artist's impact is no surprise. 'His disciples were many,' he writes, although Vasari's list included just three names.[3]

Vasari had to defend his choice of Piero. He recognized of course that he was not an artist of Leonardo's calibre, but he was the Florentine who most enthusiastically and creatively developed Leonardo's inventions. To solve his dilemma, the writer resorted to a hypothetical argument suggesting that Piero might have become an artist of Leonardo's stature and his worthy partner in developing the perfect phase of Florentine art but for his own psychological problems:

> If Piero had not been so solitary, and had taken more care of himself in his way of living than he did, he would have made known the greatness of his intellect in such a way that he would have been revered, whereas, by reason of his uncouth ways, he was rather held to be a madman.[4]

As we have already seen, Vasari was even more specific:

> After the death of Cosimo [Rosselli] . . . he kept himself
> constantly shut up, and would not let himself be seen at
> work, leading the life of a man who was less man than
> beast. He would never have his rooms swept, he would
> only eat when hunger came to him, and he would not let
> his garden be worked or his fruit-trees pruned . . . for it
> pleased him to see everything wild, like his own nature;
> and he declared that Nature's own things should be left
> to her to look after, without lifting a hand to them[5]. . . He
> would sometimes stop to gaze at a wall against which sick
> people had been for a long time discharging their spittle,
> and from this he would picture to himself battles of horse-
> men, and the most fantastic cities and the widest land-
> scapes that were ever seen; and he did the same with the
> clouds in the sky.[6]
>
> . . . [Piero] reduced himself to eating nothing but boiled
> eggs, which, in order to save firing, he cooked when he
> was boiling his glue, [presumbly in the same water?] and
> not six or eight at a time, but in fifties; and, keeping them
> in a basket, he would eat them one by one.[7]

Vasari seems to have concocted these proofs of Piero's eccentricities. As was his practice when lacking sufficient data, he
constructed artists' personalities from his interpretation of their
paintings or sculptures. Piero's paintings are often offbeat, and
this gave rise to Vasari's conception of his character. He established Piero as the alter-ego of Leonardo, for good and bad.[8]
Vasari wanted to cast Piero in negative terms because he had not
lived up to his potential and, in the biographer's view, had failed
Florentine art. To make his case, Vasari sought out tropes that
can be traced to Latin authors well known in the fifteenth and

sixteenth centuries, or to notable contemporaries like Leonardo, and simply applied them to Piero. Moreover, he deliberately converted these anecdotes, which had been formerly employed as praise, to opposite effect in order to discredit Piero.

The story about Piero being inspired by the random patterns of spit left on walls or by clouds in the sky derives directly from Leonardo's similarly worded advice about stimulating creativity. Note that Vasari's adaptation of it to Piero becomes more graphic and grotesque ('a wall against which sick people had been for a long time discharging their spittle'); Leonardo's notebooks recording his recommendation to artists is couched in more refined terms:

> I cannot forbear to mention . . . a new device . . . extremely useful in arousing the mind to various inventions. And this is, when you look at a wall spotted with stains, or with a mixture of stones, if you have to devise some scene, you may discover a resemblance to various landscapes . . . or . . . battles and figures in action; or strange faces and costumes.[9]

Leonardo's counsel on how to fire the imagination is likely to have been part of the artistic lore of Florence in his day and may have been known to contemporaries like Piero. It derives from Alberti's treatise on sculpture (*De statua*, 1464), where the theorist counsels the artist:

> Those [who were inclined to express and represent the bodies brought forth by nature] would at times observe in tree trunks, clumps of earth, or other objects of this sort certain outlines (*lineamenta*) which through some light changes could be made to resemble a natural shape.[10]

He alluded to such random inspiration to be found by the artist in nature again briefly in his treatise on painting (*De pictura*, 1450): 'Nay, nature herself seems to take delight in painting, as when she depicts centaurs and the faces of bearded kings in cracked blocks of marble.'[11]

Vasari was a learned man, deeply versed in literature and theory. He would have been aware of Alberti's writings. It is also likely that he knew how the northern Italian artist Mantegna had adopted chance cloud shapes to meaningful effect when he painted *St Sebastian* in 1456–9.[12] In that painting, Mantegna inserted an imagined rider on horseback made of clouds in the sky above the tortured saint. The equestrian figure functions to suggest Sebastian's erstwhile identity as a member of the pagan emperor's Praetorian Guard before he was discovered to be a covert Christian.

Vasari probably was also acquainted with Leonardo's elaboration of Alberti's ideas by word of mouth from fellow artists or from the unpublished manuscript compilation of Leonardo's writings by his student Francesco Melzi, which was brought to him by Gian Paolo Lomazzo (1538–1592).[13] Vasari's application of these theories to Piero twists time-honoured artistic concepts into an example of Piero's disgusting behaviour.

Indirectly, it is also a version of another interpretation of the 'image made by chance' tale. It goes back to Pliny's *Natural History* (XXXV, 102–3), where the Roman author applied it admiringly to the Greek painter Protogenes.[14] Pliny commended the artist's spontaneous naturalism by citing this tale. As he tells it, Protogenes, frustrated at his unconvincing efforts to recreate the foaming saliva of a dog, threw his sponge at his painting, leaving chance to produce the effect of nature. In this rendition, the artist took advantage of good fortune and contributed nothing. That lazy lack of imagination roused Leonardo's ire, as seen in his adaptation of the Protogenes anecdote to Botticelli. In his notebooks,

Leonardo snidely remarked that Botticelli proudly claimed that, rather than studying nature, the artist could achieve the same results 'by merely throwing a sponge soaked in a variety of colours at a wall', adding, 'there would be left on the wall a stain in which could be seen a beautiful landscape'.[15] Vasari did not charge Piero with painting without painstaking analysis and careful transcription of nature. As we have seen, he admired Piero's landscapes. However, no matter how creatively Piero transformed the age-old spittle markings, lurking behind the language in Vasari's account is another proof of Piero's eccentric, even repulsive artistic practices.

A similar pattern is found with the anecdote of the exclusive diet of fifty eggs boiled at a time. Again, the original protagonist is Protogenes and the author is Pliny (*Natural History*, XXXV, 102). Just before the 'image made by chance' tale, Pliny recounts how, when executing his most acclaimed painting, Protogenes lived on soaked lupins. The artist's choice of cuisine was purposeful: lupins satisfied his thirst and hunger, allowing him to work non-stop and to avoid 'blunting his sensibilities by too luxurious a diet'. Pliny did not comment specifically on such behaviour, but his entire report about Protogenes' accomplishments, especially this painting, is adulatory, so we must assume that he endorsed the artist's practice as a sign of focus and dedication to his career. As far as I know, the anecdote was neither visualized nor repeated in another artist's biography, but Vasari transformed Pliny's moral tale by implying gratuitously that Piero's similar behaviour was strange.

The anecdote about Piero not pruning his trees or tending his garden because he believed that nature should be left wild and not cared for by man harks back to Lucretian philosophy. These habits could be interpreted to suggest that the artist made a conscious choice to live the natural lifestyle advocated by Lucretius. A leading expert on the writer noted that Piero's preference for wild nature, and even his diet of hard-boiled eggs, conformed to Lucretian ideas about how humans should coexist with the natural world, including by being vegetarians.[16] This argument presupposes that Piero learned enough about Lucretius' ideas in preparation for painting scenes like the two so-called *Hunt* scenes (see illus. 7 and 9) and the *Forest Fire* panel (see illus. 10) that he chose to absorb them into his own way of living. He may well have. Such an assessment of the artist's sensitivity to the latest cultural phenomenon of Lucretian philosophy is a long way from Vasari's charge that he was a 'beast'.

Vasari recorded his ambivalent judgement of Piero in his editions of the *Lives* in the mid-sixteenth century. It was a retrospective evaluation and obviously did not influence artists who were Piero's contemporaries or immediate successors. However, Vasari's narrative charted and shaped the historiography of the centuries he covered for later periods. His arguments about the superiority of sixteenth-century art, or the Third Style or High Renaissance, presumed that preceding artists' work was largely outmoded. Not until the twentieth century were Vasari's vivid anecdotes about Piero's strange ways found attractive and reinterpreted as praise by the Surrealists, who seized upon the most lurid details in Vasari's biography as proof that Piero was a 'spiritual ancestor' of their movement.

Factors that did have an immediate impact on Piero's standing in the artistic scene around 1500 include the scope of his artistic activity. It took place entirely in Florence, so artists and patrons were not exposed to his art unless they visited the city. Even in Florence, no painter was a long-time apprentice in his workshop and, as a result, none closely and consistently imitated Piero's style or inventions. Despite being trained in fresco painting at the Sistine Chapel, Piero chose not to paint in the popular medium, which closed off many commissions to him and meant that young painters had to look elsewhere to learn that technique. His decision also led to a loss of public visibility for his paintings as most fresco commissions were in the heavily trafficked areas of churches and civic buildings.

Patrons in the next generation were not as enthusiastic about commissioning for their private residences pagan subjects drawn from Lucretius and Ovid, so there was no market for the type of storytelling at which Piero excelled. The rise of masters like Michelangelo and Raphael, who could digest and inventively extend Leonardo's inventions, led to a whole new style in art (what Vasari called the Third Style and considered perfect). It ultimately submerged artists like Piero, who could not fully convert to its lessons. Even though Vasari had named Piero as a leader in that style, the biographer came to question his judgement and equivocated about Piero's achievements because of what he considered the painter's psychological and social problems. In a sense Piero lived at the wrong time and in the wrong place to become a major influence. Nevertheless, a wide range of artists were impressed by his inventions, reflected them in their art and made them part of the Florentine vocabulary. As a result, Piero had a widespread but relatively superficial impact, even in his native city.

Piero's *Madonna and Child with Sts Onuphrius and Augustine* of about 1480 (see illus. 4) can serve as an example. Leonardo's student Lorenzo di Credi reused the composition for his *Sacred Conversation with Sts Julian and Nicholas of Myra* (1494, illus. 62), once the central panel of an altarpiece in the church of Cestello, Florence, rather than Piero's model, Cosimo Rosselli's altarpiece (see illus. 5). He repeated its vibrant blue sky, monochrome background architecture and emphatic cast shadow, all of which impart more energy to the composition and direct attention to the Virgin and Child and saints who venerate them.

Piero's *Incarnation with Sts Catherine of Alexandria, Margaret, John the Evangelist, Peter, Filippo Benizzi and Antoninus* (see illus. 34) provides another salient example of his inventions' appeal, as several other

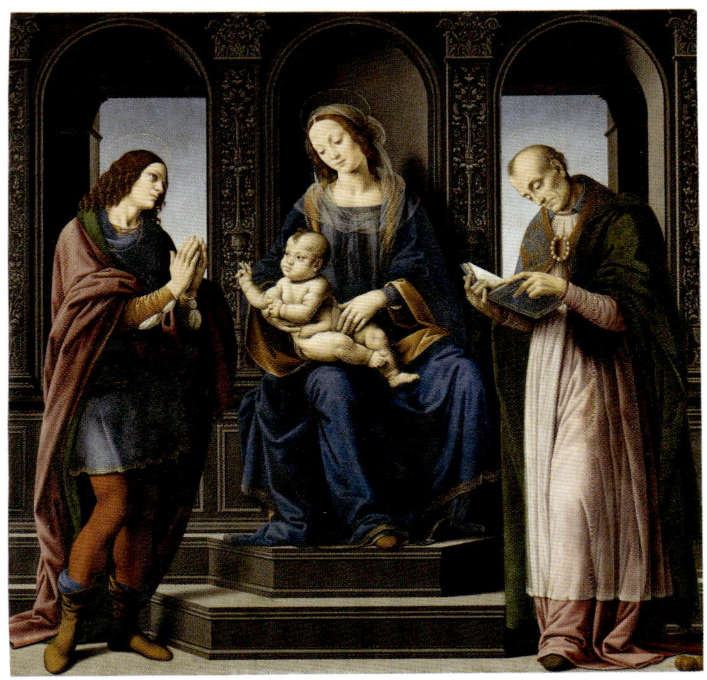

painters took up and embroidered his ideas. The basic composition
of the Madonna standing on a central pedestal amid adoring
saints and angels was reworked several times. Albertinelli (1474–
1515), who trained alongside Piero in the workshop of Cosimo
Rosselli and so knew Piero well, adapted the *Incarnation*'s arrangement ingeniously. In 1506, collaborating with another Florentine
painter named Franciabigio (1482–1525) on an altarpiece for the
church of Santa Trinità in Florence, they transformed the solitary
Virgin with the Holy Spirit above her into the *Madonna Holding the
Blessed Christ Child with Sts Jerome and Zenobius* (1506, illus. 63). Like
Piero, they used the pedestal's base to expand the subject. Piero
had painted the illusion of a sculpted low relief of the Annunciation,
which was the prelude to the Incarnation of Christ. Albertinelli

62 Lorenzo di Credi, *Sacred Conversation with Sts Julian and Nicholas of Myra*, 1494,
oil on panel.

and Franciabigio confected a sculpted low relief of Adam and
Eve to convey the theological idea that the Virgin and Christ are
the 'new Adam and Eve' who cleansed humankind of the original
sin brought on it by the first couple. They reduced the number of
Piero's kneeling and standing saints to just the front two kneeling
figures of St Jerome and the Florentine bishop St Zenobius, to
focus attention on the central group.

In 1494 Albertinelli formed a partnership with Fra Bartolomeo,
so called because he had become a follower of Savonarola in the
1490s and joined his order as a Dominican friar in 1500. The pair
renewed their association in the early sixteenth century after the
Dominican Order, recognizing the value of a trained artist who

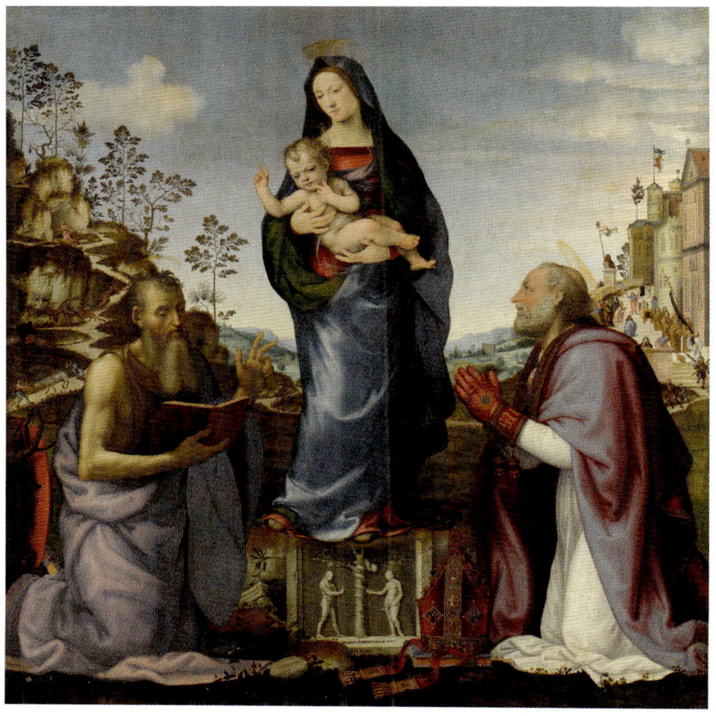

63 Mariotto Albertinelli and Franciabigio, *Madonna Holding the Blessed Christ Child
with Sts Jerome and Zenobius*, 1506, oil on canvas.

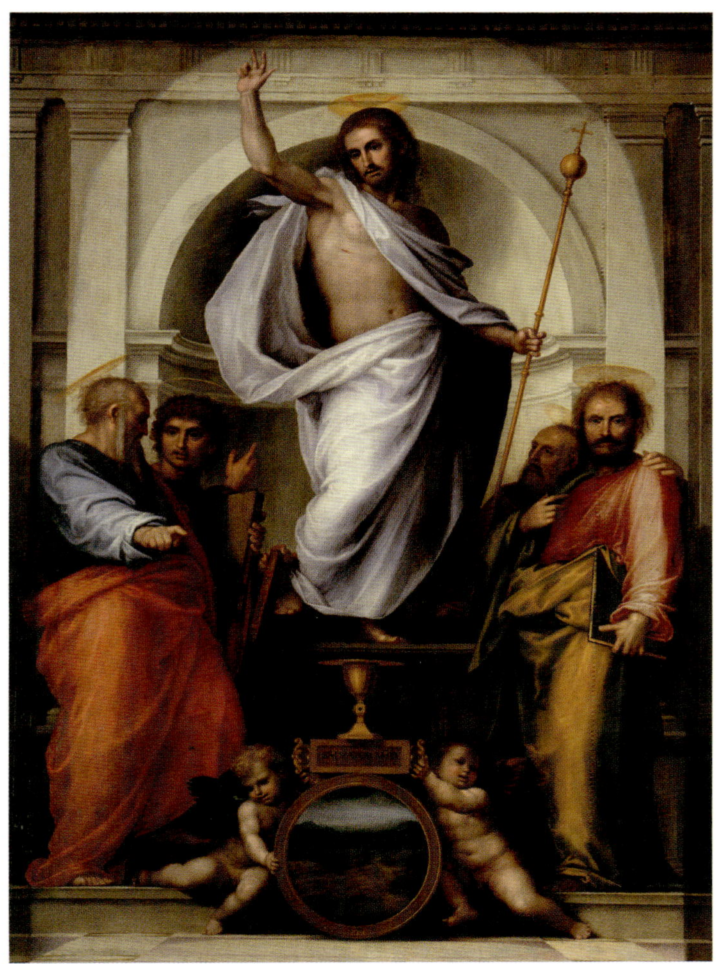

could create religious images, insisted Fra Bartolomeo return to painting. Like Albertinelli, Fra Bartolomeo had been originally trained by Cosimo Rosselli, and so had worked alongside Piero in his earliest years as an artist. Fra Bartolomeo's *Christ with the Four Evangelists* of 1516 (illus. 64) shows the enduring attraction of the

64 Fra Bartolomeo, *Christ with the Four Evangelists, c.* 1516, oil on canvas.

composition Piero devised. Here the central figure, Christ, is elevated on a pedestal and surrounded by worshipping figures situated before an architectural niche that suggests a small chapel. In the friar's variant, an apparition of the standing Christ surmounts a base composed of a chalice and a view of the world's landscape. The subject is another version of the Salvator Mundi theme, as the inscription above the vista reveals. Christ holds a long rod topped by a globe and cross, the other necessary components of Salvator Mundi iconography. The surrounding saints gesture excitedly in reaction to the saviour's appearance. The size, three-dimensionality and idealization of the figures, their poised gestures and the sense of atmosphere and modelling created by light and shade betray that Fra Bartolomeo looked beyond Piero to other artists such as Leonardo and Raphael.

The only prominent painter whom Vasari names as a student of Piero is Andrea del Sarto: 'I have heard from the lips . . . of Andrea del Sarto, who was Piero's disciple.'[17] Sarto followed Piero's *Incarnation* as had Franciabigio, Albertinelli and Fra Bartolomeo. His *Madonna of the Harpies* (illus. 65) dates from about 1515–17, or contemporaneously with Fra Bartolomeo's *Christ with the Four Evangelists*. The painter adopts the device of a fictive stone pedestal to elevate and draw attention to the central figures of the standing Virgin and Child. Sarto modifies the format by introducing a three-dimensional base that is decorated with what appear to be harpies as well as an inscription prayer to the Virgin and identification of Sarto as the artist, with the date of 1517. The inclusion of harpies may allude to their role in the perpetual torture of suicides, as in Dante's *Inferno* (Canto XIII). The position of the Virgin and Child atop them suggests that the holy figures would counter the harpies' menace to the penitent faithful for this sin and others. Like Fra Bartolomeo, Sarto transfers the image into an architectural interior and reduces the adoring saints to two, in this case Francis on the left and John the Evangelist on the

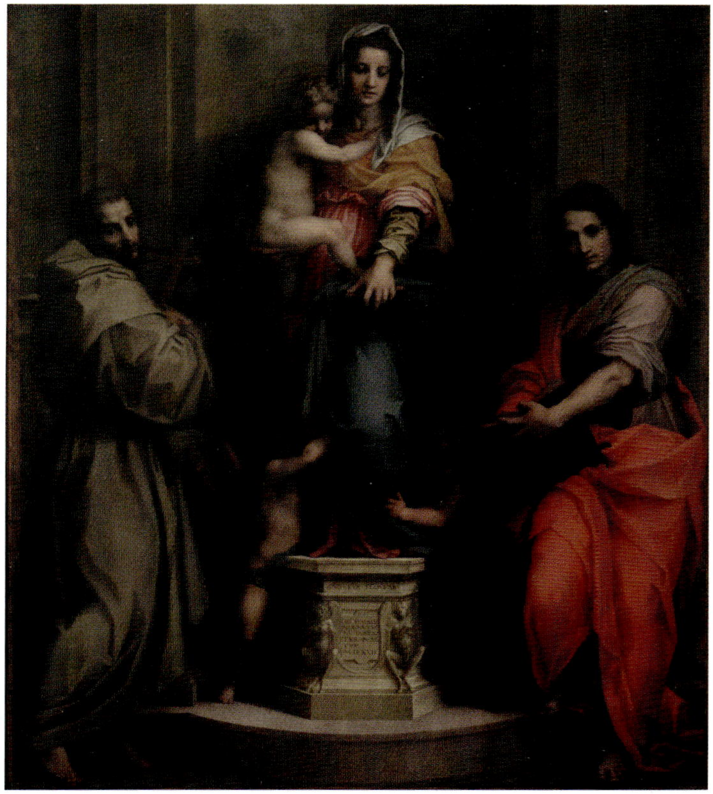

right. He adds two straining angels that grab and support the
Virgin's legs. Like Fra Bartolomeo, Sarto has clearly gone beyond
Piero and absorbed Raphael's and Leonardo's lessons of idealized
monumental figures made three-dimensional through light and
shade modelling. His figures are posed in a unified rhythm and
movement around the Virgin and Child, a compositional feature
also typical of Leonardo and Raphael.

   An entirely dissimilar type of influence can be traced in Piero's
images for private devotion. His *St John the Evangelist* (see illus. 52)

65 Andrea del Sarto, *Madonna of the Harpies*, c. 1515–17, oil on panel.

seems to have inspired Sarto's half-length image of St John the Baptist (*c.* 1523, illus. 66). Sarto's Baptist, like Piero's Evangelist, is seen close up, so that his body is cut off at the lower abdomen. Both saints are posed against a neutral ground to enhance our focus on them. Their attributes are included: John the Evangelist's poisoned chalice and the snake symbolizing that poison; John

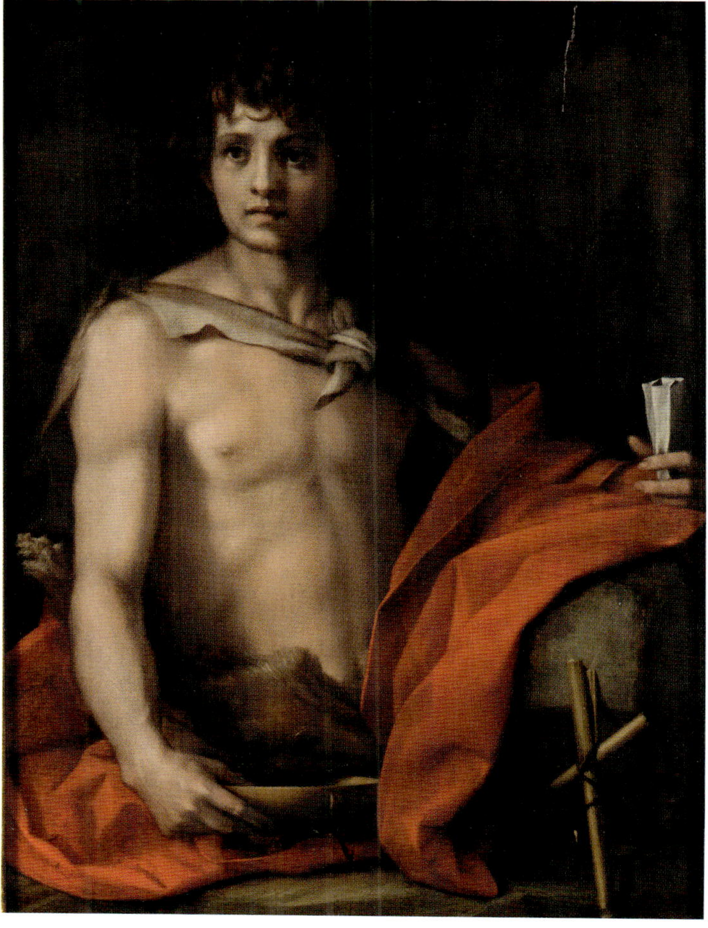

66 Andrea del Sarto, *St John the Baptist, c.* 1523, oil on panel.

the Baptist's reed cross, whose arms are tied together by a leather thong; the simple bowl with which he baptized Christ; and his camel-skin loincloth, connoting the years he spent in the wilderness. He holds a folded paper that conceals its contents but is likely to recall the words of his destiny to announce Christ's coming. John's muscular, nude body with its twisting pose evokes Michelangelo's figures. The emergence of his form from shadow is symbolic of how he foretells Christ, who is the light and will redeem humanity, but the artistic technique Sarto uses in merging form into atmosphere also provides ample proof of his study of Leonardo's famous *sfumato*, or smoky shadow. The painting reveals a much greater command of convincing three-dimensional volume and movement, and light and shade, than Piero had mastered.

Another of Piero's private devotional paintings was studied by fellow Florentine artists. His *Madonna and Child with Two Musician Angels* (see illus. 57) caught the eye of Franciabigio, whose *Madonna and Child* (c. 1523, illus. 67) borrows the baby's distinctive features: the plump, rubbery body, lack of a neck, large and rather square head, fleshy nose, mass of curly hair and, most of all, his surprisingly wide-mouthed grin.

Sarto's *Mystical Marriage of St Catherine* of circa 1512 also picks up the delirious smiles of Piero's Christ Child and two angels in the *Madonna and Child with Two Musician Angels* and adds to their strangeness by pitting with shadow the eyes and mouth of Christ, John the Baptist and angels.[18]

Although Vasari records Andrea del Sarto only as a 'disciple' of Piero's, he does tell the story of how the young Pontormo spent brief intervals in a few workshops when he arrived in Florence. He first went to Leonardo, then to Albertinelli, then to Piero di Cosimo and, finally, in 1512, to Sarto's workshop. He does not mention the length of Pontormo's stay with these masters other than to indicate that he did not stay long with Sarto. Pontormo and Piero must have remained in some contact, however, because

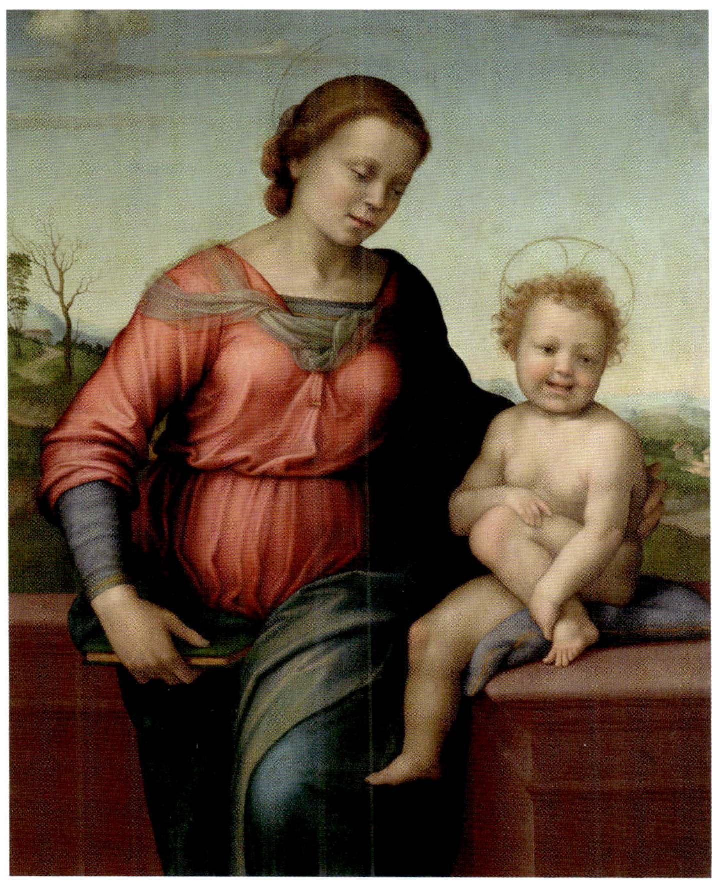

after Piero's death, Pontormo rented his house.[19] Pontormo's own oddness must have made him a kindred spirit!

However long Pontormo stayed with Piero, some of his paintings reveal that he looked seriously enough at the older artist's inventions to become intrigued by his imagination, which he exploited in his own unorthodox style. Pontormo's altarpiece the *Madonna and Child with Sts John the Evangelist, Joseph, the Young John*

67 Franciabigio, *Madonna and Child*, c. 1523, oil on panel.

the Baptist, Francis and James, or the *Pala Pucci* (1518) for the church of San Michele Visdomini in Florence (illus. 68) takes up the unusual facial features and emotionalism of the Christ Child in Piero's devotional painting (see illus. 57). They are repeated not only in Pontormo's Christ Child but in the young St John the Baptist and the two angels around the altarpiece. The larger scale of the altarpiece intensifies their effect. Pontormo expands the emotional effects of Piero's technique of conveying the child's slippery positioning on the Virgin's lap, a means the earlier artist used to create

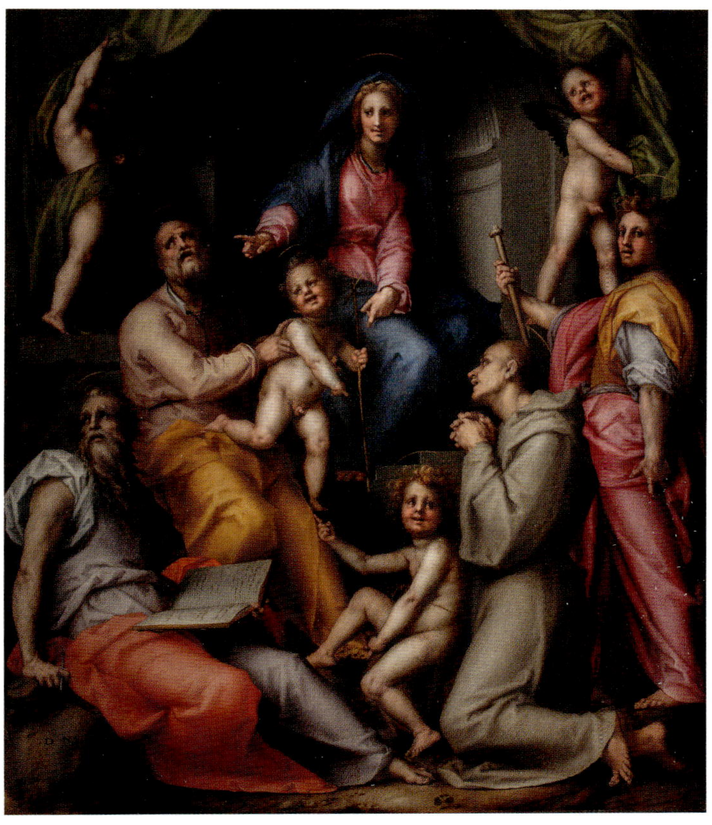

68 Jacopo da Pontormo, *Madonna and Child with Sts John the Evangelist, Joseph, the Young John the Baptist, Francis and James*, or the *Pala Pucci, c.* 1518, oil on panel.

compositional dynamism. Pontormo's Christ seems to be dancing down Joseph's leg. Pontormo increases the number of young nude figures to four; he paints them all in twisting transition and places them within a shadowy setting with erratic light that emphasizes change. He composed the group in a circular shape around the Virgin and Child, contributing to the sense of movement. In this way he destabilized the basic vocabulary of Piero's painting, and most other earlier paintings, which had been known for their dominant central axis, symmetry and balance.

Pontormo also appreciated Piero's iconographical inventiveness in secular domestic painting. He never did the pagan literary subjects that comprised Piero's production in this type of commission, but in Old Testament narratives he adopted the same methods. Pontormo collaborated with Sarto, Franciabigio and other Florentine artists to complete a series of fourteen paintings that trace the life of Joseph for the important Florentine banker and patron Pier Francesco Borgherini to commemorate his marriage to Margherita Acciaiuoli in 1515. The series was for their nuptial chamber and, in the tradition of such scenes, was aimed primarily at the instruction of the bride. They were originally set into the wall panelling and furniture in the couple's bedroom at the Borgherini Palace in Florence. The decoration was more complex than Piero's shorter series of panels, which were usually set into the walls of his patrons' residences and not part of the furniture. It also centred on the Old Testament patriarch Joseph, an unprecedented subject in this context.[20]

One of Pontormo's four paintings for the series depicts the biblical narrative in which Joseph reunites with his family in Egypt, usually called *Joseph with Jacob in Egypt* (c. 1518–19, illus. 69). Pontormo developed the story through the means of multiple sequential episodes located out of order around the panel. He jettisoned the order Piero had imposed on his multiple sequential narratives in *Perseus Liberating Andromeda* (see illus. 6), which followed each

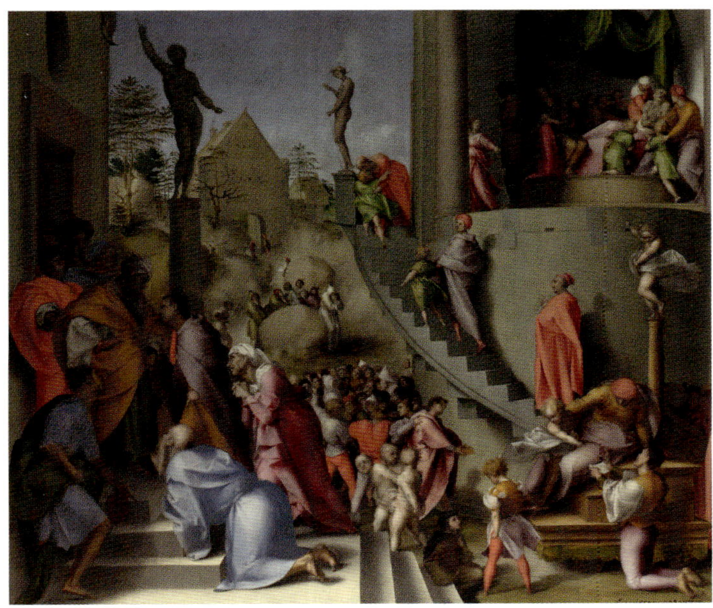

other in a counter-clockwise position. Piero had spotted the various episodes enacted by small figures throughout the landscape in that painting, enveloping them within the setting's natural forms, whereas here Pontormo uses the built environment, not natural settings, to situate and embed them. Like Piero, Pontormo repeats the protagonists as needed to recount the story. He transforms standard architectural features to make them a stage set to hold narratives. The bedroom in which Jacob dies is circular and lacks a wall, so that we can see within. A winding outdoor staircase provides prominence to Joseph's and his son's upward climb towards Jacob's deathbed. Joseph's wife embraces their other son at the top of the stairs. At the deathbed, Joseph and his son receive Jacob's blessing. The stepped platform on the left of the panel is too big to serve as a stepped entry to the building, but it works to elevate into our focus many large figures. The important

69 Jacopo da Pontormo, *Joseph with Jacob in Egypt*, c. 1518–19, oil on panel.

episode is the next one, which features the confrontation between Joseph and the Pharoah, whom Joseph asks for permission to bury his father in Canaan. An audience, composed mostly of his brothers, looks on. Whereas Piero created a charming fairy tale of Ovid's story of Perseus and Andromeda, Pontormo, using some of Piero's storytelling methods, painted a scene of disorientating architecture, an urban setting and differently sized figure groups to deconstruct narrative and pictorial logic. He nevertheless created a fascinating visualization of Genesis; the biblical narrative was skilfully dramatized in a new way. Not just the structure but the strident colours and illogical placement of light and shade in Pontormo's cycle dismay but intrigue viewers, who are sometimes bewildered by these radical new narrational techniques but come to recognize that being forced to adjust to them yields new perceptions.

In its structure and violent narrative, Pontormo's *Martyrdom of the Ten Thousand* (c. 1530, illus. 70) is most akin to Piero's *Battle of the Lapiths and Centaurs* (see illus. 8). Pontormo's painting represents the legend of the 10,000 martyrs, who were Roman soldiers led by St Acacius to convert to Christianity. As a result, they were crucified on Mount Ararat by order of the Roman emperor. Pontormo arranged this narrative as Piero had the *Lapiths and Centaurs*. One episode is given pre-eminence in the foreground: for Piero it is the centauress who cradles her dying mate; for Pontormo it is the Roman emperor who commands the murder of all the Christian converts. Pontormo seems to adopt Piero's use of a surrounding landscape of contrasting colour to set off the episode from the surrounding tumult. He also emphasizes the emperor by his large size and quiet pose, just as Piero enhanced the tender final embrace of the centaur couple. Furthermore, Pontormo structured the surrounding violent scenes in pockets of separate combat in the landscape, another narrative device he may have borrowed from Piero.

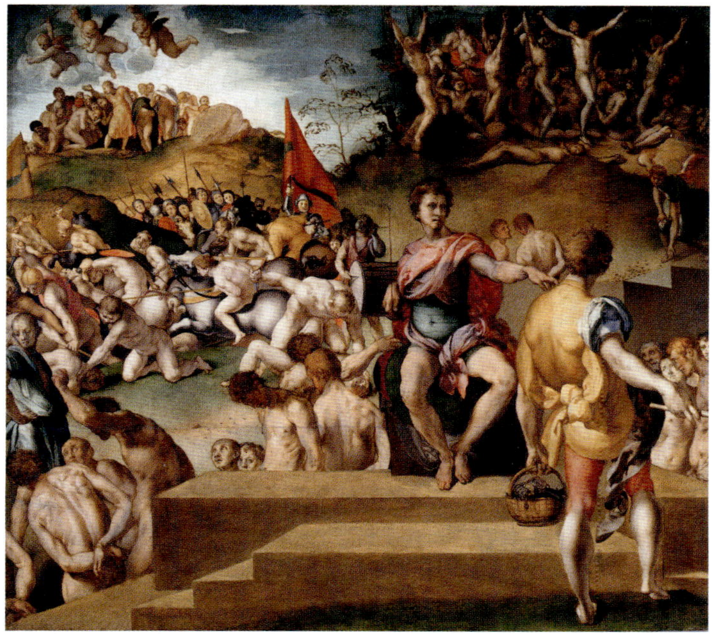

The final example of Piero's influence that I would like to
highlight is the surprising impact his painting of Simonetta
Vespucci (see illus. 29) seems to have had on Michelangelo's
so-called 'divine heads', or *teste divine* drawings: highly finished
black chalk drawings given as presents to Michelangelo's close
associates. In one of them, Michelangelo makes a direct connection
to Piero by creating a bust-length Cleopatra whose breast is being
bitten by an asp (illus. 71). As has been discussed, Piero's painting
had been identified in Michelangelo's lifetime as an image of
Cleopatra. Whereas Piero's painting showed a harmless snake
slithering around his sitter's neck, Michelangelo fulfils the plot
of Cleopatra's suicide as the asp burrows its fangs into her flesh.
Cleopatra's hairstyle is as complexly ornate as Simonetta's, but
she twists her head forward so that we view her expression full

70 Jacopo da Pontormo, *Martyrdom of the Ten Thousand*, *c.* 1530, oil on panel.

face as she stoically submits to her fate. One of her braids has come undone and winds around her shoulders, not unlike the asp. It signals her undoing.

Another similar drawing, given to Gherardo Perini, Michelangelo's model, in 1522, poses the female like Piero's precedent.[21] The central, most finished figure is a bust-length view of a bare-breasted woman in profile. Her form is established between the

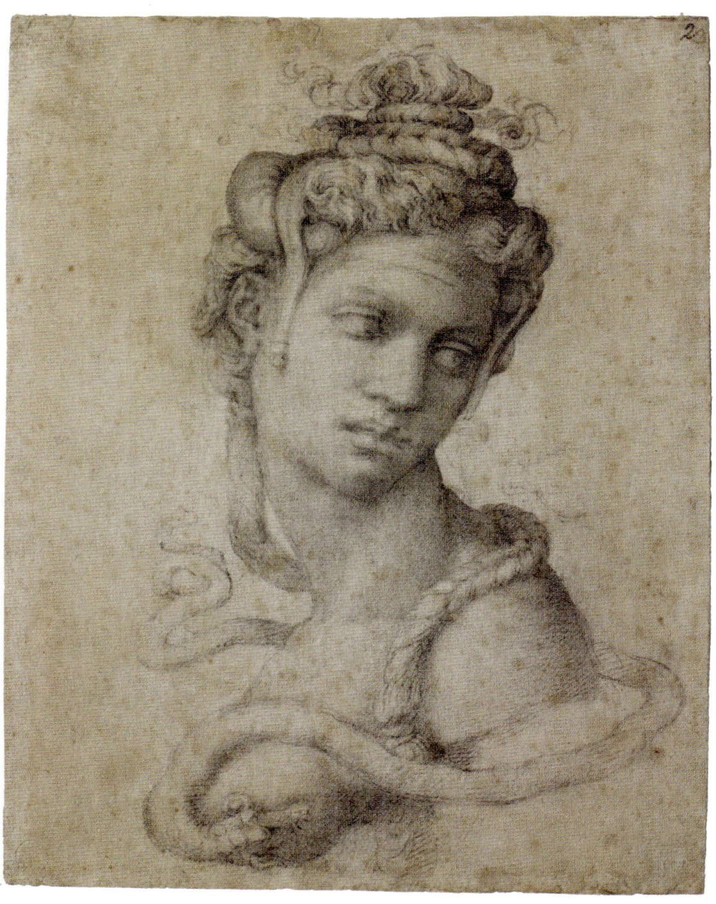

71 Michelangelo, *Presentation Drawing of Cleopatra*, c. 1533–4, black chalk.

head of a lightly drawn child and an old man, but she dominates the drawing. The woman's pose is akin to Piero's Simonetta, as is the extravagant swept-up hairstyle embellished by multiple braided tresses. Michelangelo coifs his figure with a prominent, fantastic serpentine headpiece worn at the back of the head. The decoration emphasizes this area, just as Piero had with the winding braids setting off the back of Simonetta's head.

There are many other paintings and drawings that show Piero's influence on contemporary or later artists. The above sampling is a selection to suggest the range of subject-matters and narrative and artistic techniques borrowed from his paintings, and the widely different artists on whom he had an impact. It is a fraught enterprise to single out Piero's influence on a fellow painter or draughtsman, since so many of his contemporaries had experience in multiple artists' workshops and thus were exposed to the same or similar inventions filtered through diverse agents. Nevertheless, as acknowledged by Vasari, Piero played an important role in the transition of Florentine art into the sixteenth century and in shaping the next phase of Renaissance art. He helped lead the way from the old-fashioned style of his master, Cosimo Rosselli, to the revolutionary Pontormo, who overturned many of the standards of Florentine Renaissance art.

Conclusion

So great a lover of solitude that he knew no pleasure save that of going off by himself with his thoughts . . . after the death of Cosimo [Rosselli], when he kept himself constantly shut up.

GIORGIO VASARI, *Lives*

He would not have assistants standing round him, so that his misanthropy [*bestialità*[1]] had robbed him of all possible aid.

GIORGIO VASARI, *Lives*

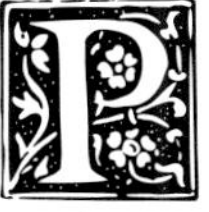

Piero di Lorenzo, later di Cosimo, may have been misanthropic or brutish, an outlier who drove off assistants, but newly found evidence erodes Vasari's claims.[2] As we have seen, he collaborated with other artists on ceremonial art for pageants. He also joined teams of craftsmen working to create the decorations for the triumphal entry of Pope Leo X into Florence in 1515.[3] In addition, he joined the two major organizations for painters, where he interacted with others. He was also part of a confraternity based at Santissima Annunziata, which he put in charge of his funeral and burial.[4] The artist bequeathed the generous sum of 35 gold florins to the confraternity, of which not less than 10 was to be spent on his funeral rites. Piero requested that the confraternity bury him in its communal tomb and that all members and clergy of Santissima Annunziata attend his funeral at his parish church of San Pier Maggiore. He furthermore stipulated that an annual mass in his honour be said on the feast day of his patron saint, St Peter, for 25 years after his death. The document attests to Piero's wealth and piety, countering Vasari's inferences that Piero rejected the period's expectations about Christian practices. It directly contradicts Vasari's claims that Piero was too strange to attract associates and to gain commissions. He served on a large committee to determine the final site of Michelangelo's *David*. Piero also benefited from a neighbour's solicitude over a sustained period: he retained enough of his neighbour's concern that the man kept him supplied with food and necessities while he was well and until his death. In addition to the neighbour, an artist who lived with Piero helped take care of him.[5]

Even if his relations with assistants were unsuccessful, Piero was a canny and successful artist. He skilfully tracked what patrons wanted and kept abreast of – sometimes ahead of – their requirements and his contemporaries' inventions. To some extent, his persona may have been self-created to attract notice. If any of the stories Vasari recounts about him are true and not just applied to him by that writer from Graeco-Roman sources, Piero also knew how to invent an attention-grabbing public persona. He may have been a pioneer of techniques associated with later artists, employed to keep themselves in the limelight and attract commissions. His career poses many puzzles, and this has led to misunderstandings. He was something of a prodigy – Vasari singled out his contributions at the early age of about twenty to the paintings on the Sistine Chapel walls assigned to Cosimo Rosselli. In his day Rosselli was well regarded, but in historical hindsight he seems a conservative, rather mediocre painter. With Rosselli as his mentor, Piero had a long way to go to win ranking in the vanguard of Florentine art.

Meagre documentary evidence has been so far uncovered about the artist in other regards. There is some data about Piero's birth and death dates and aspects of his genealogy, the evolution of his name, his work as a manuscript illuminator; the dates he apprenticed with Rosselli, joined the Company of St Luke painters' association (again at twenty) and the painters' guild, as well as the years in which he executed certain altarpieces. There seems to be no way to understand fully Piero's metamorphosis from a pupil of the conventional artistry of Rosselli into a much more progressive painter. The force of Piero's independent personality certainly played a role. That Piero went on to influence Andrea del Sarto and Pontormo, who were giants in the innovative style of sixteenth-century Florentine art and vastly different from Rosselli, seems stunning.

In part, it was due to Piero's shrewdness. Recognizing the burgeoning market for small secular painting in oil for private residences, a type of commission Rosselli avoided, Piero worked hard to become the favourite painter of wealthy and sophisticated Florentine merchants who wanted such decorations for their homes. He painted Graeco-Roman mythologies and legends with originality, verve and wit, delighting his patrons. His painted images whetted his contemporaries' fascination with ancient authors – some long known, such as Ovid, Vitruvius, Virgil and Aristotle; others newly recovered, such as Empedokles and Lucretius – and elevated that enthusiasm to an intense pitch. He succeeded in creating visual renditions of still other authors as diverse as Philostratus, Plutarch and Theocritus.

The complexities of Piero's secular subject-matter immediately introduce us to recurring interrelated problems in studying his paintings: their topics can be unusual, even unprecedented, and patrons' motivations in asking for them unclear. We know that two of his patrons, Piero del Pugliese and Filippo Strozzi the Younger, owned copies of Lucretius' *De rerum natura*, but access to Empedokles is more difficult to trace and may be indirect. Often Piero had few or no artistic models from which to develop his visual renditions of the texts, and there is no evidence that he researched them himself. A tantalizing clue, the sole case in which we can track his borrowing from an earlier secular source, is his painted cover of *Allegory* (see illus. 31). The detail of a rearing horse in that painting seems to be based on a drawing on parchment for an illumination in a manuscript of Virgil's *Aeneid* attributed to Apollonio di Giovanni (1414–1465), a foremost miniaturist and painter of domestic furnishings, such as *cassoni*, or marriage chests. Apollonio's drawing depicts a stallion rearing and twisting in the same way as in Piero's painting.[6] This suggests that his patrons may have given him access, at least on some occasions, to their incunables of Graeco-Roman authors. As previously noted, Piero must have had a particular affinity for manuscript illumination – the painstaking detail of his independent paintings suggests as much. Documents describe him as a miniaturist himself, although no examples of his work in that medium have been identified. The information provides a key potential conduit between Piero's knowledge of Graeco-Roman texts, which were all the rage at the end of the fifteenth century, other artists' illustrations of them in manuscripts and incunables and his own imaginative reinterpretations of the tales as domestic panel paintings.

Despite the lacunae in our understanding of his background and preparation, Piero's success in secular commissions was unquestionably remarkable: such paintings totalled almost 40 per cent of his artistic production of fewer than fifty securely attributed paintings over a career of almost four decades. This is a very high number of secular paintings, given that most of the period's art was geared to religious purposes. He dominated the market in mythological and legendary painting.

The well-established tale of his creation of the two pre-Lenten Triumph of Death pageants, the first sponsored by the Strozzi family in 1507 and the second of about 1512, provides the most informative guide to Piero's creative process and the reception of his production. For this yearly ritual he employed traditional symbols: black-draped oxen to transport tombs, a costumed figure of Death wielding a scythe and skeletons within tombs surrounding the carriage of Death. Piero, however, transformed all precedents for such celebrations. He animated the ensemble in a novel and terrifying way: at every stop of the procession, the doors on the tombs opened, bodies emerged and skeletons sang the mournful, penitential *Miserere*, chilling the audience with the spectre of their imminent deaths. According to Vasari, onlookers remembered their horror and morbid fascination long afterwards.

Piero was astute in another way. He followed closely the innovations in contemporary art. Only one of his narrative paintings, the *Venus, Mars and Cupid* (see illus. 15), seems to rival deliberately another artist's version of a closely similar subject (see illus. 16). As alike as his and Botticelli's panels are in theme and composition, Piero makes his interpretation more down-to-earth and less idealized, which may reflect Piero's antipathy towards human beings. Venus leans back in a graceless fashion; Venus' body is not idealized according to the admired Graeco-Roman models; Cupid's teeth show unattractively; and the painting is cluttered with symbols. The model of Botticelli's idealized heads of women (see illus. 30) was also important for Piero's adaptation of the type in his painting of Simonetta Vespucci (see illus. 29). Whereas Botticelli's females seem seductive with their long, dishevelled hair, Piero's Simonetta looks innocent, youthfully pert, and aloof from and unsullied by the audience's gaze.

Filippino Lippi sometimes worked for the same patrons as Piero, and his compositions for altarpieces and private devotional paintings were a model. Piero seems to have copied Filippino's *Madonna Holding the Reading Baby Christ* (see illus. 48) for the Strozzi family in his version of the subject (see illus. 47), although he changed the resplendent lapis lazuli blues of the Madonna's robes in Filippino's painting to lugubrious greys, perhaps to hint at the Virgin's sorrow regarding her son's future. He also modified the background vista from a scene of Strozzi property and their slaves to a more standard Netherlandish type of landscape vista.

Piero must have also looked carefully at drawings and paintings by Leonardo, even though we cannot trace how he had access to them. In a rare instance, his borrowing was direct: he transformed a drawing by Leonardo for the lascivious myth of *Leda and the Swan* (see illus. 60) to create the sinuous poses of angels and the Christ Child in a painting for private devotion (see illus. 57). He also turned to *The Benois Madonna* (see illus. 38) and a sculpture of the laughing Madonna and Child (see illus. 59), sometimes ascribed to Leonardo, to create the disconcerting grins of the figures in this painting. There are other instances of specific borrowings from Leonardo, but the most important lessons Piero learned from the older artist were how to use oil paint to create subtle gradations of light and shade to nuance expression and to create three-dimensional forms whose borders merge into the surrounding atmosphere. In addition, he picked up Leonardo's use of his fingers to manipulate paint to gain surface texture. Piero may have been the first artist after Leonardo to exploit the technique extensively and dramatically, as in *A Satyr Mourning over a Nymph* (see illus. 3), where he varied the sense of light and air currents in the sky through a series of overlapping, parallel dragging motions of his fingers.

The itinerant Leonardo offered the example of the subtleties afforded by painting in oil, but Piero probably learned the basics of how to use the technique from the colony of German and Netherlandish artists headquartered in Florence. Recognizing the advantages of oil painting and the rising appreciation of the technique on the part of Florentine collectors, Piero studied examples by the best practitioners, especially Hugo van der Goes and Hans Memling, whose panels were avidly admired by Florentines. Part of Piero's appeal to patrons may have been his skilful exploitation of the advantages of oil.

The analogy with Leonardo stands out most clearly in Piero's absorption in the natural world. Vasari must be right in describing Piero's passionate study of the creatures, landscapes and natural phenomena around him, because abundant evidence of that fascination is provided by his paintings. A comparable roster of drawings after nature matching those extant by Leonardo does not survive to prove what Vasari writes, but it can be inferred from the finished product of Piero's paintings. There are instantly identifiable animals and birds of all types, blazing spontaneous fires, serene seasides, luminous skies and threatening storm clouds.

Most of Piero's paintings were standard subjects, such as altarpieces, private devotional paintings and a limited number of portraits. So far as we know, they were all well received. In the mid-sixteenth century, Vasari collected most of the information about this aspect of his career, proving that many of Florence's leading families – the Strozzi, Capponi, Sangallo, Vespucci, del Pugliese and Tedaldi, but never the Medici – offered him patronage and collected his paintings. Even in Vasari's day, there is no evidence that the Medici owned anything other than drawings by Piero. Nevertheless, to have won prominent commissions from so many foremost families of his native city, Piero must have satisfied their stipulations and desires.

Piero was savvy about the current art scene in another way. Recognizing the growing popularity among Florentine patrons for *tondi*, he created at least twelve panels in the format. The surviving dozen represent about 20 per cent of his total extant production. Later generations frequently copied them, and they became the most influential category of his painting career. The *tondi* became enduring agents of Piero's popularity.

His grand altarpieces hung in important public institutions, like those controlled by the Servites (Santissima Annunziata), the Augustinians and Florentine Republic (Santo Spirito) and the Arte della Seta (Ospedale degli Innocenti), and in several minor Dominican sites outside Florence. Piero's authorship, and often the works' dates, can be verified against documentary evidence, making the altarpieces key markers of his career's development and the only available scaffolding on which to attempt to reconstruct Piero's chronological evolution. Hypotheses about the dating for the rest of his commissions must be fitted into this framework. Piero's interpretations of religious themes were doctrinally correct, even erudite, but he peppered them discreetly with slyly witty details that enlivened – and extended, or, depending on the viewer, distracted from – their serious message.

The subject-matter and format of the altarpieces provide other important insights into Piero's career: they follow period norms, confirming that Piero had a sense of decorum. He distinguished between the strictures attendant on altarpieces created for public religious sites and the panels planned for domestic residences and selected audiences. He also understood the need to meet patrons' expectations in public and private sites, where their commissions might be rejected by religious authorities or private patrons, or be censured. In most of these religious paintings, however, Piero managed to sprinkle into the secondary areas delightful digressions – whether drying laundry, errant pigs, acrobatic monkeys or burl-disfigured trees – that amused their audiences and enlivened serious religious content.

Piero could create in an altarpiece many levels of symbolism that readily adapted to the demanding programmes his commissioners wanted visualized and so gain their satisfaction. To fit their needs he created compositions with saintly protagonists who could be readily identified by believers and were also devotionally and visually engaging. This level of interpretation satisfied all types of worshippers.

There were other levels accessible to the more knowledgeable. In predellas, or the background of a work, he introduced scenes that demanded reflection or learning. To take an example, in the altarpiece for the Dominican church at Lecceto (see illus. 40), the attributes and dress of the four main saints, Peter, John the Baptist, Dominic and Nicholas, make them easily identifiable. The predella narratives extend the implications of the main panel, as is the norm. They portray a combination of legends that religious viewers would have recognized immediately and others that they would have found unfamiliar. The first scene on the left, the successful trial by fire of Dominic's texts (which did not burn because they were sanctioned by God), is a standard theme. On the other hand, the second predella panel depicts the story of Christ consoling John on the death of his mother, St Elizabeth, an extremely unusual subject that derives from several New Testament apocryphal books. The scene at the right, where St Nicholas chops down a tree sacred to Diana to demonstrate his powers over paganism, is equally rare. The scenes of John the Baptist and Nicholas would have been familiar only to a small, learned audience.

A second case is the altarpiece from Santo Spirito, the *Visitation with Sts Nicholas of Bari and Anthony Abbot* (see illus. 33), which was a frequently represented scene because it underscored the miraculous nature of Mary's and Elizabeth's pregnancies. Isolating the two standing women from their usual narrative context and placing two reading, seated old men before them changes the depiction to a two-part representation of the men commenting on the meaning of the women's encounter, which is uncommon.

Many ancillary scenes are distributed throughout the background. They are all familiar narratives, but Piero plays with the viewers, forcing them to scrutinize the painting to find the stories and put them into narrative order. This may be an example of

Piero's whimsy or a calculated display of originality that he intended the viewer to admire, but it could also reflect the painting's multiple audiences. The learned members of the Order of St Augustine frequented the church's choir, where this altarpiece stood. To their initiated eyes, many of the altarpiece's peculiarities could be understood through sophisticated biblical and extra-biblical exegesis. Piero seems to have cleverly taken the subjects that needed to be included and spelled out different messages with them for a lay audience and for the Augustinians, thereby satisfying the learned audience of friars and delighting all viewers by his unorthodox presentation of well-known stories.

He added humorous or surprising touches, such as Anthony Abbot's pig, trotting unfettered in the middle-ground. Escaping from the tumult of the Massacre of the Innocents is an incongruous white four-legged creature, which could be Christ represented as the Lamb of God, eluding an early death. The facade of the building where the massacre takes place has pole railings at each level: on one is draped a drying dish cloth while on another, higher up, a monkey parades nonchalantly. What is their meaning, or are they just whimsical, eye-catching details?

In the right background of the *Incarnation with Sts Catherine of Alexandria, Margaret, John the Evangelist, Peter, Filippo Benizzi and Antoninus* altarpiece (see illus. 34) for the church of Santissima Annunziata, tiny figures of Mary and Christ on a donkey follow Joseph's lead. They seem miraculously helped along a narrow mountain path by foliage that bends in the direction of their destination, following descriptions in apocryphal texts. The strange rendition of Egypt as a walled, medieval hilltop town in Europe may represent a site important to the Servite Order and serve here as a symbolic respite for the family. The Tedaldi family commissioned the *Incarnation* altarpiece in the church of the Servites, but the altarpiece may have had special meaning for Piero: he belonged to a confraternity attached to the church and planned to be buried there himself. (His plans were not carried out, perhaps because he died of the plague and his interment had to be rushed.[7]) We can not tell if Piero's funerary intentions play into the painting's depiction of the *Incarnation* or its ancillary narratives in any way.

A less complex sense of humour is seen in the early plague painting the *Madonna and Child with Sts Lazarus and Sebastian* (see illus. 36). Piero gives special energy to the painting's totemic powers against the plague by picturing a dog enthusiastically licking the wounds of St Lazarus, so intent on cleaning them that his tongue hangs out.

Piero turned to humour in his secular scenes as well. He leavened the horrifying mayhem in his representation of the earliest history of humankind (see illus. 7) with touches of his typical caprice. He painted a monkey, which has climbed high in a foreground tree to escape the chaos, twisting its head to confront the viewer, as if to ask what he thinks of the spectacle. One of the humans, in hand-to-hand combat, is draped in a lion's skin replete with tail and testicles, ironically commenting on his borrowed masculinity. It inverts the well-known myth of Hercules, who miraculously defeated the Nemean lion as one of his twelve impossible labours and afterwards wore its skin. Piero's figure, who struggles with his opponent and ridiculously wears a lion's pelt, testicles and all, is no heroic Hercules. In the so-called *Return from the Hunt* (see illus. 9), a man swimming in the water before the boats pops up his head to confront our gaze, as if sharing an enigmatic commentary on all this 'more civilized' activity. These details seem added to delight the scrutiny of the patron or his guest, who carefully studies the paintings, and to provoke reflection about the reality of human progress as it develops between the two scenes.

Even in his portraits there are the witty and amusing details that are the hallmarks of Piero's inventiveness. In the double portrait of *Giuliano da Sangallo* and *Francesco Giamberti* (see illus. 23), he played to the pride of the family. They had recently adopted the new name of Sangallo, and Piero honoured that by painting hanging 'roosters', or *galli*, from a clothes line outside the church built by Giuliano da Sangallo and where his father, Francesco Giamberti, played the organ, thereby paying tribute to the talents of father and son both.

In addition to glimpses of unexpected humour, another distinguishing feature of Piero's paintings is the author's palpable sympathy with animals. Just as he activated the vegetation in the *Incarnation* altarpiece to shelter and guide the Holy Family along their way, Piero included animals and birds as major characters in his visual tales. Vasari waxed enthusiastic about Piero's empathy, writing that he had 'a certain subtlety in the investigation of some of the deepest and most subtle secrets of nature'.[8] More than just simple personal kinship with animals, Piero is reflecting contemporary debates around animal sensibilities and their ability to respond to, and with, feelings. Piero's interpretation of animals distinguishes him from other contemporary artists, even Leonardo. He is innovative in his sensitivity to the possible range of animal emotions. Piero effectively marshals animals as a perceptive audience to his paintings' drama. Understanding that humans can sometimes be more vulnerable to animals than to other humans, he uses the animals' expressions and reactions to what is taking place to engage the viewers of his paintings and to cue their responses. In some cases, Piero visualizes the opinion that animals are superior to humans. Perhaps the dislike of human company that Vasari ascribed to Piero ('If Piero had not been so solitary'), however exaggerated, had its roots in Piero's preference for animals.[9] In imbuing animals with personalities and a sensitive range of feelings, and in his implicit distaste for humans, Piero goes beyond the ever sociable and gracious courtier Leonardo.

One sees these features throughout Piero's paintings. Some, such as the scenes of early humankind (see illus. 7 and 9) or *The*

Forest Fire (see illus. 10), are effectively tales of animals. They feature more animals or hybrid animal characters than they do humans. These figures articulate emotions as intensely as humans, whether ferocity or, in the case of *The Forest Fire*, fear, by fleeing in species-specific gaits and by using their voices to bellow, cry or, in the case of the mother bear, growl a warning to her cubs to follow her.

In secular paintings like *The Battle of the Lapiths and Centaurs* (see illus. 8), Piero shows surprising sympathy for the wrong side. The half-animal centaurs were usually considered inferior to humans because they were only partly human. In the tale of the battle with the human Lapiths, the centaurs committed the social breach of trying to abduct the Lapith women. Nevertheless, Piero trains the painting's spotlight on a distraught centauress who mourns her dead lover. The pair are isolated on a prominent knoll in the centre foreground. She is lost in her deep affection and distress and oblivious to the surrounding horrors of battle. In *Perseus Liberating Andromeda* (see illus. 6), Piero makes the sea monster more like a child's toy than a frightful dragon and lingers over the details of its death, so that the viewer focuses on it – and mourns. The bleeding dragon lists to the side, shoots a long stream of saliva from its nose, dribbles from its mouth and rolls up its eyes. Perseus seems more like a small dancer atop the dragon than a hero, and the counter-clockwise circle of the multi-scene narrative of Andromeda loses the audience's attention. Andromeda is completely upstaged.

In *A Satyr Mourning over a Nymph* (see illus. 3), mammals, hybrid animals and birds are the dead woman's solitary grievers. A dog and a satyr stand watch over the nymph as though at a wake. The satyr's crouching position and gentle support of the nymph's body, the dog's fixed gaze on her unmoving form, underscore their watchful sadness. They have apparently rushed to the place where she fell before any humans have realized the consequences of her wounds. Whatever story is represented, the sequence of response to her death is clear. The animals' tender sadness expresses their understanding of the meaning of her loss and is profoundly moving to viewers of the painting. Piero marshals the landscape behind the death scene as a complementary protagonist: its smooth, flat planes create a melancholic but beautiful and peaceful setting to calm the tragedy. In revolutionary fashion, Piero used his fingers to shape aspects of the background and skyscape to augment this effect.

Piero skilfully differentiated species and their growth to embellish his narratives in paintings like the monumental *tondo* the *Adoration of the Child* (see illus. 49). The holy figures are set in a landscape crowded with plants, animals and insects. Their abundance suggests that the patron chose Piero because of his reputation for a sensitivity to nature. No other artist paralleled the theological implications of the transformations of Christ's body to the biological stages of growth in nature in specimens such as tadpoles and dandelions. Piero's painting suggested that tadpoles' metamorphosis into frogs could be viewed as an animal analogy to the word of God transformed into flesh in the form of Christ's conception. Reinforcing this theological premise through the phenomena of nature, the dandelion clock symbolizes another type of indirect generation, in this case, by the wind. These comparisons are not simply eye-catching wonders of nature. They vivify profound theological arguments about the world of nature as God's creation and thus are suitable parallels to the Nativity of Christ. One can imagine Piero studying these phenomena in his outdoor investigations. Vasari emphasized his delight with the oddities he found in the natural world. Piero may have himself made the connection between the natural and theological worlds. The unusual connection of frogs and dandelions to Christ seems more likely to have been suggested by someone versed in theology. Like all viewers of the painting, Piero must have experienced watching these changes in the animal and plant worlds, but he alone (or perhaps his patron) thought of comparing them to ineffable Christian mysteries.

This book has paid little attention to the development of Piero di Cosimo's style, a topic that is normally the bread and butter of art historians. There are solid reasons behind the choice. Few of Piero's paintings are dated, which means that establishing a chronology is a largely subjective endeavour. As Vasari opined, Piero changed his style in almost every painting.[10] Almost half of his paintings recount mythological stories, with many active, small-scale figures scattered throughout a landscape. By contrast, his religious commissions depict large and stationary figures, few in number and positioned close to the viewer. Over the course of his long career, Piero's religious painting underwent impressive development. His earliest work adopted the rigidly posed figures in symmetrical compositions of Cosimo Rosselli: the characters lacked poignant engagement with the subject's narrative possibilities and did not move viewers' emotions. Over time, Piero developed the three-dimensionality and grace in their implied movement and evoked more thoroughly their theological meanings.

If tracing the evolution of his style is treacherous, recognizing paintings by Piero is not. They have a consistent and distinct pictorial charm and iconographical inventiveness that I have attempted to capture here. These qualities suggest what he offered to his student Pontormo. Using his miniaturist's eye, Piero devised details of uncanny reality and vividness that jolt the viewer with their intensely scrutinized physical presence – but then combined them fancifully. He studied the techniques of Netherlandish and German painters to achieve this realism but then took them to a different end. His ability to convey empathy with animals is unparalleled during the fifteenth and sixteenth centuries, as is his technique of often transferring to them the role of expressing feelings and acting as his narratives' protagonists. Whether Piero's attentive sympathy to animals is the inverse of an antipathy towards humans, whom he frequently paints in a less idealized manner than his contemporaries, cannot be proved, but it is a tempting hypothesis.

Although *The Forest Fire* (see illus. 10) is a one-off, it stands as a landmark in the history of landscape painting because of its focus on the natural world. It is the first depiction of a carefully detailed vista of animals, birds, trees and plants that allocates to humans only a minor role. In that painting especially, but also to a lesser extent in the other two panels representing the early history of humankind, Piero made a bravura display of painting's possibilities, surpassing any earlier Renaissance painter and indeed Apelles himself. Piero evoked powerfully the transitory effects experienced by the senses of sight, hearing, touch, smell and taste: the visual effects of the fire and the fleeing animals and birds, the crackling sounds of burning wood, the frightened cries of animals, the smell of smoke so pungent it could almost be tasted, the changing lights and colours of a spreading fire and even the ores melted out of the earth by the terrible heat, which could be touched and utilized when cooled. He so effectively conjured these effects that the viewer could easily imagine the sensory repercussions of the narrative through what could be observed in the work.

Although Piero painted what is one of the most extraordinary images of idealized feminine beauty in the fifteenth century in his fantasy image of Simonetta Vespucci, his typical females are otherwise unusual in their rather homely types. Even when visualizing the supremely beautiful goddess Venus, Piero veered away from his contemporary Botticelli's idealized type of Graeco-Roman perfection. His Venus is almost ungainly, but nevertheless she has allured and seduced Mars, and controls him. Perhaps that was Piero's point: to convey that her sexual powers are irresistible no matter her physical form.

As we have seen, Vasari had numerous criticisms of Piero. He considered him a sort of genius *manqué*, an artist of the greatest talent who never realized his potential because of his peculiar behaviour. Nevertheless, the influential biographer named him a founder of the last and perfect third phase of Italian art, or what is now often called the High Renaissance. This book has aimed to reinforce the unique aspects of Piero's painting that warranted Vasari's positive judgement: his inventiveness and whimsy; his unusual abilities to jump between media and translate learned texts into compelling images; his command of his contemporaries' innovations; and his talent for enlivening orthodox religious imagery with humorous, incidental details. Vasari's ambivalence about Piero led him to adopt a series of anecdotes that Graeco-Roman sources applied positively to famous Greek artists and curdle them into criticism of Piero. They had the desired effect of diminishing Piero's reputation. Modern audiences, however, question the negative side of Vasari's subjective judgement, as the flurry of publications and exhibitions devoted to the artist since 2006 indicate. This text joins in their redressing of critical opinion: to an unknowable extent, Piero may have been a genius *manqué*, but he played an important role in the development of the art of the next generation of the city's painters, at the same time as he won over patrons with his originality and playful humour. That magic still casts its spell on audiences today.

CHRONOLOGY

1462	Piero is born to Lorenzo di Piero d'Antonio, a small toolmaker or blacksmith, and Alessandra
1480	A tax return lists Piero, aged eighteen, as an apprentice in Cosimo Rosselli's studio
1481–2	Works on the Sistine Chapel frescoes in the Vatican Palace as an assistant to Rosselli
1482	Joins the Compagnia di San Luca (Company of St Luke), a Florentine artists' confraternity
1489	Piero di Gino Capponi pays a frame-maker for a frame for the altarpiece of the *Visitation with Sts Nicholas and Anthony Abbot*, once in the Capponi Chapel, Santo Spirito, indicating that Piero's painting dates from 1489–90
1491	A will dated 21 September 1491 (Archivio di Stato, Florence, Notarile Antecosimiano 16841) alludes to 'Piero Laurentii Pieri miniatore' as a witness, suggesting that the artist, better known as Piero di Cosimo, was a manuscript illuminator
1493	A contract dated 11 September 1493 (Archivio di Stato, Florence, Notarile Antecosimiano 11685) alludes again to 'Piero Laurentii Pieri miniatore' as a witness. Piero del Pugliese orders a sacred conversation altarpiece (*Madonna and Child Enthroned with Sts Elizabeth of Hungary, Catherine of Alexandria, Peter and John the Evangelist*) from Piero for the Ospedale degli Innocenti, Florence
1499	Piero is again listed in the Company of St Luke
1504	Piero is selected to sit on the committee of artists who will decide on the placement of Michelangelo's *David*. Piero joins the Arte dei Medici e Speziali (Guild of Doctors and Apothecaries), also open to painters

1507	Commissioned by Lorenzo and the younger Filippo Strozzi to provide costumes and staging for the pre-Lenten Triumph of Death pageant as part of the city's carnival
1510	The younger Filippo Strozzi is documented as paying Piero six large *fiorini* of gold for part of a room (probably including the *Perseus Liberating Andromeda* panel)
c. 1512	Another documented carnival pageant, probably the one described by Vasari, is executed by Piero and his students Andrea del Sarto and the little-known Andrea di Cosimo Feltrini
1515	Piero, along with Pontormo and others, creates paintings for Pope Leo X's triumphal entry into Florence
1518	Recognizing his grave illness, Piero leaves 35 florins to the Confraternity of the Santissima Annunziata for his funeral and burial
1521	Piero leaves 50 florins to his neighbour out of his estate for his many kindnesses over an unspecified time in supplying him with food and clothing
1522	Piero dies of the plague at the age of sixty. He is buried in Florence by members of the Confraternity of the Santissima Annunziata at the church of San Pier Maggiore

REFERENCES

Introduction

1 Giorgio Vasari, *Lives of the Most Eminent Painters, Sculptors and Architects* [1568], trans. Gaston du C. de Vere [1912–15] (ebook, London, 2009), vol. IV, p. 125.
2 George Eliot, *Romola*, ed. Dorothea Barrett (London, 1996), p. 186.
3 Georges [Georg] Pudelko, 'Piero di Cosimo, peintre bizarre', *Minotaure*, XI (1938), p. 22.
4 I thank Betsy and Joan Rosasco for this reference.
5 Robert Langton Douglas, *Piero di Cosimo* (Chicago, IL, 1946), and Jean-Louis Vaudoyer, 'Piero di Cosimo', in *L'Art est délectation* (Paris, 1968), pp. 61–79.
6 Sharon Fermor, *Piero di Cosimo: Fiction, Invention and Fantasia* (London, 1993), and Dennis Geronimus, *Piero di Cosimo: Visions Beautiful and Strange* (New Haven, CT, 2006).
7 Gretchen Hirschauer and Dennis Geronimus, eds, *Piero di Cosimo: The Poetry of Painting in Renaissance Florence*, exh. cat., National Gallery of Art, Washington, DC (2015), and Elena Capretti et al., eds, *Piero di Cosimo, 1462–1522: Pittore eccentrico fra Rinascimento e Maniera*, exh. cat., Galleria degli Uffizi, Florence (2015).
8 Stephanie J. Craven, 'Three Dates for Piero di Cosimo', *Burlington Magazine*, CXVII/870 (1975), p. 575.
9 Vasari, *Lives*, vol. IV, pp. 128–9.
10 Ibid., p. 129.
11 Luigi Lazzerini, '"Bizzarrissime fantasie": Piero di Cosimo's Pageant Wagon of the Dead and Girolamo Savonarola', in *Renaissance Studies in Honor of Joseph Connors*, ed. Machtelt Israëls et al. (Florence, 2013), pp. 95–101.
12 Geronimus, *Piero di Cosimo: Visions Beautiful and Strange*, p. 13.

13 See the Chronology of major secure dates in Piero's life in this book, p. 208.

14 Ianthi Assimakopoulou, 'Piero di Cosimo's Nymph and the Hallmark of Artemis', in *Piero di Cosimo: Painter of Faith and Fable*, ed. Dennis Geronimus and Michael W. Kwakkelstein (Leiden, 2018), p. 133.

15 Serena Padovani, 'La mostra su Piero di Cosimo: Una proposta per il suo percorso nel contesto contemporaneo', in *Piero di Cosimo, 1462–1522*, ed. Capretti et al. (2015), p. 29.

16 Vasari, *Lives*, vol. IV, pp. 126–7.

17 Ibid., p. 127.

1 Mythologies

1 Carlo Gamba, 'Piero di Cosimo e i suoi quadri mitologiche', *Bollettino d'arte*, 30 (1936–7), pp. 54–6.

2 Erwin Panofsky, *Studies in Iconology: Humanistic Themes in the Art of the Renaissance* [1939], 3rd edn (New York, 1967), pp. 33–67.

3 Ibid., pp. 38–9.

4 The latter painting is owned by the John and Mable Ringling Museum of Art, Sarasota, Florida. Claudia Cieri Via, 'Per una revisione di primitivismo nell'opera di Piero di Cosimo', *Storia dell'arte*, XXIX (1977), pp. 5–9.

5 Serena Padovani, 'La mostra su Piero di Cosimo: Una proposta per il suo percorso nel contesto contemporaneo', in *Piero di Cosimo, 1462–1522: Pittore eccentrico fra Rinascimento e Maniera*, ed. Elena Capretti et al., exh. cat., Galleria degli Uffizi, Florence (2015), pp. 32–3.

6 Giorgio Vasari, *Lives of the Most Eminent Painters, Sculptors and Architects* [1568], trans. Gaston du C. de Vere [1912–15] (ebook, London, 2009), vol. IV, p. 131.

7 Dennis Geronimus, *Piero di Cosimo: Visions Beautiful and Strange* (New Haven, CT, 2006), pp. 150–61.

8 Daniel Arasse, 'Piero di Cosimo, l'excentrique', in *Le Sujet dans le tableau: essais d'iconographie analytique*, ed. Daniel Arasse (Paris, 1997), p. 55.

9 Vasari, *Lives*, vol. III, p. 222.

10 J. K. Cadogan, *Domenico Ghirlandaio: Artist and Artisan* (New Haven, CT, 2000), pp. 287–8.

11 Geronimus, *Piero di Cosimo: Visions Beautiful and Strange*, pp. 158–9.

12 Alcimar do Lago Carvalho and Inácio Schiller Bittencourt Rebetez, 'Moth of Venus, Caterpillar of Christ: Piero di Cosimo's Insects and

Their Possible Meanings', *Figura: Studies on the Classical Tradition*, VII/I
(2019), p. 19.

13 Sarah Blake McHam, 'The "Fantasia" of the Cricket in Piero di
Cosimo's *Vulcan and Aeolus*', in *Piero di Cosimo: Painter of Faith and Fable*,
ed. Dennis Geronimus and Michael W. Kwakkelstein (Leiden,
2018), pp. 91–2.

14 Roberta J. M. Olson, '*Rara Avis*: Piero di Cosimo and the Birds He
Painted', in *Piero di Cosimo*, ed. Geronimus and Kwakkelstein, p. 103.

15 Pliny the Elder, *Natural History*, ed. H. Rackham, Loeb Classical
Library (Cambridge, MA), XXXV, 112–14 (vol. CCCXCIV, pp. 343–5).

16 McHam, 'The "Fantasia"', pp. 92–4.

17 David Bellingham, 'Aphrodite Deconstructed: Botticelli's *Venus and
Mars* in the National Gallery, London', in *Brill's Companion to Aphrodite*,
ed. Amy C. Smith and Sadie Pickup (Leiden, 2010), p. 349.

18 All quotations from Lucretius derive from *The Nature of Things*, trans.
A. E. Stallings; intro. Richard Jenkyns (London, 2007).

19 E. Capretti, '"Fece in Fiorenza molti quadri a più cittadini, sparsi
per le loro case": *Venere, Marte, e Cupido* e altri dipinti da camera con
"storie di favole"', in *Piero di Cosimo, 1462–1522*, ed. Capretti et al.,
pp. 95–6.

20 Biblioteca Apostolica Vaticana, Fondo Barberiniani, Latini 154
[IX.23].

21 Ada Palmer, *Reading Lucretius in the Renaissance* (Cambridge, 2014), p. 48.

22 Norberto Massi, 'Lorenzo Lotto's New York "Venus"', in *Watching
Art: Writings in Honor of James Beck*, ed. Lynn Catterson and Mark Zucker
(Todi, 2006), pp. 167–70.

23 Arasse, 'Piero di Cosimo, l'excentrique', p. 50.

24 Olson, '*Rara Avis*', p. 118, quoting Pliny the Elder, *Natural History*,
X.104.

25 Carvalho and Schiller Bittencourt Rebetez, 'Moth of Venus',
pp. 27–31.

26 Vasari, *Lives*, vol. IV, p. 132.

27 Botticelli's *Lamentation* of 1490–92 is in the Alte Pinakothek,
Munich, inv. no. 1075.

28 Guy Hedreen, 'The Question of Centaurs', in *Piero di Cosimo: Painter
of Faith and Fable*, ed. Dennis Geronimus and Michael Kwakkelstein
(Leiden, 2015), pp. 198–208.

29 Guy Hedreen, 'The Question of Centaurs: Lucretius, Ovid and
Empedokles in Piero di Cosimo', in *Piero di Cosimo*, ed. Geronimus
and Kwakkelstein, p. 207.

30 Vincenzo Farinella, '"Il dolce miele delle muse": Piero di Cosimo
    e la tradizione lucreziana a Firenze', in *Piero di Cosimo, 1462–1522*,
    ed. Capretti et al., pp. 113–14.

31 Irving Lavin, 'Cephalus and Procris: Transformations of an Ovidian
    Myth', *Journal of the Warburg and Courtauld Institutes*, XVII (1954),
    pp. 266–72.

32 Dennis Geronimus, 'Satiro che piange', in *Piero di Cosimo, 1462–1522*,
    ed. Capretti et al., pp. 276–9.

33 Ianthi Assimakopoulou, 'Piero di Cosimo's Nymph and the Hallmark
    of Artemis', in *Piero di Cosimo*, ed. Geronimus and Kwakkelstein, p. 139.

34 Ibid., p. 141.

35 Vasari, *Lives*, vol. IV, p. 127.

36 Ibid., p. 133.

37 Dennis Geronimus, 'Beautiful Monsters: The Language of Empathy
    and Grief in Piero di Cosimo's Representations of Animals and
    Human–Animal Hybrids', in *Piero di Cosimo*, ed. Geronimus and
    Kwakkelstein, p. 161.

38 Geronimus, *Piero di Cosimo: Visions Beautiful and Strange*, p. 131.

39 Nathaniel Wolloch, *Subjugated Animals: Animals and Anthropocentrism
    in Early Modern European Culture* (Amherst, NY, 2006), pp. 14–26.
    Briefly, Geronimus, 'Beautiful Monsters', p. 160.

40 Wolloch, *Subjugated Animals*, p. 26; Katharine Park, 'Psychology,
    the Organic Soul', in *The Cambridge History of Renaissance Philosophy*,
    ed. C. Schmitt et al. (Cambridge, 2008), part 2, pp. 465–7.

41 Leon Battista Alberti, *Theogenius*, book 2: *Opere volgari*, ed. Cecil
    Grayson (Bari, 1960–73), vol. II, pp. 90–94. I thank François
    Quiviger and David Marsh for this reference.

42 Leon Battista Alberti, *Momus*, ed. Virginia Brown and Sarah Knight
    (Cambridge, MA, 2003), book IV, 43–5, pp. 308–11.

43 Simona Cohen, *Animals as Disguised Symbols in Renaissance Art* (Leiden,
    2008), pp. 25–9; Leonardo da Vinci, *Favole e profezie: Scritti letterari*,
    ed. Giuditta Cirnigliaro and Carlo Vecce (Milan, 2019), pp. 5–19.

44 Alison Luchs, 'Creatures, Great, Small and Hybrid: The Natural
    and Unnatural Wonders in Piero's Art', in *Piero di Cosimo: The
    Poetry of Painting in Renaissance Florence*, ed. Gretchen Hirschauer and
    Dennis Geronimus, exh. cat., National Gallery of Art, Washington,
    DC (2015), pp. 62–9.

45 Elizabeth Walmsley, '"A Very Rich and Beautiful Effect":
    Piero's Painting Technique', in *Piero di Cosimo: The Poetry of Painting*,
    ed. Hirschauer and Geronimus, pp. 72–81; Larry Keith,

'A Sky of 500-Year-Old Fingerprints', www.nationalgallery.org.uk, 28 April 2022. I thank Elizabeth Walmsley for telling me about Keith's restoration of the painting.

46 The *St Jerome* painting is in the Vatican Museums. Thomas Brachert, 'A Distinctive Aspect of Painting Technique in *Ginevra de' Benci* and Leonardo's Early Works', *Report and Studies in the History of Art*, III (1969), p. 85. Larry Keith kindly alerted me to Brachert's research.

47 Ibid., p. 94.

48 Stephanie J. Craven, 'Three Dates for Piero di Cosimo', *Burlington Magazine*, CXVII/870 (1975), pp. 575–6.

49 Vasari, *Lives*, vol. IV, pp. 139–40.

50 Geronimus, *Piero di Cosimo: Visions Beautiful and Strange*, pp. 109–10.

51 Craven, 'Three Dates', p. 576.

52 Vasari, *Lives*, vol. IV, pp. 130–31.

53 Elizabeth McGrath, 'The Black Andromeda', *Journal of the Warburg and Courtauld Institutes*, LV (1992), pp. 1–18.

54 Sergio Tognetti, 'The Trade in Black African Slaves in Fifteenth-Century Florence', in *Black Africans in Renaissance Europe*, ed. T. F. Earle and K.J.P. Lowe (Cambridge, 2005), pp. 221, 223.

55 Jonathan K. Nelson, 'Ethiopian Christians on the Margins: Symbolic Blackness in Filippino Lippi's *Adoration of the Magi* and *Miracle of St Philip*', *Renaissance Studies*, XXXV/5 (2021), p. 859.

56 Georges [Georg] Pudelko, 'Piero di Cosimo, peintre bizarre', *Minotaure*, XI (1938), p. 19.

57 Georgette Camille, 'Piero di Cosimo', *Documents*, II/6 (1930), p. 334: 'Piero di Cosimo, véritablement, par misanthropie ou une con naissance magique de la nature, ait préféré le commerce des bêtes à celui des hommes.'

58 Vasari, *Lives*, vol. IV, p. 131.

59 Ibid., p. 5.

60 Ibid.

61 Ibid., p. 3.

62 Ibid., p. 7.

63 Ibid., p. 9.

2 Legendary Subjects

1 Giorgio Vasari, *Lives of the Most Eminent Painters, Sculptors and Architects* [1568], trans. Gaston du C. de Vere [1912–15] (ebook, London, 2009), vol. IV, p. 131.

2 Panofsky argued that the two narratives (see illus. 7 and 9) were
   part of a larger series of five paintings, including *The Forest Fire*
   (see illus. 10) and the two narratives of Vulcan (see illus. 12 and 13).
   He also supported the claim that Francesco del Pugliese was their
   likely patron. Only the second theory wins support today.
3 Dennis Geronimus, 'Beautiful Monsters: The Language of Empathy
   and Grief in Piero di Cosimo's Representations of Animals and
   Human–Animal Hybrids', in *Piero di Cosimo: Painter of Faith and Fable*,
   ed. Dennis Geronimus and Michael W. Kwakkelstein (Leiden,
   2018), p. 166. I thank Stephan Wolohojian and Gretchen Walter
   of the Department of European Paintings, Metropolitan Museum
   of Art, New York, for making it possible for me to study these
   paintings while they were in storage.
4 Dennis Geronimus, 'Living Landscape and Wonderment in
   Renaissance Art', in *Material World: The Intersection of Art, Science, and
   Nature in Ancient Literature and Its Renaissance Reception*, ed. Guy Hedreen
   (Leiden, 2021), pp. 200–201.
5 Maria Belozerskaya, 'Real or Imagined? Exotic Animals in Piero
   di Cosimo's Mythologies', in *Piero di Cosimo: Painter of Faith and Fable*,
   ed. Geronimus and Kwakkelstein, p. 64.
6 Ibid., p. 66.
7 Roberta J. M. Olson, '*Rara Avis*: Piero di Cosimo and the Birds He
   Painted', in *Piero di Cosimo*, ed. Geronimus and Kwakkelstein, p. 124.
8 Catherine Whistler and David Bomford, '*The Forest Fire*' by Piero di
   Cosimo (Oxford, 1999), pp. 20–21.
9 Ibid., p. 5.
10 Vasari, *Lives*, vol. IV, p. 131.
11 Whistler and Bomford, *Forest Fire*, p. 11.
12 Guy Hedreen, 'The Question of Centaurs: Lucretius, Ovid and
   Empedokles in Piero di Cosimo', in *Piero di Cosimo*, ed. Geronimus
   and Kwakkelstein, pp. 201–2.
13 Scott Nethersole, *Art and Violence in Early Renaissance Florence* (New
   Haven, CT, 2018), p. 237.
14 Vincenzo Farinella, '"Il dolce miele delle muse": Piero di Cosimo
   e la tradizione lucreziana a Firenze', in *Piero di Cosimo, 1462–1522:
   Pittore eccentrico fra Rinascimento e Maniera*, ed. Elena Capretti et al.,
   exh. cat., Galleria degli Uffizi, Florence (2015), p. 107.
15 Alison Brown, 'Lucretius and the Epicureans in the Social and
   Political Context of Renaissance Florence', *I Tatti Studies in the Italian
   Renaissance*, IX (2001), p. 56.

16   Vasari, *Lives*, vol. IV, pp. 126–7.
17   Arthur O. Lovejoy and George Boas, *Primitivism and Related Ideas in Antiquity* (Baltimore, MD, 1935), p. 222.
18   Brown, 'Lucretius and the Epicureans', p. 12, n. 3.
19   Dennis Geronimus, 'No Man's Lands: Lucretius and the Primitive Strain in Piero's Art and Paintings', in *Piero di Cosimo: The Poetry of Painting in Renaissance Florence*, ed. Gretchen Hirschauer and Dennis Geronimus, exh. cat., National Gallery of Art, Washington, DC (2015), p. 55.
20   Eve Borsook, 'Filippo Strozzi and the Two Plinys: Civic Pride, Diplomacy, and Private Taste in Quattrocento Naples and Florence', *I Tatti Studies in the Italian Renaissance*, XXIII/1 (2020), pp. 77–99.
21   Brown, 'Lucretius and the Epicureans', p. 56; Alison Brown, *The Return of Lucretius to Renaissance Florence* (Cambridge, MA, 2010), pp. 1–2, notes 48 manuscript copies in Latin and 7 different printed editions in the fifteenth century.
22   Ada Palmer, *Reading Lucretius in the Renaissance* (Cambridge, 2014), pp. 4, 98.
23   Brown, 'Lucretius and the Epicureans', pp. 41–2.
24   Ibid., p. 40.
25   Vespucci, Letter V 'Mundus Novus' to Lorenzo di Pierfrancesco de' Medici, p. 50, quoted in Stephen J. Campbell, 'Giorgione's *Tempest*, *Studiolo* Culture, and the Renaissance Lucretius', *Renaissance Quarterly*, LVI/2 (2003), p. 323.
26   Amerigo Vespucci, *Letters from a New World: Amerigo Vespucci's Discovery of America*, ed. Luciano Formisano (New York, 1992), p. 50.
27   Ibid., p. 64.
28   He lists deer, lions, wild boars and monkeys, and notes that there were no domestic animals. Ibid., p. 31.
29   Ibid., p. 73.
30   Ibid., p. 32.
31   Ibid., p. 33.
32   Hedreen, 'The Question of Centaurs', p. 198.

3 Portraits

 1   Duke Valentino is Cesare Borgia. Giorgio Vasari, *Lives of the Most Eminent Painters, Sculptors and Architects* [1568], trans. Gaston du C. de Vere [1912–15] (ebook, London, 2009), vol. IV, p. 126.

2 Jodi Cranston, *The Poetics of Portraiture in the Italian Renaissance*
   (Cambridge, 2000), p. 66.

3 Duncan Bull, 'Portrait of Giuliano da San Gallo' and 'Portrait
   of Francesco Giamberti', in *Piero di Cosimo: The Poetry of Painting in
   Renaissance Florence*, ed. Gretchen Hirschauer and Dennis Geronimus,
   exh. cat., National Gallery of Art, Washington, DC (2015),
   cat. no. 4.

4 Dennis Geronimus, *Piero di Cosimo: Visions Beautiful and Strange*
   (New Haven, CT, 2006), p. 45.

5 Vasari, *Lives*, vol. IV, p. 134.

6 Paula Nuttall, *From Flanders to Florence: The Impact of Netherlandish
   Painting, 1400–1500* (New Haven, CT, 2004), p. 37.

7 Bull, 'Portrait', *Piero di Cosimo: The Poetry of Painting*, cat. no. 4.

8 Cranston, *Poetics*, p. 100.

9 Doris Carl, 'New Documents for Piero di Cosimo's Portrait of
   Francesco di Bartolo Giamberti', *Burlington Magazine*, CLVII/1342
   (2015), p. 4.

10 Nuttall, *From Flanders to Florence*, pp. 254–62. For the Medici
   collections, see also pp. 105–17.

11 Carl, 'New Documents', pp. 5–7.

12 Vasari, *Lives*, vol. IV, p. 194.

13 Ibid., p. 191.

14 Jill Burke, *Changing Patrons: Social Identity and the Visual Arts in Renaissance
   Florence* (University Park, PA, 2004), pp. 85–96.

15 Alessandro Cecchi, 'Piero di Cosimo e Filippino Lippi, affinità e
   differenze', in *Piero di Cosimo: 1462–1522: Pittore eccentrico fra Rinascimento
   e Maniera*, ed. Elena Capretti et al., exh. cat., Galleria degli Uffizi,
   Florence (2015), pp. 123–33.

16 Allison Levy, 'Framing Widows: Mourning, Gender, and Portraiture
   in Early Modern Florence', in *Widowhood and Visual Culture in Early
   Modern Europe*, ed. Allison Levy (London, 2003), p. 224.

17 Serena Padovani, 'Ritratto femminile', in *Piero di Cosimo, 1462–1522*,
   ed. Capretti et al., cat. no. 39.

18 Erin J. Campbell, 'Prophets, Saints, and Matriarchs: Portraits of Old
   Women in Early Modern Italy', *Renaissance Quarterly*, LXIII/3 (2010),
   pp. 822–4.

19 Vasari, *Lives*, vol. IV, p. 134.

20 Béla Jozsef Demeter, 'Reappraising Piero di Cosimo's Serpents:
   The Role of Vipers in Renaissance Florence', *Renaissance Studies*,
   XXXII/4 (2017), pp. 642–5.

21 Ibid., pp. 647–9.
22 Ibid., p. 646.
23 Ibid.
24 Geronimus, *Piero di Cosimo: Visions Beautiful and Strange*, p. 67.
25 Eve Borsook quoted ibid., p. 68.
26 Vasari, *Lives*, vol. IV, p. 134.
27 Gabriele Donati, 'Francesco da San Gallo, Paolo Giovio, e la "Simonetta" di Piero di Cosimo', *Prospettiva*, 101 (2001), p. 82.
28 Ibid., pp. 82–3.
29 Adrian W. B. Randolph, 'Performing the Bridal Body in Fifteenth-Century Florence', *Art History*, XXI/2 (1998), pp. 185–9.
30 Carole Collier Frick, 'Fashion and Adornment', in *A Cultural History of Hair in the Renaissance*, ed. Edith Snook (London, 2019), p. 58.
31 Geronimus, *Piero di Cosimo: Visions Beautiful and Strange*, p. 59.
32 Charles Dempsey, *The Portrayal of Love: Botticelli's 'Primavera' and Humanist Culture at the Time of Lorenzo the Magnificent* (Princeton, NJ, 1992), pp. 120–21.
33 Ibid., pp. 116–17, 120–21, 124–5; Judith Rachel Allen, 'Simonetta Cattaneo Vespucci: Beauty, Politics, Literature, and Art in Early Renaissance Florence', PhD thesis, University of Birmingham (2014).
34 David Alan Brown, *Virtue and Beauty: Leonardo's 'Ginevra de' Benci' and Renaissance Portraits of Women* (Washington, DC, 2001).
35 Frick, 'Fashion and Adornment', p. 53.
36 Allen, *Simonetta*, p. 220.
37 Friedrich Ohly, 'Tau und Perle: Ein Vortrag', in *Festschrift für Ingeborg Schröbler zum 65. Geburtstag*, ed. Dietrich Schmidtke and Helga Schüppert (Tübingen, 1973), pp. 406–9.
38 Gretchen Hirschauer, 'Allegoria', in *Piero di Cosimo, 1462–1522*, ed. Capretti et al., cat. no. 11.
39 Roberta Milliken, *Ambiguous Locks: An Iconology of Hair in Medieval Art and Literature* (Jefferson, NC, 2012), pp. 23–30.
40 Ibid., p. 108.
41 Mirella Levi d'Ancona, *The Garden of the Renaissance: Botanical Symbolism in Italian Painting* (Florence, 1977), pp. 197–9.
42 Geronimus, *Piero di Cosimo: Visions Beautiful and Strange*, pp. 73–4.
43 Alison Luchs, 'Allegory', in *Piero di Cosimo: The Poetry of Painting*, ed. Hirschauer and Geronimus, cat. no. 17. See there the illustration of Apollonio's drawing, which is now in the Biblioteca Riccardiana, Florence.

4 Altarpieces

1 Dennis Geronimus, *Piero di Cosimo: Visions Beautiful and Strange* (New Haven, CT, 2006), p. 188.

2 Nicoletta Pons, 'Madonna col bambino . . .', in *Piero di Cosimo, 1462–1522: Pittore eccentrico fra Rinascimento e Maniera*, ed. Elena Capretti et al., exh. cat., Galleria degli Uffizi, Florence (2015), cat. no. 3; Alcimar do Lago Carvalho and Inácio Schiller Bittencourt Rebetez, in 'Moth of Venus, Caterpillar of Christ: Piero di Cosimo's Insects and Their Possible Meanings', *Figura: Studies on the Classical Tradition*, VII/2 (2019), p. 15, link it to the plague of 1479–80.

3 Carvalho and Schiller Bittencourt Rebetez, 'Moth of Venus', pp. 14–15.

4 Sheila M. F. Torres et al., 'Salivary Proteomics of Healthy Dogs: An In Depth Catalog', *PLOS ONE*, XIII/1 (2018), doi:10.1371/journal. pone.0191307.

5 Geronimus, *Piero di Cosimo: Visions Beautiful and Strange*, p. 186.

6 Jacobus de Voragine, *The Golden Legend*, trans. Granger Ryan and Helmut Ripperger (New York, 1969), pp. 109–10.

7 Paula Nuttall, 'Piero di Cosimo and Netherlandish Painting', in *Piero di Cosimo: Painter of Faith and Fable*, ed. Dennis Geronimus and Michael W. Kwakkelstein (Leiden, 2018), pp. 216–17.

8 Paula Nuttall, *From Flanders to Florence: The Impact of Netherlandish Painting, 1400–1500* (New Haven, CT, 2004), p. 123.

9 Giorgio Vasari, *Lives of the Most Eminent Painters, Sculptors and Architects* [1568], trans. Gaston du C. de Vere [1912–15] (ebook, London, 2009), vol. IV, p. 131.

10 Jill Burke, *Changing Patrons: Social Identity and the Visual Arts in Renaissance Florence* (University Park, PA, 2004), pp. 210–11.

11 Gretchen Hirschauer in Gretchen Hirschauer and Dennis Geronimus, eds, *Piero di Cosimo: The Poetry of Painting in Renaissance Florence*, exh. cat., National Gallery of Art, Washington, DC (2015), cat. no. 3.

12 Joan Evans, *Magical Jewels of the Middle Ages and the Renaissance, Particularly in England* (New York, 1976), p. 72.

13 Friedrich Ohly, 'Tau und Perle: Ein Vortrag', in *Festschrift für Ingeborg Schröbler zum 65. Geburtstag*, ed. Dietrich Schmidtke and Helga Schüppert (Tübingen, 1973), pp. 406–9.

14 Michèle Casanova, 'Il lapislazzuli nell'antico oriente', in *Lapislazzuli: Magia del blu*, ed. Maria Sframeli et al. (Livorno, 2015), p. 52.

15 Valentina Conticelli, 'Pillole per la malinconia e amuleti d'amore:
    Note sulle virtù mediche e magiche della pietra lapislazzuli',
    in *Lapislazzuli*, ed. Sframeli et al., p. 83. The manifold religious
    associations of lapis lazuli led to these magical and medical relations.
16 Maria Sframeli, 'Il Lapislazzuli alla corte dei Medici: ". . . se ne faccino
    vasi belli e bacini ed altri lavori"', in *Lapislazzuli*, ed. Sframeli et al., p. 71.
17 C. Willemijn Fock, 'Vases en lapis-lazuli des collections
    médicéennes du seizième siècle', in *Münchner Jahrbuch der Bildenden
    Kunst* (1976), pp. 119–54.
18 Mirella Levi d'Ancona, *The Garden of the Renaissance: Botanical Symbolism
    in Italian Painting* (Florence, 1977), pp. 20, 201.
19 Nuttall, *From Flanders to Florence*, p. 61.
20 Bianca Hatfield Strens, 'L'arrivo del trittico Portinari a Firenze',
    Commentari, n.s., XIX (1968), pp. 315–19.
21 Nuttall, *From Flanders to Florence*, p. 61.
22 Dennis Geronimus and Louis A. Waldman, 'Children of Mercury:
    New Light on the Members of the Florentine Company of St Luke
    (*c.* 1475–*c.* 1525)', *Mitteilungen des Kunsthistorischen Institutes in Florenz*,
    XLVII/1 (2003), pp. 119–20.
23 Robert Koch, 'Flower Symbolism in the Portinari Altarpiece',
    Art Bulletin, XLVI/1 (1964), pp. 70–77.
24 Slavomir Čéplö, 'The Life of John the Baptist by Serapion', *New
    Testament Apocrypha: More Noncanonical Scriptures*, 1 (2016), pp. 282–3.
25 Elena Capretti, 'Gli Albigesi bruciano i libri di San Domenico, etc.',
    in *Piero di Cosimo, 1462–1522*, ed. Capretti et al., cat. no. 6.
26 Holly Flora, *The Devout Belief of the Imagination: The Paris 'Meditationes
    Vitae Christi' and Female Franciscan Spirituality in Trecento Italy* (Turnhout,
    2009), illus. 39, for the manuscript in the Bibliothèque Nationale de
    France (Ital. 115, f. 46v).
27 Burke, *Changing Patrons*, p. 65.
28 Elena Capretti, 'Antefatti della Controriforma in Santo Spirito:
    tipologia, iconografia e sviluppo dell'altare, dalla "Visitazione" di
    Piero di Cosimo all'altare Maggiore del Caccini', in *Altari e immagini
    nello spazio ecclesiale: Progetti e realizzazioni fra Firenze e Bologna nell'età della
    Controriforma*, ed. Anna Forlani Tempesti (Florence, 1996), p. 46.
29 Stephanie J. Craven, 'Three Dates for Piero di Cosimo', *Burlington
    Magazine*, CXVII/870 (1975), p. 572.
30 Laura Cavazzini, 'Un documento ritrovato e qualche osservazione
    sul percorso di Piero di Cosimo', *Prospettiva*, LXXXVII–LXXXVIII
    (1997), p. 125.

31 Burke, *Changing Patrons*, pp. 67–77.
32 Antonia Fondaras, 'Hope and the Virtues: Piero di Cosimo's *The Visitation with Saints Nicholas of Bari and Anthony Abbot*', in *Augustinian Art and Meditation in Renaissance Florence: The Choir Altarpieces of Santo Spirito, 1480–1510* (Leiden, 2020), p. 167.
33 Ibid., pp. 189–92.
34 Ibid., pp. 192–5.
35 Capretti, 'Antefatti', pp. 48–9.
36 Geronimus, *Piero di Cosimo: Visions Beautiful and Strange*, p. 202.
37 Capretti, 'Antefatti', p. 46.
38 Kirk Ambrose, 'Spectacles and Prosthetic Visions in Fourteenth- and Fifteenth-Century Art', in *The Lives and Afterlives of Medieval Iconography*, ed. Pamela A. Patton and Henry D. Schilb (University Park, PA, 2021), pp. 101–26.
39 Fondaras, 'Hope and the Virtues', p. 173.
40 Katie A. Zins, 'St Augustine among the Mendicants: The Order of Augustinian Hermits and Early Renaissance Art in Italy', PhD thesis, Pennsylvania State University (2016), p. 188.
41 Ibid., pp. 9–22.
42 Ibid., pp. 8–9.
43 Fondaras, 'Hope and the Virtues', p. 189.
44 Ibid., pp. 175–89.
45 Vasari, *Lives*, vol. IV, p. 126.
46 Elena Capretti, 'L'altare del Pugliese nella chiesa dello Spedale degli Innocenti: un esempio di dialogo fra pittura e scultura', in *Piero di Cosimo*, ed. Geronimus and Kwakkelstein, p. 39.
47 Ibid., p. 48.
48 Nicoletta Pons, 'Madonna col bambino . . .', in *Piero di Cosimo, 1462–1522*, ed. Capretti et al., cat. no. 18.
49 Nuttall, 'Piero di Cosimo', pp. 213–14.
50 Geronimus, *Piero di Cosimo: Visions Beautiful and Strange*, p. 206.
51 Ibid.
52 J. K. Cadogan, *Domenico Ghirlandaio: Artist and Artisan* (New Haven, CT, 2000), p. 261.
53 Geronimus, *Piero di Cosimo: Visions Beautiful and Strange*, p. 206.
54 Adrian W. B. Randolph, 'Performing the Bridal Body in Fifteenth-Century Florence', *Art History*, XXI/2 (1998), pp. 188–9.
55 Karen Raber, 'Chains of Pearls: Gender, Property, Identity', in *Ornamentalism: The Art of Renaissance Accessories*, ed. Bella Mirabella (Ann Arbor, MI, 2012), p. 159.

56 Burke, *Changing Patrons*, pp. 135–7.
57 They may have been the pair of angels in the Victoria and Albert Museum, London, attributed to the workshop of Andrea della Robbia or possibly his son Giovanni (inv. nos 7615–1861 and 7614–1861), or like them.
58 Capretti, 'L'altare del Pugliese', pp. 53–7.
59 Ibid., pp. 39–59.
60 Daniela Parenti, 'Incarnazione di Gesu . . .', in *Piero di Cosimo, 1462–1522*, ed. Capretti et al., cat. no. 38.
61 Vasari, *Lives*, vol. IV, p. 132; Sharon Fermor, *Piero di Cosimo: Fiction, Invention and Fantasia* (London, 1993), p. 134.
62 Parenti, 'Incarnazione di Gesu . . .', cat. no. 38.
63 Maurice B. McNamee, *Vested Angels: Eucharistic Allusions in Early Netherlandish Painting* (Leuven, 1998), pp. 123, 129.
64 Alessandra Galizzi Kroegel, 'From *Ancilla Domini* to *Madonna del Parto*: Observations on Piero di Cosimo's Marian Imagery', in *Material World: The Intersection of Art, Science, and Nature in Ancient Literature and Its Renaissance Reception*, ed. Guy Hedreen (Leiden, 2021), pp. 32–4.
65 Sally J. Cornelison, *Art and the Relic Cult of St Antoninus in Florence* (Farnham, 2012), p. 103, n. 22.
66 Geronimus, *Piero di Cosimo: Visions Beautiful and Strange*, p. 210.
67 Vasari, *Lives*, vol. IV, p. 130.
68 Geronimus, *Piero di Cosimo: Visions Beautiful and Strange*, p. 210.
69 Daniela Parenti, 'Piero di Cosimo nelle collezioni medicee', in *Piero di Cosimo, 1462–1522*, ed. Capretti et al., p. 172.
70 Alison Luchs, 'Creatures, Great, Small and Hybrid: The Natural and Unnatural Wonders in Piero's Art', in *Piero di Cosimo: The Poetry of Painting*, ed. Hirschauer and Geronimus, p. 68.

5 Private Devotional Paintings

1 Jill Burke, *Changing Patrons: Social Identity and the Visual Arts in Renaissance Florence* (University Park, PA, 2004), p. 96.
2 Paula Nuttall, *From Flanders to Florence: The Impact of Netherlandish Painting, 1400–1500* (New Haven, CT, 2004), p. 93.
3 Alessandra Galizzi Kroeger, 'From *Ancilla Domini* to *Madonna del Parto*: Observations on Piero di Cosimo's Marian Imagery', in *Material World: The Intersection of Art, Science, and Nature in Ancient Literature and Its Renaissance Reception*, ed. Guy Hedreen (Leiden, 2021), p. 23.

4 John Kent Lydecker, 'The Domestic Setting of the Arts in
   Renaissance Florence', PhD thesis, Johns Hopkins University,
   Baltimore, MD (1987), p. 65.
5 Roberta J. M. Olson, *The Florentine Tondo* (New York, 2000); Dennis
   Geronimus, *Piero di Cosimo: Visions Beautiful and Strange* (New Haven,
   CT, 2006), p. 164.
6 Geronimus, *Piero di Cosimo: Visions Beautiful and Strange*, pp. 283–5.
7 Virginia Brilliant, 'The Adoration of the Child', in *Piero di Cosimo:
   The Poetry of Painting in Renaissance Florence*, ed. Gretchen Hirschauer
   and Dennis Geronimus (Washington, DC, 2015), cat. no. 9.
8 Giorgio Vasari, *Lives of the Most Eminent Painters, Sculptors and Architects*
   [1568], trans. Gaston du C. de Vere [1912–15] (ebook, London,
   2009), vol. IV, p. 133.
9 Giancarlo Fiorenza, 'Tadpoles, Caterpillars, and Mermaids: Piero
   di Cosimo's Poetic Nature', in *Gifts in Return: Essays in Honour of Charles
   Dempsey*, ed. Melinda Schlitt (Toronto, 2012), p. 158.
10 Alison Luchs, 'Creatures, Great, Small and Hybrid: The Natural
   and Unnatural Wonders in Piero's Art', in *Piero di Cosimo: The Poetry of
   Painting*, ed. Gretchen Hirschauer and Dennis Geronimus, pp. 63–4.
11 Fiorenza, 'Tadpoles', p. 154.
12 Ibid., p. 163.
13 Brilliant, 'The Adoration of the Child', cat. no. 9.
14 Maurice B. McNamee, *Vested Angels: Eucharistic Allusions in Early
   Netherlandish Painting* (Leuven, 1998), pp. 123, 129.
15 Everett Fahy, 'San Giovanni Evangelista', in *Piero di Cosimo, 1462–1522:
   Pittore eccentrico fra Rinascimento e Maniera*, ed. Elena Capretti et al., exh.
   cat., Galleria degli Uffizi, Florence (2015), cat. no. 30.
16 Béla Jozsef Demeter, 'Reappraising Piero di Cosimo's Serpents:
   The Role of Vipers in Renaissance Florence', *Renaissance Studies*,
   XXXII/4 (2017), pp. 649–50.
17 Ibid., p. 648.
18 Jacobus de Voragine, *The Golden Legend*, trans. Granger Ryan and
   Helmut Ripperger (New York, 1969), vol. I, p. 53.
19 Paula Nuttall, 'Piero di Cosimo and Netherlandish Painting', in
   Piero di Cosimo: Painter of Faith and Fable, ed. Dennis Geronimus and
   Michael W. Kwakkelstein (Leiden, 2018), p. 230.
20 Lionello Venturi quoted in Geronimus, *Piero di Cosimo: Visions Beautiful
   and Strange*, p. 184.
21 Virginia Brilliant, 'Saint John the Evangelist', in *Piero di Cosimo:
   The Poetry of Painting*, ed. Hirschauer and Geronimus, cat. no. 20.

22 Geronimus, *Piero di Cosimo: Visions Beautiful and Strange*, p. 258; Elena
    Capretti, 'Madonna con Bambino e due Angeli', in *Piero di Cosimo,
    1462–1522*, ed. Capretti et al., cat. no. 40.
23 Carmen Bambach, *Leonardo da Vinci Rediscovered*, 4 vols (New Haven,
    CT, 2019), vol. I, pp. 464–6, and illus. 1.4.117.
24 Francesco Caglioti, 'The Virgin with the Laughing Child', in
    Verrocchio: Master of Leonardo, ed. Francesco Caglioti and Andrea de
    Marchi, exh. cat., Palazzo Strozzi, Florence (2019), cat. no. 9.9.
25 The Donatello sculpture is in the collections of the Staatliche
    Museen, Berlin (inv. no. 1940). The painting by Uccello is owned
    by the National Gallery of Ireland, Dublin (inv. no. NGI.603).
26 Vasari, *Lives*, vol. IV, p. 127.
27 Ibid.
28 Nuttall, 'Piero di Cosimo', p. 220.
29 J. J. Tikkanan, 'Die Beinstellungen in der Kunstgeschichte, ein
    Beitrag zur Geschichte des künstlerischen Motive', *Acta Societatis
    Scientiarum Fennicae*, 42 (1913), pp. 3–197, and Herbert von Einem,
    'Die Medicimadonnas Michelangelos', *Rheinische-Westfälische Akademie
    der Wissenschaften. Vorträge. Geisteswissenschaften* 190, Opladen, 1973,
    pp. 15–25. I thank Betsy Rosasco for leading me to these references.

6 Piero's Artistic Legacy

 1 Giorgio Vasari, *Lives of the Most Eminent Painters, Sculptors and Architects*
    [1568], trans. Gaston du C. de Vere [1912–15] (ebook, London,
    2009), vol. IV, p. 123.
 2 Ibid., p. 133.
 3 Ibid., p. 134.
 4 Ibid., p. 127.
 5 Ibid., pp. 126–7.
 6 Ibid., p. 127.
 7 Ibid., p. 133.
 8 Daniel Arasse, 'Piero di Cosimo excentrique', in *Le Sujet dans le tableau:
    essais d'iconographie analytique*, ed. Daniel Arasse (Paris, 1997), p. 46.
 9 Jean Paul Richter, ed., *Scritti letterari di Leonardo da Vinci* (London,
    1883), part I, p. 254, no. 508. I thank François Quiviger for bringing
    this to my attention.
10 H. W. Janson, 'The "Image Made by Chance" in Renaissance
    Thought', in *De artibus opuscula, XL: Essays in Honor of Erwin Panofsky*,
    ed. Millard Meiss (New York, 1961), vol. I, p. 254. Janson is

quoting Leon Battista Alberti, *On Sculpture*, vol. I, section 28
[of book 2 of Alberti's text] as in Leon Battista Alberti, *On Painting
and Of Sculpture*, ed. Cecil Grayson (London, 1972), pp. 120–21.
Janson, p. 261, recognized that Vasari meant to attach Piero
di Cosimo to this tradition.

11 Ibid., p. 255, where he quotes Alberti, *On Painting*, book 2,
    section 28, as in *On Painting and Of Sculpture*, ed. Grayson, pp. 64–5.

12 Mantegna's painting of St Sebastian is in the Kunsthistorisches
    Museum, Vienna.

13 Carmen Bambach, *Leonardo da Vinci Rediscovered*, 4 vols (New Haven,
    CT, 2019), vol. III, pp. 578–9.

14 Sarah Blake McHam, *Pliny and the Artistic Culture of the Italian Renaissance:
    The Legacy of the 'Natural History'* (New Haven, CT, 2013), p. 341,
    cat. no. 137.

15 Martin Kemp, ed., *Leonardo on Painting* (New Haven, CT, 1989),
    p. 201.

16 Alison Brown, 'Lucretius and the Epicureans in the Social and
    Political Context of Renaissance Florence', *I Tatti Studies in the Italian
    Renaissance*, IX (2001), p. 56.

17 Vasari, *Lives*, vol. IV, p. 129.

18 The *Mystic Marriage of St Catherine* by Andrea del Sarto is in the
    Galleria degli Uffizi, Florence.

19 Louis Alexander Waldman, 'Fact, Fiction, Hearsay: Notes on Vasari's
    Life of Piero di Cosimo', *Art Bulletin*, LXXXII/1 (2000), pp. 173–4.

20 On this complex cycle, see Peter Francis Lynch, 'Patriarchy and
    Narrative: The Borgherini Chamber Decorations', PhD thesis,
    Yale University, Princeton, NJ, 1992.

21 Carmen Bambach, ed., *Michelangelo: Divine Draughtsman and Designer*,
    exh. cat., Metropolitan Museum of Art, New York (2017),
    pp. 139–42.

Conclusion

1 De Vere translated *bestialità* as 'misanthropic', which stretches the
   term's meaning figuratively. More literally, it should be defined as
   'brutish' or 'bestial'.

2 See Chronology, pp. 208–9, which is condensed from Dennis
   Geronimus, *Piero di Cosimo: Visions Beautiful and Strange* (New Haven, CT,
   2006), pp. 269–80, unless otherwise noted.

3 See Chronology, p. 209, for both festivities.

4 See Chronology, p. 208–9. Louis Alexander Waldman, 'Fact,
   Fiction, Hearsay: Notes on Vasari's Life of Piero di Cosimo',
   Art Bulletin, LXXXII/1 (2000), pp. 172–3.
5 See Chronology, p. 208. Documents discovered by Waldman,
   'Fact, Fiction, Hearsay', p. 174.
6 Alison Luchs, 'Allegory', in *Piero di Cosimo: The Poetry of Painting in
   Renaissance Florence*, ed. Gretchen Hirschauer and Dennis Geronimus,
   exh. cat., National Gallery of Art, Washington, DC (2015), cat. no. 17.
7 Waldman, 'Fact, Fiction, Hearsay', pp. 172–3.
8 Giorgio Vasari, *Lives of the Most Eminent Painters, Sculptors and Architects*
   [1568], trans. Gaston du C. de Vere [1912–15] (ebook, London,
   2009), vol. IV, p. 133.
9 Ibid., p. 127.
10 Ibid.

SELECT BIBLIOGRAPHY

Brown, Alison, 'Lucretius and the Epicureans in the Social and Political
    Context of Renaissance Florence', *I Tatti Studies in the Italian Renaissance*,
    IX (2001), pp. 11–62
Burke, Jill, *Changing Patrons: Social Identity and the Visual Arts in Renaissance
    Florence* (University Park, PA, 2004)
Capretti, Elena, et al., eds, *Piero di Cosimo, 1462–1522: Pittore eccentrico fra
    Rinascimento e Maniera*, exh. cat., Galleria degli Uffizi, Florence (2015)
Dempsey, Charles, *The Portrayal of Love: Botticelli's Primavera and Humanist
    Culture at the Time of Lorenzo the Magnificent* (Princeton, NJ, 1992)
Douglas, R. Langton, *Piero di Cosimo* (Chicago, IL, 1946)
Fermor, Sharon, *Piero di Cosimo: Fiction, Invention and Fantasia* (London,
    1993)
Fiorenza, Giancarlo, 'Tadpoles, Caterpillars, and Mermaids: Piero di
    Cosimo's Poetic Nature', in *Gifts in Return: Essays in Honour of Charles
    Dempsey*, ed. Melinda Schlitt (Toronto, 2012), pp. 153–77
Franklin, David, *Painting in Renaissance Florence, 1500–1550* (New Haven,
    CT, 2001)
Geronimus, Dennis, *Piero di Cosimo: Visions Beautiful and Strange* (New Haven,
    CT, 2006)
—, and Michael W. Kwakkelstein, eds, *Piero di Cosimo: Painter of Faith and
    Fable* (Leiden, 2018)
Hedreen, Guy, ed., *Material World: The Intersection of Art, Science, and Nature
    in Ancient Literature and Its Renaissance Reception* (Leiden, 2021)
Hirschauer, Gretchen, and Dennis Geronimus, eds, *Piero di Cosimo:
    The Poetry of Painting in Renaissance Florence*, exh. cat., National
    Gallery of Art, Washington, DC (2015)
Lucretius, *The Nature of Things*, trans. A. E. Stallings; intro. Richard
    Jenkyns (London, 2007)

McHam, Sarah Blake, *Pliny and the Artistic Culture of the Italian Renaissance: The Legacy of the 'Natural History'* (New Haven, CT, 2013)
Nethersole, Scott, *Art and Violence in Early Renaissance Florence* (New Haven, CT, 2018)
Panofsky, Erwin, *Studies in Iconology: Humanistic Themes in the Art of the Renaissance* [1939], 3rd edn (New York, 1967)
Vasari, Giorgio, *Lives of the Most Eminent Painters, Sculptors and Architects* [1568], trans. Gaston du C. de Vere [1912–15] (ebook, London, 2009)
Vaudoyer, Jean-Louis, 'Piero di Cosimo', in *L'Art est délectation* (Paris, 1968)
Whistler, Catherine, and David Bomford, *'The Forest Fire' by Piero di Cosimo* (Oxford, 1999)
Wolloch, Nathaniel, *Subjugated Animals: Animals and Anthropocentrism in Early Modern European Culture* (Amherst, NY, 2006)

ACKNOWLEDGEMENTS

Without the constant assistance of the Rutgers University Libraries, I could not have written this book during the COVID-19 pandemic. Once they partially reopened, librarians sent me books and scans from the Rutgers system or procured them from other universities.

I owe a large intellectual debt to Dennis Geronimus. I have depended on his books and articles with their authoritative command of Piero, and I am grateful he got me into writing this book. Many curators and conservators graciously answered my questions about works by Piero in their collections. They include Gretchen Hirschauer, Alison Luchs, Debra Pincus (now retired) and Elizabeth Walmsley at the National Gallery of Art, Washington, DC; Larry Keith at the National Gallery, London; Gretchen Walter and Stephan Wolohojian at the Metropolitan Museum of Art, New York; and Suzanne Hargrove and Sophie Ong at the Toledo Museum of Art. Melissa Conn, head of Save Venice Inc. in Venice, procured for me a photograph of a painting by Piero in the Cini collection that Save Venice had recently restored. Friends and colleagues offered their expertise on the wide range of topics required when studying Piero. I am particularly grateful to Patricia Fortini Brown, Andrea Campbell, Rebecca Cypess, David Marsh, Negar Rokhgar, Betsy Rosasco, Joan Rosasco, Connie and John Webster and Laura Weigert. Laura Robbins provided considerable help locating photographs, preparing the bibliography and captions list and checking the manuscript. Finally, I would like to extend my gratitude to François Quiviger, Michael Leaman, Phoebe Colley, Emma Devlin and Alex Ciobanu at Reaktion Books, who carefully oversaw this book's preparation.

PHOTO ACKNOWLEDGEMENTS

The author and publishers wish to express their thanks to the sources listed below for illustrative material and/or permission to reproduce it. Some locations of artworks are also given below, in the interest of brevity:

Ashmolean Museum, University of Oxford: 10; Basilica di Santa Maria Novella, Florence: 18; Birmingham Museum of Art, AL: 67; Casa Buonarroti, Florence: 17 (photo Sailko/Francesco Bini, CC BY 3.0), 71; Chiesa di San Michele Visdomini, Florence: 68; Chiesa dei Santi Michele Arcangelo e Lorenzo Martire, Montevettolini: 36; Denver Art Museum, CO: 25; Galleria Giorgio Franchetti alla Ca' d'Oro, Venice, photo Wolfgang Moroder (CC BY 3.0): 32; Galleria Palatina, Palazzo Pitti, Florence: 26, 64 (photo Scala, Florence), 66, 70; Galleria di Palazzo Cini, Venice: 57, 61; Gallerie degli Uffizi, Florence: 1, 6, 14, 34, 37, 39 (*middle*), 41, 65; Gemäldegalerie, Staatliche Museen zu Berlin: 15; Honolulu Museum of Art, HI: 52; Istituto Nazionale di Studi sul Rinascimento, Palazzo Strozzi, Florence: 5; The J. Paul Getty Museum, Los Angeles: 58; The John and Mable Ringling Museum of Art, Sarasota, FL: 11; © Kungliga slotten, Stockholm, photo Alexis Daflos: 47; The Metropolitan Museum of Art, New York: 2, 7, 9, 24, 28, 48, 56; Musée des Beaux-Arts de Strasbourg, photo Musées de Strasbourg/M. Bertola: 50; Musée Condé, Chantilly: 29; Musée du Louvre, Paris: 27 (photo © RMN-Grand Palais/Michel Urtado/Dist. Photo Scala, Florence), 27, 51, 62, 63; Museo degli Innocenti, Florence: 46; Museo Nazionale del Bargello, Florence, photo De Agostini/G. Nimatallah/Getty Images: 21; Museum Boijmans Van Beuningen, Rotterdam, photos Studio Tromp: 22, 60; The National Gallery, London: 3, 8, 16, 39 (*left* and *right*), 69; National Gallery of Art, Washington, DC: 19, 20, 31, 33, 45, 53, 54; National Gallery of Canada, Ottawa: 13; Ospedale degli Innocenti, Florence, photo Sailko/Francesco Bini (CC BY 3.0): 35; private collection: 4, 55; Rijksmuseum, Amsterdam: 23;

INDEX

Illustration numbers are indicated by *italics*

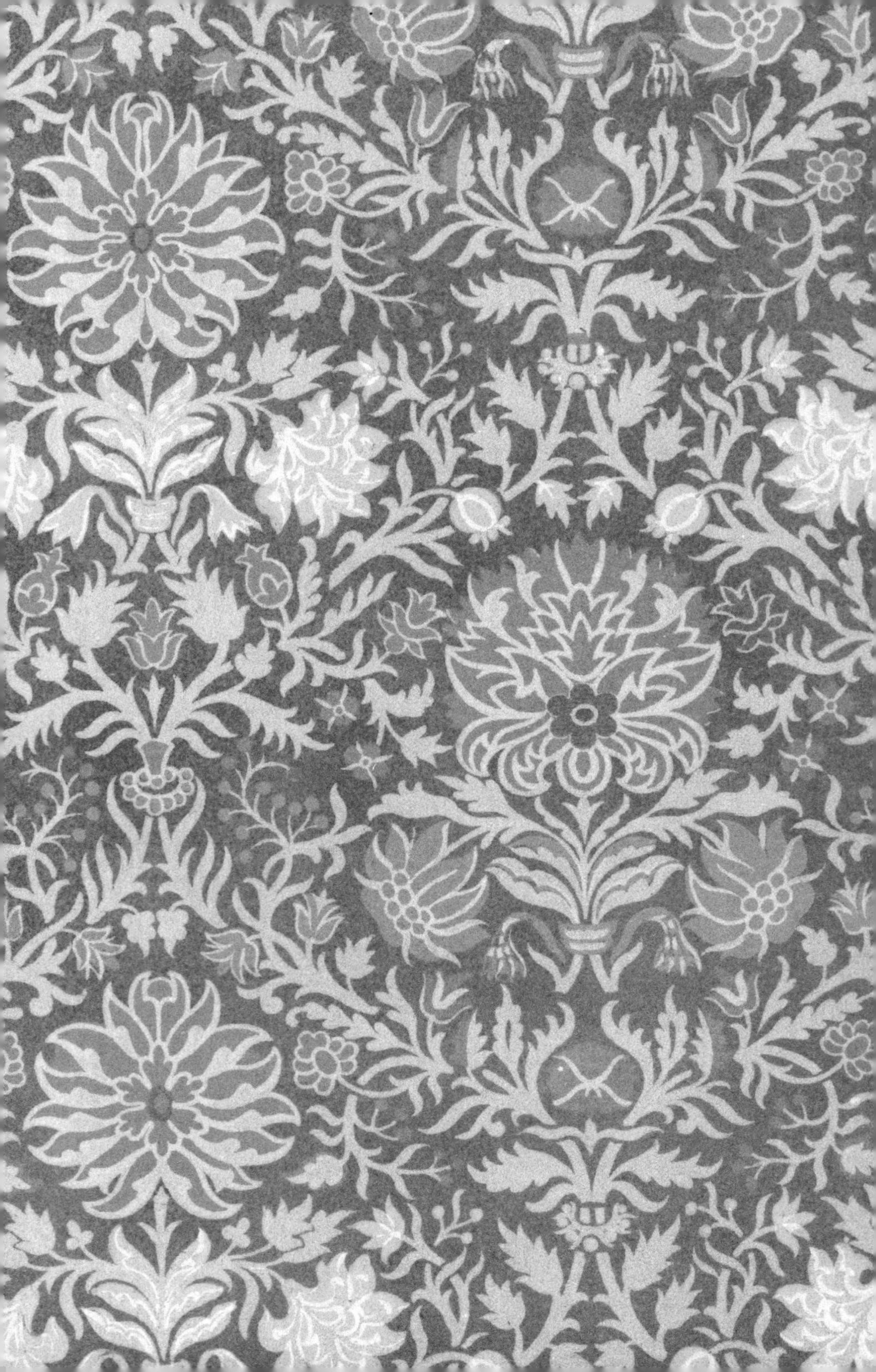